ECONOMICS & SOCIAL INSTITUTIONS

INSIGHTS FROM THE CONFERENCES ON ANALYSIS & IDEOLOGY

ROCHESTER STUDIES IN ECONOMICS
AND POLICY ISSUES

Published in cooperation with

The Center for Research in Government
Policy & Business
Graduate School of Management
University of Rochester
Rochester, New York, U.S.A.

ECONOMICS & SOCIAL INSTITUTIONS

INSIGHTS FROM THE CONFERENCES ON ANALYSIS & IDEOLOGY

Karl Brunner, editor

Martinus Nijhoff Publishing, Boston
Boston • The Hague • London

Portions of this work originally appeared in *Journal of Financial Economics*, in *Freedom in Constitutional Contract*, James Buchanan, published by Texas A & M University Press, in *Kyklos* and in *Schweizerische Zeitschrift für Volkswirtschaft und Statistik.*

Library of Congress Cataloging in Publication Data

Interlaken Seminar on Analysis and Ideology.
Economics and social institutions.
(Rochester studies in economics and policy issues)

1. Economics—Congresses. I. Brunner, Karl, 1916–
II. Title. III. Series.

HB21.I615 1979 330 79-13177

ISBN-13: 978-94-009-9259-7 e-ISBN-13: 978-94-009-9257-3
DOI: 10.1007/978-94-009-9257-3

Contents

Contributors

Hans Albert—Lehrstuhl für Soziologie und Wissenshaftslehre, Universität Mannheim

Armen Alchian—Department of Economics, University of California, Los Angeles

Peter T. Bauer—Department of Economics, London School of Economics and Political Science

Karl Brunner—Center for Research in Government Policy and Business, Graduate School of Management, University of Rochester and Universität Bern

James M. Buchanan—Center for Study of Public Choice, Virginia Polytechnic Institute and State University

Harold Demsetz—Department of Economics, University of California, Los Angeles

Gérard Gäfgen—Fachbereich Wirtschaftswissenshaften und Statistik, Universität Konstanz

Michael C. Jensen—Managerial Economics Research Center, Graduate School of Management, University of Rochester

William H. Meckling—Graduate School of Management, University of Rochester

Hans G. Monissen—Justus Liebig Universität-Giessen

Svetozar Pejovich—Department of Economics, University of Dallas

Introduction

The productive work of widely distributed academic research has contributed substantially, over the postwar period, to important advances in our understanding. It has also offered a clearer recognition of many unresolved problems. Nevertheless, the progress achieved over the last decades, exhibited by the systematic application of "theory" to actual issues and observable problems, could not overcome a pervasive sense of dissatisfaction. Some academic endeavors pursued within a traditional range of economic analysis have appeared increasingly remote from broad social issues, motivating the social and intellectual unrest experienced in recent years. Conditioned by the traditional use of economic analysis, many have naturally concluded that the "most relevant" social issues agitating our times are beyond the reach of economics. Purist advocates of a traditional view thus condemn any extension of economic analysis to social issues as an escape into "ideology". Others argue the need for an "interdisciplinary approach" involving sociology, social psychology, or anthropology as necessary strands in a useful understanding of social, institutional, and human problems of contemporary societies. We note here, in particular, the subtle attraction inherent in Marxian thought. It appears to offer a unified approach, with a coherent interpretation, to all matters and aspects of human society, including even nature. It is quite natural under the circumstances for eager young scholars, concerned with the broader social issues of our times and impressed by the allure of an encompassing vision, to turn to Marxian thought, disgruntled by the prevalent "Platonic exercise" in formal economics.

These developments are not imposed on us as our uncontrollable fate. We are offered a choice. There is an alternative to the illusion or reality of ideological miasmas, interdisciplinary convolutions, or salvation through Marxian dogma. This alternative was defined by Adam Smith's vision of economics as the social science. The successful development of a coherent analytic framework in the context of economic analysis—contrasting with shifting ad hoc constructions in social or behavioral psychology and empirical sociology, and contrasting also with the essentially programmatic and nonanalytic outlines and speculations in theoretical sociology and the pronounced analytic flaws or metaphysical intrusions in Marxian thought—suggests the useful exploration of a far-reaching intellectual program.

There are no inherent reasons for limiting the application of economic analysis to the narrow range codified by a tradition formed in this century. There are, in particular, no a priori grounds why the perception of man elaborated in economic analysis since its origins in the writings of the Scottish philosophers of the 18th century could not be usefully extended over the widest range of human experiences. This research program has been initiated by a small number of economists and has gained substantial momentum in recent years. It offers many opportunities for coping with serious social issues or institutional problems beyond the traditional marketplace. It promises, moreover, to yield useful analytic evolutions in the adaptation of inherited formulations to new ranges of human endeavors and expressions.

The Interlaken Seminar on Analysis and Ideology was conceived in 1973 as a forum encouraging an explicit and searching extension of economic analysis to the full sweep of social phenomena. The Interlaken Seminar thus addresses, in Hans Albert's words, a "sociology" with the analytic means developed by economic analysis.

The first meeting was held in 1974, and the sessions continue every year during May or June. A wide range of topics has been considered and vehemently argued in past years. A number of papers have been collected for a first volume. The authors are mostly academic economists but also include a philosopher of science and sociologist (Hans Albert). The issues covered range from economics as a social science (Hans Albert, Karl Brunner), to critical evaluations of Galbraithian notions of the world (Gerard Gäfgen, Hans Georg Monissen) and interpretation of Rawlsian ethics (James Buchanan); from social and political incentives encouraging disregard of economic analysis (Peter Bauer), to the working of specific social institutions (Armen Alchian, Michael Jensen, William Meckling, Svetozar Pejovich). The reader may not be convinced of the validity of the broader purpose of this volume and of the Interlaken Seminar. But the participants of the seminar may reasonably hope that the outcome will stimulate further probing and pondering of the basic questions.

Karl Brunner

Hans Albert

The Economic Tradition

Economics as a Research Programme for Theoretical Social Science*

Methodological Remarks

In general the growth of knowledge takes place within the framework of comprehensive *theoretical traditions* that are connected with more or less explicitly formulated *research programs.* Tradition means for knowledge about the same as capital means for the economy. Methodology has to take account of this fact.

A methodological conception can only be judged in relation to *aims*—the aims of scientific activity. These aims are controversial among scientists; therefore, we have to take sides on this question. I prefer *critical realism* as an epistemological conception, as Adam Smith did about two hundred years ago.[1] According to this view, the central aim of scientific activity is to discover the *structure of reality* by a systematic search for comprehensive, deep, and precise knowledge. It is thus necessary to strive for theories with great explanatory power; that is, theories that are as simple

---

* Presented at the Third Annual Interlaken Seminar on Analysis and Ideology, Switzerland, June 1976. I am thankful for the assistance of Marty Zupan in revising this article.

1 Adam Smith, "The Principles Which Lead and Direct Philosophical Enquiries Illustrated by the History of Astronomy," in *The Works of Adam Smith,* ed. Dugald Stewart (1811–12; reprint, Aulen: Otto Zeller, 1963), vol. 5.

as possible while explaining very much. Most methodological problems can be related to this aim.

The first problem seems to be to answer the question, Which are the properties such a theory must have? It would be plausible to say, certainly, that it has to be simple, general, and true. But with all these properties we get into difficulties, because no adequate explication exists at present. Simplicity seems to be important,[2] but it is a rather vague idea, not completely reducible to information content.[3] Generality seems to be relevant as well, but the attempt to reduce it to independence from spatiotemporal restrictions is insufficient.[4] As to *truth,* there is not only a problem of explication. Another problem seems to be even more important. If we agree that fallibilism is inherent in modern science and philosophy, then there can be *no criterion* of truth. Truth can only be a *regulative idea*—the idea of adequate representation—which leads to a particular orientation for the methodology of testing: All attempts at testing should be organized so that the "resistance of reality" is used to find out the strong and weak points of our problem solutions. It is always possible, by using alibi formulas or ad hoc assumptions, to immunize a set of propositions against criticism. But corroboration is only possible via serious attempts to test.[5]

Another problem is to formulate an adequate characterization of theories themselves. A *theory* may be conceived of as a *system of interconnected nomological statements* that depend on some *simple, unifying ideas* and are formulated in terms of a *coherent conceptual apparatus.* It implies assertions to the effect that under certain general conditions certain events are to be expected, perhaps with a certain probability. Because of their nomological content, counterfactual or subjunctive conditionals can be deduced from them (example: if in the space-time region x, y, z, t the quantity of money was increased rapidly, an inflationary develop-

---

2 Ibid.; Karl Popper, *Conjectures and Refutations* (London: Routledge & Kegan Paul, 1963), p. 241.

3 Carl Gustav Hempel, *Philosophy of Natural Science* (Englewood Cliffs, N.J.: Prentice-Hall, 1966), p. 44.

4 Karl Popper, *The Logic of Scientific Discovery* (originally published as *Logik der Forschung,* 1934) (London: Hutchinson, 1959), pp. 420–41.

5 Popper, *Scientific Discovery.*

ment would have ensured there—if we may believe Milton Friedman).

The main cognitive performance of such a theory is the *explanation* of states of affairs. An explanation involves an interpretation of the facts under consideration in such a way that they are described by means of the theoretical language and are shown to be expected on the basis of theoretical laws (nomological statements).[6] Conditions of adequacy for such explanations are controversial. They are intended to ensure the independent testability and the explanatory relevance of all the components involved in particular explanations. Even theories that, strictly speaking, are to be considered false can be used for explanations under certain circumstances—namely, if their truth content is sufficient and no better alternatives are at hand. We are often compelled to be satisfied with approximate explanations.

Other problems arise in the *application* of theoretical systems to concrete situations. Such application generally presupposes *abstractions* or *idealizations* of many kinds. A *model* of the situation has to be constructed by making a set of "assumptions" involving simplifications. Thus, a model is not identical to the theory concerned but is constructed in order to get an explanation by applying a theory. If very complex constellations of facts are to be explained, one must often begin with a relatively simple model, the assumptions of which are easily manageable. By introducing increasingly complicated assumptions one may arrive at a representation of the facts that provides an adequate explanation.[7]

Surely, for certain purposes one can also imagine particular situations for applying theoretical propositions, in which case assertions are not connected to concrete states of affairs

6 See John E. Cairnes, *The Character and Logical Method of Political Economy*, 2d ed. (1888; reprint, New York: Augustus M. Kelley, 1965), pp. 129 ff., for the correct distinction between laws and the conditions of their application.

7 With regard to Newton's explanation of planetary movements, see Imre Lakatos, "Falsification and the Methodology of Scientific Research Programmes," in *Criticism and the Growth of Knowledge*, ed. Imre Lakatos and Alan Musgrave (London: Cambridge University Press, 1970), pp. 235–36. (Cf. Alan Musgrave, "Falsification and Its Critics," mimeographed, 1971, pp. 16 ff., for a criticism of the special use made of this example in Lakatos's framework.) Following Friedrich von Wieser, one may call this procedure a "method of decreasing abstraction," but I don't know whether he used this term in exactly the same way.

in a certain space-time region.[8] By such constructions we are able to achieve explanations in principle of typical cases or explanations of ideal cases that in reality can only be approximated.[9] Ideal-typical explanation sketches of this kind can yield descriptions of what would happen if certain extreme (not realizable) conditions would prevail.[10]

Identification of the conditions relevant for explaining certain facts—that is, construction of the corresponding model—often presupposes the application of other, interpretative theories, for example, about the instruments needed for observation and measurement.[11] It is possible that defects of such interpretative theories lead to inadequate explanations, but it is also possible that we incorrectly charge interpretative theories with the defects of the explanatory theories. This is a problem with testing theories that is, usually, not considered in neoclassical empiricism.

As mentioned above, the state of theoretical development often allows only an approximate explanation by means of theories that are taken to be false. Above all, such a situation arises with regard to *idealizations.* In this case the nomological statements themselves have to be characterized as idealizations and therefore can only be approximately true. There are two possibilities, then:

1. These statements *hold* only under *ideal conditions;* that is, extreme conditions that can only be approximated in reality. (An example is Boyle's law.[12])
2. The relevant *ideal conditions* are specified in the *if clause* of the statements; that is, the statements are constructed

8 That "thought experiments" of this kind are no *substitutes* for real experiments was emphasized long ago by John Neville Keynes, *The Scope and Method of Political Economy,* 4th ed. (1917; reprint, Clifton, N.J.: Augustus M. Kelley, 1973), p. 182.

9 Karl Popper, "Rationality and the Status of the Rationality Principle," in *Le fondements philosophiques des systêmes èconomiques: Text de Jacques Rueff et essays en son honneur* (Paris: Payot, 1967); Raymond Boudon, *Education, Opportunity, and Social Inequality* (New York: John Wiley and Sons, 1974).

10 F. A. Hayek, "Degrees of Explanation," *British Journal for the Philosophy of Science 6* (1955).

11 On interpretative theories, see Lakatos, "Falsification." In recent discussions of the relation between theories and instruments, the example of optics (within astronomy) has a prominent place, for example, with respect to Galileo.

12 William F. Barr, "A Syntactic and Semantic Analysis of Idealizations in Physics," *Philosophy of Science* 41 (1974).

by the conditionalization of type (1) statements on the basis of adequate theories.[13]

As soon as a conditionalization of this kind and therefore an explanation of the ideal type (1) law are possible, the deviations occurring if the law is applied to real cases are explainable too. Thus we have at the same time an explanation of the ideal case and of the real cases, for which the first law was valid only more or less approximately. But idealizations are applicable in explanatory arguments even before degrees of idealization can be assessed in a precise way by means of a more comprehensive theory.[14] That is important, for we have reason to believe that all our theories are strictly speaking false even if they have a core of truth.

This viewpoint seems to be decisive for another methodological problem, that of assessing theories—and problem solutions in general. The history of science shows that all theoretical systems, even the most efficient theories of natural science, display certain weaknesses. For every theory there are certain *anomalies* that it is unable to master.[15] Since such anomalies can always be explained away by means of appropriate additional assumptions, it is possible in principle to immunize a theory against every possible objection, as mentioned above. On the other side, it is always possible to take such an anomaly as a counterinstance motivating a rejection of the theory. This strategy would hardly be a rational one, however, if used in general, for there are many cases in which anomalies can later be explained within the framework of the theory that initially seemed to be incompatible with them.[16] It therefore seems plausible to reject an otherwise powerful theory in the face of anomalies only if a *better alternative*—that is, a theory with greater explanatory power—is at hand.[17] This is a principle of ration-

13 Shortly after its formulation Boyle's law was recognized as an idealization, but no one was able to specify the ideal conditions of its validity. The kinetic theory of gases later made the conditionalization of this law possible.

14 Barr, "Idealizations in Physics," p. 60.

15 Thomas S. Kuhn, *The Structure of Scientific Revolutions* (Chicago: University of Chicago Press, 1962); Lakatos, "Falsification."

16 Morton Grosser, *The Discovery of Neptune* (Cambridge, Massachusetts: Harvard University Press, 1962); Joseph Agassi, "Sensationalism," in *Science in Flux* (Dordrecht, Holland: D. Reidel, 1975).

17 On the importance of alternatives, see Paul K. Feyeabend, "How to Be a Good Empiricist: A Plea for Tolerance in Matters Epistemological," in *The Delaware*

al problem-solving behavior familiar from economics. It is valid in daily life, in the realm of knowledge, and, as we shall see, with regard to the problem of social order.

Testing a theory, that is, trying to come to an adequate judgment about its efficiency, is more complicated than is usually assumed. Even if we accept explanatory power as the most important quality, there is more than one criterion that has to be taken into account; and the results of empirical investigations—for example, of experiments—have to be judged on the basis of certain traits of a nonempirical kind. If we compare theories with one another, one of them can be more *simple* than others, a second can be more *general,* a third more *precise,* a fourth more *testable* on technological grounds, and a fifth *compatible with* more of our *other views.* As to the *outcomes* of empirical investigations, they can never verify a theory, because every theory involves an infinite set of consequences; nor can they decisively falsify a theory, for a false prognosis can be a consequence of a false identification of the relevant singular conditions. There is *no secure empirical basis*—as empiricism had assumed—and there is *no complete theoretical autonomy* immunizing a view against the impact of discoveries in other realms of knowledge.

Theoretical traditions steered by more or less articulated research programs and embedded in *philosophical views* are evolving systems of knowledge, often competing with one another. They may be elaborated, modified, transferred to new fields of application, restricted, or expanded. In their development there may be progressive and degenerative shifts (as Lakatos has called them[18]). And as exemplary models—as paradigms in a non-Kuhnian sense—they may even influence the development of other realms of knowledge, as Newtonian physics with its idea of natural law was exemplary for political economy in the eighteenth and nineteenth centuries.

Seminar in Philosophy of Science, ed. B. Baumrin, vol. 2 (New York: John Wiley & Sons, Interscience, 1963).

18 Lakatos, "Falsification."

The Economic Tradition and Its Development

Economics and Its Research Program

Economics seems to be the only theoretical tradition in the social sciences that is approximately comparable to the great theoretical traditions in natural science. How can it be demarcated in a proper way? There are "formalists" who emphasize rational behavior and are inclined to make economics a part of a general logic of decision. There are "materialists" who prefer to relate it to a social sphere, the economy, where wealth or welfare is strived for. Another tendency is to identify it with "catallactics", the science of exchange (or sociology of the market). There may be a core of truth in all these definitions, but I would prefer to accentuate the central problem handled in economics. In my view, economics is the first science that has analyzed in a theoretical way comparable to natural science the problem of *social steering* (or of social control—*Problem der sozialen Steuerung*).

In the perspective of classical political economy, market processes are part of a mechanism of social control, which involves a particular *order* in social life—a mechanism governed by certain *laws* and leading to results that are relevant to the members of a society with regard to their individual life situations. According to this view, this social mechanism (1) works within the framework of a certain legal order whereby it is protected by the state, but essentially without direct interventions; and (2) operates by means of rewards and penalties of a pecuniary (or quasi-pecuniary) kind, which arise from the interactions of the individuals themselves and are causally relevant for them. It is a nonauthoritarian system of social control on the basis of voluntarily accepted contracts. Thus the classics of political economy for the first time made the problem of social control the basis of a theoretical science with the aim of discovering the laws governing the phenomena concerned. They initiated the analysis of social systems and even used the idea of negative feedback.

The research program of classical political economy may be characterized by the following ideas:

1. The assumption that there are *laws* suitable for explaining the social facts under consideration
2. *Methodological individualism;* that is, the idea of ex-

plaining these facts as resulting from the combination of individual actions under varying circumstances
3. The assumption that the *scarcity of means* for the fulfillment of human wants is an essential aspect of the states of affairs to be analyzed
4. The assumption that *self-interest* is of decisive importance for the orientation of human behavior, and the idea of *rational action* connected with this assumption
5. The idea of "canalizing" human behavior (and social processes) by the *shaping of the legal order,* the historically variable institutional arrangements of social life, so that under different legal regulations different social consequences will result.

So far, this is a quite general conception with a few simple and powerful ideas, not restricted to particular social spheres or to particular historical periods—a general sociological research program. The first result of the investigations inspired by this program was the classical theory of free competition, an analysis of the price mechanism in a society with private ownership and freedom of contract and of its effects on production, distribution, and accumulation. The behavior of entrepreneurs—striving for profit—presupposed in this theory was a special case of rational action (see (4) above) under particular institutional conditions, but there was no general theory of behavior. Also, a uniform explanation of different kinds of income was not achieved. And even with regard to the formation of prices, an exception had to be made for certain kinds of goods. The attempt to make the cost principle the basis of value theory led into a blind alley. A fundamental change seemed to be necessary.

This change took place in the course of the so-called marginal revolution, leading to *neoclassical economics.* If one looks for a clear formulation of the ideas underlying this theoretical development, one comes across the works of Jeremy Bentham, the founder of philosophical radicalism. The contribution of Bentham to the reformation of the economic research program essentially consists in his conception of human behavior based on the principle of utility. Following Bentham, it appeared to be necessary for an adequate explanation of individual behavior to go back to the needs of men and their striving for satisfaction, to identify the sanctions influencing human behavior—rewards and penalties—in connection with these needs, and to discover the relevant expectations with regard to such sanctions. The behavior to be anticipated then had to be derived from a principle of maximization. As for objections to this view, I only quote Taylor: "The real significance...of this way of thinking is that it tries *to start out by* formulating a fully general or all-inclusive *approach to* the problems of human life or conduct, so that all of the particular facts, relations, and possibilities can then be examined with the aid of, and be fitted into, this conceptual framework."[19] In any case, Bentham's conception (and similar ideas of other origin) made it possible to substitute for the assumption of self-interest in the classical economic research program a new theory of value that in principle lent itself to an interpretation of all kinds of behavior.

Neoclassical Idealizations

Of course, the Bentham-Program (as I shall call it) has not been carried through completely in the neoclassical phase, and even where it led to very interesting problem solutions these were afflicted with certain weaknesses and difficulties that were then often ascribed, incorrectly I think, to the program itself and to the theoretical tradition connected with it. The development in this phase brought about, not so much the sought-after psychological foundation of economic explanations, but among other things, a *problem shift* in the direction of *decision logic.* At the time of the marginal revolution, economists themselves had to construct the behavioral assumptions requisite for explaining complex social phenomena, because there was at this time no psychological research within the Benthamite framework. The outcome of their endeavors was the well-known formal utility theory—the "self-produced psychological basis", as Morgenstern called it,[20] although in many eyes it seems rather to be a logic of choice.

19 Overton H. Taylor, *A History of Economic Thought* (New York: McGraw-Hill, 1960), p. 128. Modern psychological theories of behavior also incorporate elements of Bentham's conception; for instance, see John W. Atkinson, *An Introduction to Motivation* (Princeton: Princeton University Press, 1964).

20 Oskar Morgenstern, "Die drei Grundtypen der Theorie des subjektiven Wertes," *Schriften des Vereins für Sozialpolitik* 183 (1931).

The most admired achievement of this phase was the *general equilibrium theory* of Léon Walras, the "magna charta of exact economics."[21] For the first time, the means of the calculus were applied to a static analysis of the whole "economic universe", the totality of the activities connected by market relations. In Walras's view, pure economics is "in essence, the theory of the determination of prices under a hypothetical régime of perfectly free competition." Its task is to state the *laws* governing *market phenomena* in the same way as Newton did it for astronomical movements and to show that "within certain limits the mechanism of free competition is a self-driven and self-regulating mechanism."[22] Walras tried to achieve the solution of this problem by setting up a system of simultaneous equations to determine the state of general equilibrium generated under free competition. He explicitly conceded that this is an "ideal" state never attainable in the real world but "normal" insofar as, under a régime of free competition, there would be a tendency to realize it.[23]

It is very interesting to see how the connection has been established between the core of this system—the set of simultaneous equations—and the phenomena to be explained. Assuming given data, the characterization of the equilibrium itself, and the determination of the corresponding values for the equations, posed a purely mathematical problem. But the thesis that there is a tendency in this direction (a tendency to equilibrium) can be regarded as a hypothesis, to be tested by empirical investigations. This employment of the idea of equilibrium (die *Nomologisierung* dieser Idee) involved a genuine claim of explanation in the Walrasian conception. To show its justification Walras made some heroic *idealizations* to eliminate all possible frictions affecting the requisite market movements. Strictly speaking, in his model a mechanism is imagined that *would* bring about the postulated state *if* it would be realizable and *if* it would operate as its inventor had assumed. Above all, the problem of infor-

21 Joseph A. Schumpeter, *Geschichte der volkswirtschaftlichen Analyse,* 2 vols. (Gottingen: Vanderhock and Rupprecht, 1965), vol. no. 2: 1177 English ed., *A History of Economic Analysis* (New York: Oxford University Press, 1954).

22 Léon Walras, *Elements of Pure Economics;* or, *The Theory of Social Wealth* (1874), trans. William Jaffé (New York: Augustus M. Kelley, 1969), pp. 40, 305.

23 Ibid., pp. 224, 380.

mation is completely evaded in this model. Moreover, institutional arrangements relevant for the working market mechanisms are neglected almost completely (apart from certain fictitious assumptions). Finally, by presupposing utility functions as given, the problem of motivation, including the problem of a possible change of need structures, has been eliminated as well. Thus it may be only a slight exaggeration to say that the Walrasian attempt to explain the market system takes place in a *cognitive, motivational, and institutional vacuum.*[24]

Considering that in Walrasian analysis all real sociological problems are avoided by making suitable idealizations and that even psychology is reduced to the well-known maximization thesis for given utility functions (apart from the corresponding thesis for entrepreneurial profit, similar to the classical idea), it is at least very plausible, then, that in this case the *classical problem of social control* in decentralized systems, a problem of theoretical science, has been replaced by a *formal problem of collective choice.* This is especially plausible if one bears in mind the normative use of the idea of equilibrium (die *Axiologisierung* dieser Idee) in the thesis of the collective maximization of wants. It is not surprising, therefore, that systems of this kind can be treated as *neutral* with regard to the social order, so that it is possible to project them without difficulty into a socialist society.[25] Exactly this is to be expected because the institutional, motivational, and cognitive-informative aspects of the price mechanism are hardly touched upon in this kind of analysis. This encourages the illusion that by taking over the marginalist conception—as a logic of collective choice—it is possible to make a socialist economy work in a "rational" way as formulated by the theoreticians of capitalism.[26]

---

24 Schumpeter, who admired Walras's system more than all other achievements of economic analysis, nevertheless came to the conclusion that it may, in the final analysis, be nothing but a huge research program. Schumpeter, *Volkswirtschaftliche Analyse*, vol. 2: 1246.

25 See Enrico Barone, "Ministry of Production in the Collectivist State," in *Collectivist Economic Planning*, ed. F. A. Hayek (London: George Routledge & Sons, 1935); Joseph A. Schumpeter, *Capitalism, Socialism and Democracy* (New York: Harper & Brothers, 1942); and the critical remarks in James M. Buchanan, *Cost and Choice* (Chicago: Markham, 1969), pp. 96–98.

26 See Ronald L. Meek, "Marginalism and Marxism," in *The Marginal Revolution in Economics*, ed. R. D. Collison Black, A. W. Coats, and Craufurd D. W. Goodwin

The example of Walrasian analysis has to a large extent dominated the development of economic thinking in the neoclassical phase. More than 60 years after Walras, John Hicks made an attempt of a similar kind based on Paretian value theory and including the problems of capital and interest as formulated by Knut Wicksell. He emphasized the *formal* character of his theory as a pure logical analysis of capitalism without reference to *institutional controls* of any kind.[27] But even admitting the difference between the Walrasian and the Marshallian approach, one has to say that at least with respect to idealization the Walrasian system is no exception. The model of natural science influenced economic thinking from the beginning, so that the usual idea of scientific law, the ideal of explanation connected with it, and the method of working with idealizations have been accepted in it for a long time.[28] In my view, there is no reason to regret this influence. Later methodological discussions, after the Second World War, come back to the problem of idealization, especially under the influence of Friedman's thinking.[29]

There seems to be a consensus about the fact that the model of perfect competition can at best be used for an approximate explanation of real cases (see the first section above) and that a more comprehensive theory with greater

(Durham, North Carolina: Duke University Press, 1973). In view of the fact that Marxism has never been able to make reasonable proposals for the regulation of a centralized economy, Meek's fusion of Marxism and marginalism may appear to be a useful strategy. But it only takes advantage of the model-platonism of neoclassical thinking, with its vacuum-idealizations.

27 John R. Hicks, *Value and Capital*, 2d ed. (Oxford: Oxford University Press, Clarendon Press, 1946), pp. 6–7.

28 See Cairnes, *Political Economy*, pp. 68, 104 ff.; J. N. Keynes, *Political Economy*, pp. 217 ff. 247–48; Carl Menger, *Gesammelte Werke*, ed. F. A. Hayek, 2 vols. (Tübingen: J. C. B. Mohr (Paul Siebeck), 1969), vol. II: 75 ff.; Vilfredo Pareto, *Manual of Political Economy* (1927), translator Ann S. Schweir (New York: Augustus M. Kelley, 1971), pp. 12–13; Frank H. Knight, *Risk, Uncertainty, and Profit* (1921; reprint, New York: Augustus M. Kelley, 1964), pp. 76 ff., where he speaks explicitly of "idealizations."

29 Milton Friedman, "The Methodology of Positive Economics," in *Essays in Positive Economics* (Chicago: University of Chicago Press, 1953). With regard to Friedman's position, see also Terence W. Hutchison, *The Significance and Basic Postulates of Economic Theory*, 2d ed. (New York: Augustus M. Kelley, 1960), pp. xii ff.; Ernest Nagel, "Assumptions in Economic Theory," *American Economic Review* 53 (1963): 211 ff.; Karl Brunner, "'Assumptions' and the Cognitive Quality of Theories," *Synthese* 20 (1969): 501 ff.; Barr, "Idealizations in Science," pp. 268 ff.

explanatory power—a theory that could be used to derive the respective degree of approximation of this model for every case—is unavailable.[30] For those who are trying to find such a theory, it surely would be interesting to discover for which cases the model is valid as a more or less sufficient approximation. The model itself seems to provide no indication of how to find out under which *real* conditions its nomological content (referring to the tendency toward a state of equilibrium) has *explanatory relevance.*[31] The assertion that it has such relevance if the corresponding "assumptions" are satisfied is either (1) a purely *logical* statement—that is, if these assumptions are to be identified with the supreme hypotheses of the system itself;[32] (2) a highly *problematic* statement—if the explicit if-components (antecedent clauses) of these hypotheses are meant;[33] or (3) a completely *useless* statement—if it refers to the so-far-unknown conditions under which the idealizations are true.[34] He who prefers the answer that this model has explanatory relevance whenever "free competition" is realized, in a loose institutional sense,

30 The dilemma of the Friedman-Samuelson controversy about these questions is expressed by Lawrence A. Boland: "I think, first of all, the perfect competition theory of the firm is simply false, and secondly, the imperfect competition theory, which is merely a generalization of the former, is at best pointless." "Conventionalism and Economic Theory," *Philosophy of Science* 37 (1970): 244. In other words, the latter achieves its "realism" by making ad hoc adaptations, raising its level of complexity to an extent that makes genuine explanations impossible. Boland's solution is a radical one—to reject as uninteresting the whole problem of evaluating theories. See Boland, "Methodology as an Exercise in Economic Analysis," *Philosophy of Science* 38 (1971): 105 ff., where certain analogies between welfare economics and philosophy of science are emphasized.

31 All other problems are "internal" ones of a logical or mathematical character; here, we can agree to the argument of F. A. Hayek, "Economics and Knowledge," *Economica* 4 (1937). See also Hutchison, *Economic Theory*, pp. 104 ff.; his arguments do not depend on the strong version of falsificationism that he had adopted at this time.

32 See Knight, *Risk, Uncertainty, and Profit*, pp. 76–93, on the assumptions of the theory of competition; and see the interpretation in Barr, "Idealizations in Science," pp. 266–67.

33 For instance, if one reformulates the proposition "All persons act with complete rationality" as a conditional, we have: $(x)\ (Px \rightarrow Rx)$, with Px (x is a person) as the if-component. It is easily seen that the model must be applicable, then, to all social phenomena, without restriction, as far as this proposition is concerned.

34 The usual formulations often contain no hints as to essential differences between kinds of assumptions. But within methodological individualism it is reasonable to at least make a distinction between general behavioral assumptions as *theoretical* propositions with nomological content and the other assumptions describing conditions of application that are *historically variable.*

probably would get into difficulties with regard to the anomalies coming to light in this case. At least a list of typical anomalies would be desirable then. Obviously, these problems are closely connected with the problem of empirical testability (and testing) of pure economics, which I prefer to avoid here.[35]

The Present Problem Situation in Pure Economics

Theoretical institutionalism

The development of neoclassical economics was accompanied by continuous criticism from heterodox theoreticians, partly appealing to the classical tradition, partly framing new arguments (Marxism, institutionalism, historicism, etc.). Mostly they tried to identify weaknesses in neoclassical thinking—gaps, anomalies, inconsistencies—but without presenting a full-fledged alternative (see my methodological remarks above). In addition, they often tried to identify defects of the market mechanism—that is, properties that contradicted its performance characteristics postulated in the model of competition. In both cases, the procedure followed was *criticism without analysis of alternatives,* so no consequences could be derived for a rational policy (in theory or in practice).

Only the "Keynesian Revolution" offered both: a *criticism* of neoclassical thinking connected with a *theoretical alternative*—albeit within the framework of Bentham's program—and proposals for institutional changes on the basis of theoretical investigations. But it seems to be a bit difficult to find out exactly what this revolution meant.[36] Sometimes the

35 See Emile Grunberg, "Notes on the Verifiability of Economic Laws," *Philosophy of Science* 24 (1957); Spiro J. Latsis, "Situational Determinism in Economics," *British Journal for the Philosophy of Science* 23 (1972), especially p. 219: ". . . the simplicity and ideal character of the model makes it difficult to locate and identify anomalies; for the fundamental assumptions and the initial conditions which have to be fulfilled, if the model is to be tested, are never exactly realized; and there is little guidance to indicate how much divergence is tolerable." Textbooks that analyze such questions are very rare; one of them is Richard G. Lipsey, *An Introduction to Positive Economics* (London: Weidenfeld & Nicolson, 1963) —for instance, pp. 55, 99–101, 266.

36 Craufurd D. W. Goodwin distinguishes between three revolutions in economic thinking—the Smithean, the marginal, and the Keynesian—and compares their significance. "Marginalism Moves to the New World," in *Marginal Revolution,* ed. Black, Coats, and Goodwin, pp. 382 ff. The marginal revolution seems to be a more purely academic and professional phenomenon than the other two.

impression given is that it consisted only in an enrichment of the existent conceptual apparatus of economic thinking, devised to be able to formulate macroeconomic problems in an easier way, so that the problem solutions offered by Keynes can be seen as special cases of neoclassical theory. General equilibrium theory of the Walrasian kind would then be in a position after all to digest Keynesian anomalies, for example, equilibrium with underemployment. But this interpretation doesn't quite seem to be in harmony with the intentions of Keynes, who didn't aim at representing such a special case but was looking for a really *general theory,* a fusion of price theory and monetary theory.[37] Now Keynesian analysis surely emphasized particular institutional aspects of economic processes—for example, the institutionally conditioned difference of savers and investors—but it didn't come to a solution of institutional problems as such.

As stated above, the significance of a particular legal order for the control of market processes was obvious for classical political economy. The system of "natural liberty" was explicitly presented as an alternative to other systems.[38] But there was no analysis of the impact on market phenomena of different specific legal arrangements, apart from taxes and duties as interventions of the government. In *neo*classical thinking the problem of legal regulations, and therewith the problem of institutions, vanished almost completely from theoretical analysis; and, as mentioned above, heterodox thinkers found in this problem a suitable starting point for their criticisms. But there were exceptions showing that, contrary to the usual objections to *methodological individualism* in present sociological discussion, this approach, connected with economic analysis from the beginning, is quite compatible with *theoretical institutionalism.* That is, it makes possible explanations of social phenomena that take account of institutional arrangements and even expla-

37 John Maynard Keynes, *The General Theory of Employment, Interest and Money* (London: Macmillan, 1936), p. vii. Axel Leijonhufvud, *Keynes and the Classics,* Institute of Economic Affairs Occasional Paper 30 (London, 1971), criticizes the "neoclassical synthesis," which has maintained the compatibility of the Keynesian and neoclassical approaches. See also Leijonhufvud, *On Keynesian Economics and the Economics of Keynes* (London: Oxford University Press, 1968).

38 Adam Smith, *An Inquiry into the Nature and Causes of the Wealth of Nations* (1776) (London: J. M. Dent & Sons LTD, 1910).

nations of the origin and change of institutions.[39] Therefore, in my view it is only a consistent continuation of an approach inherent in classical economics—and somewhat, but not wholly, neglected in neoclassical thinking—that contemporary theoretical economics is now entrusted with an investigation of property rights, for example.[40]

The possibility of mastering the problem of institutions within the framework of an individualistic approach is based on viewing institutional arrangements as determinants of the incentive structures effective in individual behavior;[41] for these together with other factors, for example, relevant properties of the actual situations concerned, determine which (positive or negative) sanctions the individual can expect. Of course, such incentives are effective only on the basis of individual utility functions representing the internal need structures of individuals.[42] By this approach, the dual behavioral assumptions characteristic of neoclassical economics are abandoned and replaced by the assumption of utility maximization for individuals in all positions. Profit maximization can be derived under special circumstances. This is an important step in the direction of Bentham's program, for organizations of all kinds are now analyzable in an individualistic manner.

---

39 See Menger, *Grundsätze der Volkswirtschaftslehre* (English ed., *Principles of Economics* (Glencoe, Illinois: Free Press, 1950), in *Gesammelte Werke*, ed. Hayek, 1: 55 ff; David Hume, *Ein Traktat über die menschliche Natur (A Treatise on Human Nature*, 1739–40) (Hamburg: Meiner Vertag, 1973), 3: 235 ff. In both cases, scarcity and property are related to each other. See also Menger, *Untersuchungen über die Methode der Sozialwissenschaften* und der politischen Ökonomie (English ed., *Problems of Economics and Sociology* (Urbana, Illinois: University of Illinois Press, 1963)), in *Gesammelte Werke*, ed. Hayek, 2: 171 ff., 271 ff., for attempts to explain the development of money and other institutions on the basis of individualism.

40 See Armen A. Alchian, *Pricing and Society*, Institute of Economic Affairs Occasional Papers 17 (London, 1967); James M. Buchanan, "Economics and Its Scientific Neighbors," in *The Structure of Economic Science*, ed. Sherman R. Krupp (Englewood Cliffs, New Jersey: Prentice-Hall, 1966). An adequate explanation of social phenomena appears to be possible only if the structure of property rights is taken into account.

41 See Eirik Furubotn and Svetozar Pejovich, eds., *The Economics of Property Rights* (Cambridge, Massachusetts: Ballinger Publishing Company, 1974), p. 1.

42 John W. Atkinson, "Towards Experimental Analysis of Human Motivation in Terms of Motives, Expectancies and Incentives: in J. W. Atkinson, ed., *Motives in Fantasy, Action and Society* (Princeton: D. von Nostrand Company, 1958), pp. 359 ff.

By seeing institutions in this way we have a starting point for attempting a structural reduction *(strukturelle Relativierung)* of neoclassical idealizations. It is possible now, at least partly, to state explicitly the ideal conditions under which the phenomena represented in the model of perfect competition can be expected to come about—namely, if owing to the prevailing legal arrangements and factual circumstances, particular kinds of costs vanish completely.[43] By considerations of this kind it seems to be possible in principle to discover under which (institutional and other) circumstances an approximate satisfaction of the corresponding assumptions is to be expected. More than before, an assessment of the explanatory value of this model and of the limitations of its applicability is in sight.

Expectations and behavioral assumptions

A very important problem remains, however, and it plays a considerable role in discussions of the difficulties of the neoclassical approach. Let's go back to the Walrasian system, which displayed in an impressive way the *interdependence* of all social processes in a system of decentralized, that is, individually independent, decision making. Considering that individuals' decisions refer to an important extent to future results and that these results are dependent on the decisions of other market participants, the assumption of adequate information for any of them would imply that every participant is informed about the decisions of all other participants.[44] Under these conditions, however, the state of equilibrium postulated in Walrasian analysis couldn't be derived at all, for instead of the assumed state of perfect competition there would appear a universal oligopoly.[45] In other words, from the assumption of perfect competition

43 Necessary conditions for profit-maximizing behavior of managers are stated in J. Moore, "Managerial Behavior in the Theory of Comparative Economic Systems," in *Economics of Property Rights*, ed. Furubotn and Pejovich, pp. 327 ff.

44 The importance of uncertainty and of the problem of expectations was emphasized very early by Frank H. Knight, *Risk, Uncertainty, and Profit*, pp. 197 ff. For an analysis of the attendant difficulties for equilibrium analysis, see Oskar Morgenstern, "Vollkommene Voraussicht und wirtschaftliches Gleichgewicht," *Zeitschrift für Nationalokonomie* 6 (1935); and Hutchison, *Economic Theory*, pp. 84 ff.

45 In my view, this follows from the analysis of Morgenstern, "Vollkommene Voraussicht," so that my corresponding criticism is thus far justified. See my *Ökono-*

together with the assumption of adequate information, we can infer the existence of a universal oligopoly, that is, a consequence incompatible with one of the initial assumptions. Therefore, the system of propositions considered must be inconsistent. That leads to the problem of how to formulate adequate assumptions about the distribution of information.

That it is necessary to make some assumptions about expectations had become obvious in the thirties. John Hicks tried to solve this problem, but in a formal way, that is, defining the concept of the elasticity of expectation and discussing the logically possible cases (a "taxonomic" approach).[46] In this way he attempted a transition to the analysis of dynamic problems. One of the more interesting consequences of his investigations was that cumulative processes à la Wicksell couldn't be excluded any more. But Hicks had to rely on ad hoc assumptions to deduce some interesting consequences. Thus it was quite evident that the means of neoclassical thinking weren't sufficient to explain the mode of operation of the market system. One of the more important reasons seems to be that the behavioral assumptions involved didn't take account of the cognitive aspects of individual decision making.[47]

If one considers the Keynesian criticism of neoclassical thinking, similar consequences appear. The mechanism of control assumed in this conception included only devices operating, as it were, with negative feedback, so that all deviations from equilibrium lead to immediate corrections. All market participants have to adapt their situations only to the system of equilibrium prices, presumably known by a fictitious process of tâtonnement. Since in a realistic analysis this system cannot be presupposed as known, it is to be

---

mische Ideologie und politische Theorie (Göttingen: Schwarz & Company, 1954), pp. 59–60. See also G. B. Richardson, *Information and Investment* (London: Oxford University Press, 1960), pp. 32 ff., where the same problems are discussed. "Oligopoly" refers to the phenomenon of an oligopolistic kind of interdependence here, not to competition among a few.

46 Hicks, *Value and Capital*, pp. 204 ff.

47 See ibid., p. 337, where Hicks objects to Samuelson's analysis of the mechanics of markets, contending (correctly, I think) that "for the understanding of the economic system we need something more, something which does refer back, in the last resort, to the behavior of people and the motives of their conduct;" and he also means, as far as I can see, the cognitive component (expectations).

assumed that there are price decisions under imperfect information; so market processes with positive feedback are possible, leading to larger deviations from equilibrium.[48] Thus, under the usual maximization assumptions, the factual state of information can lead to reactions causing cumulative processes. (Nota bene: the central problem here is not a problem of information *costs* but one of information *content*). Keynesian analysis seems to show that reactions of this kind are characteristic for complex market systems, rendered possible by the use of money and credit.

As mentioned above, the central problem of classical political economy was that of control in decentralized social systems (market systems), and the price mechanism was seen as a mechanism of control. In this view, two functions were assigned to *prices*—an *incentive* function and an *informative* function—and their adequate fulfillment was presupposed under conditions of free competition.[49] Now, the evasion of information problems in neoclassical thinking made the second of these functions disappear. Fulfillment of the information function is, however, one of the necessary conditions for an adequate fulfillment of the incentive function (i.e., both functions are closely connected). The real question, then, concerns the extent to which the actual price situation secures whatever information the actors need in order to discover the (alternative) positive or negative sanctions to be expected from present decisions. More generally, the question is how the horizon of expectations relevant for current decisions is influenced by price changes and other events. Individuals don't react to "data" known to the economist but react to situations interpreted by themselves.

Facts of this kind were used to overthrow the usual analysis of competition and its conception of equilibrium.[50] In the new approach, competition itself is seen as a process of acquisition and distribution of information, market partici-

---

48 Leijonhufvud, *Keynes and the Classics*, pp. 27–32, discusses the issue of deviations from equilibrium under the negative-feedback assumption and with the possibility of positive feedback.

49 Leijonhufvud, *Keynesian Economics*, p. 393; Albert, *Ökonomische Ideologie*, p. 109.

50 F. A. Hayek, "The Use of Knowledge in Society," in *Individualism and Economic Order* (Chicago: University of Chicago Press, 1948); Israel Kirzner, *Competition and Entrepreneurship* (Chicago: University of Chicago Press, 1973).

pants being continuously induced to revise their decisions. The cognitive aspects of the processes concerned are made a theoretically essential element of these events. Entrepreneurs are assigned the function of steering market processes so that they tend to a hypothetical state of equilibrium, defined in a new way.[51] Although this interpretation of market phenomena seems to be more realistic in many respects than the neoclassical one, one point may be a bit problematic. If we can assume that the reactions of market participants, in order to be sufficient to lead toward an equilibrium, have to be adequate in *kind, direction,* and *extent,* it is hardly plausible that entrepreneurs always (or in general) make decisions resulting in such reactions.[52] The question then arises, Under which circumstances can we expect that there are entrepreneurs reacting in an adequate way? And a further question may be lurking behind: How is it possible to explain market phenomena without explicitly taking account of the cognitive aspects of behavior in the relevant assumptions?

The "institutional revolution" in pure economics has undubitably rehabilitated one of the important ideas of the economic research program (see (5) in the earlier characterization of that program) and has emphasized the general significance of this approach for social science. But in one respect there remain serious problems. The psychological basis of the theory consists of individual utility functions compatible with a large range of need structures. For the explanation of actions, essentially all kinds of penalty-reward systems seem to be admitted. But in order to explain the processes concerned, in each case the specification of these utility functions has to be managed without theoretical assistance by using plausible considerations of all kinds. As long as one is able to assume the constancy of these functions, some interesting consequences can be derived,[53] but strictly

---

51 Kirzner, *Competition and Entrepreneurship,* pp. 72 ff.

52 Kirzner seems to assume this without further ado: "For me the changes the entrepreneur initiates are always toward the hypothetical state of equilibrium. . . ." Ibid., p. 73. Perhaps this is not meant to state a part of the definition of *entrepreneur* but to propose a hypothesis (liable to testing).

53 Thus it may not be justified to say that utility theory is without nomological content (because of the postulated convexity of indifference curves, or behavior-lines), but an empirical test of it would be very difficult because it presupposes the identification of the relevant utility functions or at least a determination of their constancy over time. See my "Zur Theorie der Konsumnachfrage," *Jahrbuch für Sozialwissenschaft* 16 (1965).

speaking that means to introduce an ad hoc assumption. And the problem of changes in the relevant need structures, under the influence of experiences, for example, seems to be unsolvable within the framework of the present theory.[54]

Needless to say, if one is interested in solving such problems, one needs a theory of behavior—one that does not confine itself to specifying preference structures in a general way but takes account of cognitive factors. Individual behavior is not simply determined by an "objective" situation, to be constructed without regard to individual possibilities of perception.[55] In this respect, it is not uninteresting that modern psychological theories of behavior partly operate with ideas quite similar to those of Bentham,[56] which were developed into a "logic of choice" in the neoclassical phase. The tendency in this phase to dissociate economics from psychological investigations depended a great deal on the conviction that the postulated general state of equilibrium could be determined by recourse to certain formal properties of the preference structures. This attempt to solve the problem of explaining market phenomena has led into a blind alley, however, and now, when the fiction of an institutional vacuum is vanishing, contentment with the cognitive and motivational deficit in economics will have to yield as well.[57] For example, the occurrence of a competi-

---

54 See Nicholas Georgescu-Roegen, "The Theory of Choice and the Constancy of Economic Laws," *Quarterly Journal of Economics* 64 (1950); idem, "Choice, Expectations, and Measurement," ibid. 68 (1954).

55 Therefore, Kirzner's attitude toward psychology (the usual neoclassical attitude) seems a bit doubtful. See Kirzner, *Competition and Entrepreneurship*, p. 73: "For the purposes of the economist it is not necessary to explore the psychology of the learning process, which is the result of market experiences.... But it is necessary to build formally into our theory the insight that such learning processes can be relied upon." The question that may arise is, under what conditions we may *rely* on such processes.

56 Atkinson, *Introduction to Motivation;* idem, "Change of Activity," in *Human Action*, ed. Theodore Mischel (New York: Academic Press, 1969).

57 Especially for the solution of problems of economic development, for instance, the relevance of research on achievement motivation should not be underrated. Investigations of this kind show that certain conjectures of Schumpeter on the connection of success motivation and entrepreneurs' striving for profit seem to be adequate in cases where need for achievement is high. Schumpeter, *Theorie der wirtschaftlichen Entwicklung* 5th ed. (Berlin: Duncker & Humbolt, 1926), pp. 138–39 (English ed., *Theory of Economic Development* (Cambridge, Massachusetts: Harvard Economic Studies Series, 1934)); David C. McClelland, *The Achieving Society* (Princeton: Princeton University Press, 1961), pp. 233 ff. On the question of applying psychology in economic analysis, see Schumpeter, *Wirtschaftliche Entwicklung*, pp. 131 ff.

tive pressure, presupposed without argument in many investigations, may depend not only on *institutional* conditions but also on the existence of a reservoir of *persons* motivated in a particular way—persons prepared to interpret the institutional arrangements mentioned as incentive structures and able to make their decisions by means of adequate interpretations of the market situation.

The now-recognized role of information in behavior indicates that an adequate theory of human action—necessary for the solution of the problem of social control—must involve a realistic theory of *knowledge*.[58] Philosophically educated people may smile at this idea, because they "know" that "epistemology," the theory of knowledge, is not an empirical science but a part of philosophy—a discipline "above" the sciences. I don't like to quarrel with these people, but I do wish to emphasize that for *critical realism* (of the kind I have adopted) cognition is a real problem-solving activity and that even for the solution of epistemological problems a realistic analysis of this activity may be useful. If we accept *fallibilism* as a part of our philosophy it is because by doing so we take account of the real human condition in knowledge. I suppose that it would be very strange to forget this aspect of our situation when constructing a realistic theory of action.

If one compares psychological explanations of human behavior it is often very easy to identify epistemological elements stemming from different philosophical conceptions.[59] There are traditions of learning theory involving elements of the *passivist* epistemology of empiricism, with the tendency to analyze man as a reactive-inductivist animal. On the other hand, there are traditions—for example, the "Würzburg school," whose founder, the philosopher and psychologist Oswald Külpe (a critical realist), emphasized the importance of "set" for perception and cognition—that accentuate the role of autonomous factors and defend a more *activist* conception of man as a hypothetico-imaginative organism. In

58 The attempt to do justice to the problem of information by an excursion into epistemology is a quite unusual event; for an exception, see Knight, *Risk, Uncertainty, and Profit*, pp. 197 ff., where the problem of uncertainty is treated as a central problem of economics; see also G. L. S. Shackle, *Decision, Order, and Time in Human Affairs* (Cambridge: Cambridge University Press, 1961); idem, *Epistemics and Economics* (Cambridge: Cambridge University Press, 1972).

59 Theodore Mischel, "Scientific and Philosophic Psychology," in *Human Action*, ed. Mischel.

modern psychology the view seems to be gaining ground that the behavioral relevance of cognitive (and autonomous) factors has been largely underrated, just as in neoclassical economics. Even for the analysis of daily life it seems to be fruitful to take account of the fact that man is a "theoretical animal," an animal, fabricating, adopting, and using "theories" that are effective in action.[60] We are entitled to assume that the horizon of expectations (often mentioned in economic investigations), which is relevant for decisions of all kinds, is determined among other things by the theoretical views of the actors, as we always assume in methodological analyses of the problem of prediction.[61] There is no reason to start with totally different pictures of man in epistemology, psychology, and economics. In all these disciplines we are confronted with a fallible theoretical animal trying to solve problems in a situation characterized by scarcity and uncertainty.

Economics as a general paradigm for social science

We have seen that the economic research program, as described above, doesn't involve any restriction to particular social spheres, for example, a demarcable realm of "the economy." This fact has become clearer than before by the investigations of contemporary theoretical institutionalists. The problem of social control now comes into sight in full generality, a development intimated before in the discussion about the social order. One implication is that control systems previously ascribed to the realm of politics are to be investigated by applying the individualistic method connected with economic analysis.[62] This is, indeed, increas-

60 See J. M. Keynes, *General Theory*, pp. 383–84, and F. A. Hayek, "The 'Facts' of the Social Sciences," *Ethics* 54 (1943), for expressions of quite the same idea as the so-called Thomas Theorem of sociology: "If men define situations as real, they are real in their consequences." Robert K. Merton, "The Self-Fulfilling Prophecy," in *Social Theory and Social Structure*, revised ed. (Glencoe, Illinois: Free Press, 1957), p. 421.

61 This is the context in which the problem of self-fulfilling or self-destroying prophecies arises. Bertrand Russell, *German Social Democracy as a Lesson in Political Tactics* (1896). As far as I can see, the first theoretical analysis of this problem is to be found in Oskar Morgenstern, *Wirtschaftsprognose* (Vienna: Julius Springer, 1928). Later the problem was analyzed by Popper, Topitsch, Merton, Grunberg and Modiglianai, Simon, Buck, and others.

62 The view that a sociological analysis of a socialist economy would have to start with the actions of individuals (the types of functionaries) was already held by

ingly done. A fully developed economic theory has to incorporate a theory of the central political system of control—that is; a theory of the state (but not of the normative kind) or, if you like, a theory of socialism.[63] With such a move, the problem of *economic* order is extended to the general problem of *constitution*.[64] At the same time, we now have to accept without reservation an idea for a long time defended by Ludwig von Mises, namely, that economics is nothing but the theoretically most developed part of sociology.[65] The difference between theoretical economics and other social sciences consists, then, not in the diversity of their respective ranges of objects, but in the fact that the theoretical and methodological ideas of the economic tradition lead to a particular kind of problem analysis that is applicable to all these realms, although it is thus far unusual in the other social sciences.

The idea that the conceptual apparatus of economics predetermines the analysis of a particular realm—"the economy," in the usual sense—is due to a misinterpretation widely disseminated even among economists. One usually starts with the assumption that the task of economics is to analyze the production, distribution, and consumption of scarce goods and derives the consequence that it must be a discipline restricted in the above-mentioned way. But the *concept of a good* here to be considered is a very comprehensive one. It refers to all aspects of human life that can be evaluated with regard to a *decision* (a choice between alternative

---

Max Weber, *Wirtschaft und Gesellschaft* (English ed. of pt. 1, *The Theory of Social and Economic Organizations* (New York: Free Press, 1947)), 3d ed. (Tübingen: J. C. B. Mohr, 1947), p. 9.

63 If we accept Alchian's statement that "government is socialism, by definition." Armen A. Alchian and William R. Allen, *University Economics*, 3d ed. (Belmont, California: Wadsworth, 1972), p. 627. The influence of the state on the content of property rights is alone sufficient to show that a theory of the state is desirable for economics, as Eirik Furubotn and Svetozar Pejovich have argued. "Property Rights and Economic Theory," *Journal of Economic Literature* 10 (1972): 1140.

64 See F. A. Hayek, *The Constitution of Liberty* (Chicago: University of Chicago Press; London: Routledge & Kegan Paul, 1960); James M. Buchanan and Gordon Tullock, *The Calculus of Consent* (Ann Arbor: University of Michigan Press, 1962); Buchanan, *The Limits of Liberty* (Chicago: University of Chicago Press, 1975).

65 Ludwig von Mises, *Epistemological Problems of Economics* (originally published as *Grundprobleme der Nationalökonomie*, 1933) (Princeton: Princeton University Press, 1960); Alfred Bohnen, *Individualismus und Gesellschaftstheorie* (Tübingen: J. C. B. Mohr (Paul Siebeck), 1975).

courses of action). Analyzing the usual definitions of this concept in economics, one finds that at least two elements are involved: a *power* component and a *value* component. It refers to aspects of situations *evaluated* with regard to possibilities of action (e.g. the *power* to realize individual aims).[66] A person's endowment of scarce goods determines his possibilities of action (range of power), which are evaluated with regard to his aims. Of course, one has to take account of the chances of transformation, partly determined by the prevailing institutional arrangements, to give an adequate analysis of these possibilities. The existing legal order plays an important role in the determination of these individual ranges, by protecting some modes of behavior and by discouraging others with (negative) sanctions; so it is necessary to take account of it in the explanations concerned.

In view of the above, we have to admit that, if traditional economic concepts are used, for instance, to analyze certain interactions as exchanges of help and approval,[67] it is *not* problematic transfer of economic terminology to a "foreign" realm. On the contrary, it follows exactly the rules of economic language, for help and approval are scarce goods in every society and (like time[68]) must be rationed in some way. The persons involved might prefer to invest their time and energy in other kinds of behavior if they evaluated the situation differently. Theoretical economics analyzes all social phenomena from the viewpoint of scarcity, and we can admit that, because of the human condition (the general structure of situations in human life), this viewpoint is applicable everywhere in social life.[69] Social regulation of indi-

---

66 The power component is often differentiated, so that the individual's information about possibilities of using services is given special attention. See Menger, *Volkswirtschaftslehre,* 1:3; or Eugen von Böhm-Bawerk, "Rechte und Verhältnisse vom Standpunkte der volkswirtschaftlichen Guterlehre" (1881) in *Gesammelte Schriften,* ed. Franz X. Weiss (Vienna and Leipzig: Hölder-Pichler-Tempsky, 1924), pp. 18 ff. (In the latter work, the importance of rights for the concept of goods is also elucidated.) See also Richard von Strigl, *Die ökonomischen Kategorien und die Organisation der Wirtschaft* (Jena: Gustav Fischer, 1923), where a good is defined as a complex of alternative employment possibilities.

67 George C. Homans, *Social Behavior: Its Elementary Forms* (New York and Burlingame, California: Harcourt, Brace, & World, 1961).

68 Staffan B. Linder, *The Harried Leisure Class* (New York: Columbia University Press, 1970).

69 Indeed, the viewpoint is to be found in other disciplines referring to human actions. The "principle of the limit of actions" is introduced as the most simple law of

vidual behavior, and thus the course of social processes, depends to an important degree on the striving of all participants after scarce rewards. The classic had already emphasized that pecuniary rewards (so-called material incentives) are by no means the only ones effective in human behavior.[70] That economic thought has focused up to now mainly on pecuniary incentives is due, not to inherent limitations of this tradition, but to the importance of such factors for the functioning of complex modern societies and to the fact that the "measuring rod of money" seemed to make important aspects of social life accessible to measurement. The real difficulty for the further development of economics is the absence of an elaborated theory of behavior taking account of *all kinds* of rewards (and penalties) effective in human action and of the role of cognitive factors.

Rational Politics: Adam Smith contra Karl Marx

As mentioned above, it is a principle of rational problem-solving behavior to compare concrete, realizable alternatives if a decision is to be made. This principle is applicable to the problem of choice between theories in science, where criteria like explanatory power are relevant for this comparison. It is applicable in daily life, as economists have emphasized for a long time. But it is also applicable to problem solving in politics, especially in deciding on an adequate social order. In such decisions it is not interesting to compare alternatives of an ideal kind, which are not realizable; and it is equally uninteresting to compare the existing order with a utopian scheme, contrasting the ideal properties of the last with the weaknesses of the status quo. And it is extremely dangerous to project a utopian state into history as an allegedly necessary development, motivating people by this procedure to think that present achievements could not be endangered by dubious political measures.

---

sociology in Hans L. Zetterberg, *Social Theory and Social Practice* (New York: The Bedminster Press, 1962), p. 74. A similar assumption is stated in Atkinson, "Change in Activity," p. 108. For an analysis of the relation between scarcity and power, see Heinrich Popitz, Prozesse der Machtbildung (Tübingen: J. C. B. Mohr, 1968).

70 Smith, *Wealth of Nations*, pp. 89 ff.; John Stuart Mill, *Principles of Political Economy* (1848; reprint, New York: Augustus M. Kelley, 1965), p. 390.

What can *science,* including social science, contribute to such decisions? Depending on its nomological content, theoretical science can show real possibilities and can show that certain properties, which may be evaluated positively in relevant value systems, are really incompatible, thus making more realistic the analysis of the alternatives considered. In this way science can give real content to the idea of scarcity, which implies the often-neglected simple truth that not all good things are compatible in reality. Applied science (technology, including social technology) can at best show *possible courses of action* and—with regard to the problem of social order—*possible kinds of institutional arrangements* and their *general mode of functioning.* If a science of legislation is possible at all, it must at least contain a social technology of this kind. Going back two hundred years, we find a book which at that time was looked upon as an important contribution to the science of legislation—Adam Smith's *Wealth of Nations.*[71] It contained a rudimentary analysis of alternative social systems and of their comparative performance in terms of certain criteria.[72] Smith was not eager to formulate laws of development to predict the course of history in an absolute way, as Karl Marx tried to do later; that is, he did not insist on making historical prophecies. He preferred to show, on the basis of relevant laws, the comparative functioning of alternative social arrangements, thus to make possible a free and informed decision. This conception of science helping politics is, in my view, as acceptable today as it was two hundred years ago.[73] The role of rational argument in politics is not to attempt to demonstrate that one is in tune with the meaning of history —on the side of the victorious forces—but to attempt to exhibit in the clearest possible way the realizable alternatives and to show their strengths and weaknesses.

71 See Dugald Stewart, "An Account of the Life and Writings of Adam Smith, in *Works of Adam Smith,* ed. Stewart, vol. 5: 480–84.

72 This has been correctly emphasized by Rutledge Vining, *Economics in the United States of America* (Paris: UNESCO, 1956), p. 14.

73 See my *Trakat über rationale praxis,* Tübingen: J. C. B. Mohr, 1978.

Karl Brunner**

Milton Friedman in Our Time*

The story of the Nobel Prize in economics for 1976 has entered history. The reasons officially presented by the committee need not be repeated. I had the honor and pleasure of describing Milton Friedman's contributions to monetary theory, aggregative analysis, and statistical theory in *Science* at the time. They have been discussed by many others, and they are, in any case, so well known and so much in the mainstream of economics as to obviate further discussion at this time, in this place, and for this group.

The significance of the event is, however, not exhausted by the professional achievements listed and their public recognition. Our attention should probe beyond the normal rites of a Nobel Prize award with the usual reports and columns in the newspapers. Public and private comments revealed deep ambivalence in social science and expressed pervasive ambiguities among its practitioners. This ambivalence and ambiguity was reflected in "sophisticated reservations" discriminating between Friedman the scholar and Milton the ideologue. We should also note the mindless hate and thoughtless abuse directed at Friedman by groups promising salvation through political action. These phenomena

* Presented at the Luncheon Honoring the Nobel Laureate for 1976, Annual Meeting of the American Economic Association, December 29, 1977.

** The statement was prepared during a visit at the Hoover Institution. My discussions with Allan H. Meltzer and William Meckling shaped the statement and influenced its content. The disgruntled reader should still feel entitled, however, to hold the author responsible. Special acknowledgment inserted after the lecture: I wish to express my appreciation to the "demonstrators" outside the Grand Ballroom in the New York Hilton Hotel for the zeal exhibited in supplying confirming evidence for my argument.

surrounding the event deserve our serious attention. Their exploration may appear less professional than examination of inflation, unemployment, output gaps, and stimulus packages. Such a judgment would actually form an integral part of the very problem to be pondered. The attitudes and behavior noted above are social phenomena that challenge the intellectual pretension of social science. The reservations among professionals and the abuse from the "new churches" should be recognized as symptoms of fundamental social issues of our time: the struggle for assessable knowledge as a basis for judgment, and the survival of freedom. The importance of these issues justifies my exploration of neglected aspects associated with the Nobel Prize award made in 1976.

The year of the award was also the anniversary year of Adam Smith's great work. This coincidence determines the central theme of my argument. The *Wealth of Nations* offered a remarkable cognitive vision. The broad sweep of the book launched economics on the road to becoming *the* social science. A wide range of social phenomena was approached with a unifying analysis. It was the perception of man introduced in the writings of the Scottish philosophers that provided coherence and structure to such a broad examination of social arrangements. This perception offers an understanding of man that contrasts with the Christian tradition in philosophy and theology. The Christian tradition, expressed by Christian theology and Marxian doctrine, offers two conflicting but essentially metaphysical views of man that pervasively shape our political thinking. Man is seen either as basically evil, requiring constraints or properly conceived authoritarian institutions imposing suitable guidance, or as inherently good and noble, deserving liberation from institutions repressing his "natural humanity".

The Scottish philosophers discarded this tradition and presented in basic outline a historical view of man's fundamental pattern of behavior. Man emerges in their writing as a social organism resourcefully searching for opportunities and learning to cope with a changing environment according to *his* interests and understanding. It is a view that emphasizes that, though man adapts to change, the *basic* patterns of man's behavior are *not* changed by "social engineering". The *specific* behavior and adjustments, fostered by diverse institutions, are the result not of good or bad men but of the rational response of men to the institutions under which they live. The poor correlation generally observed between the intention of "social engineering" and its outcome is made intelligible by the work of Adam Smith and the Scottish philosophers.

Subtle ramifications of the Christian heritage permeate our political thinking and the vision of man advanced in the social sciences. This heritage influences sociopolitical views claiming the occurrence of radically different *basic* behavior under market and nonmarket institutions. A pervasively influential strand of the heritage claims in particular that market institutions obstruct the evolution of higher human values and corresponding attitudes. Man's inherent humanity can be liberated, on the other hand, by substituting appropriate political institutions for market arrangements.

The Scottish philosophers broke with this religious tradition, and Adam Smith's work opened the door to a social science. The underlying perception of man supplied coherent explanations of social phenomena without invoking a metaphysical penumbra of social entities. The subsequent development of economics formalized the basic human behavior envisioned by the Scottish philosophers but also substantially narrowed the vision of "economics". A new intellectual tradition evolved, and it legislated that social, political, and institutional phenomena remain beyond the scope of "economics". The social sciences thus encouraged views of man reflecting an eclectic institutional relativism imbued occasionally with residues of the metaphysical heritage. The prevalent attitude essentially rejected, and still seems to reject, the integrating program of the *Wealth of Nations.*

Milton Friedman challenged this attitude. His violation of professional consensus was hardly the result of a deliberate program. It evolved naturally from a determined cognitive approach to economic analysis. The challenge appeared most vividly in the context of innumerable discussions in class or among groups of colleagues and was also expressed by a persistent concern about policy in a wider and a narrower sense of the word. A recognition that assessable knowledge progresses with bold and imaginative extensions of analysis subsuming a broadening field of apparently unrelated phenomena under a unified framework naturally questioned the inherited social customs of the profession. There is nothing inherent in "economic analysis" that precludes its useful application to the widest range of social phenomena. Moreover, no useful alternative analysis had been developed for the range of social phenomena beyond "economics". Friedman's sense of relevance and his understanding of the potential usefulness of economic analysis led him to the view introduced by Adam Smith but abandoned or forgotten by the profession.

The cognitive vision embedded in Friedman's work collides with major intellectual positions and well-established customs of our time. It offers a rational alternative to the inherently metaphysical view of man propagated by socialist thought. It also offers an alternative interpretation of a broadly conceived social reality. Advocates of an essentially religious approach sense the danger posed by a serious commitment to assessable cognition. Their hate and virulence is naturally directed to the most widely known contemporary practitioners of Adam Smith's intellectual heritage. Friedman's intuitive grasp that economic analysis offers a meaningful approach to man's social experience unavoidably brings him face to face, under the circumstances, with hostile accusations of ideological distortions. A confinement to analytic problems with little bearing on social reality neither endangers major beliefs nor challenges prevailing attitudes of our time. But the ideological accusations made by advocates of socialist beliefs should be properly understood. The condemnation follows from an essentially Marxian interpretation of "ideology". The term refers, in the Marxian sense, to any view of social reality that is in conflict with Marxian thought. Alternative views are necessarily the product of a "false consciousness" shaped by the institutions and social conditions of capitalism. Beyond and outside the Marxian insights into the "laws of social reality" appears the realm of ideological products. The ideological character is determined relative to the obvious truth of Marxian beliefs. Rejection of the Truth and insistence on "ideological distortions of reality" obstructs the eschatological evolution of history and reflects a mind diseased by capitalist oppression. Virtue thus requires, in a sense well appreciated by the Grand Inquisitor, appropriate political action.

The conflict called ideological is not limited to differences with the socialist conception of the world. Members of our profession or the wider intelligentsia attribute to Friedman an "ideological dimension". But the socialist condemnation and the professional judgment have different sources and are based on different conceptions. The reservations occasionally voiced by members of academia express, I suspect, a subtle conditioning by accustomed professional practices. "Economics" seems confined by "ontological gods" to the study of markets and market transactions. Established professional practice legislates the division of the social sciences into various unrelated branches and the separation of practitioners into guilds. Forcefully imaginative and innovative application of economic analysis beyond the accustomed range and the resulting conflict with sociology, political science, behavioral psychology, or "history" create unease and uncomfortable doubts.

The problem arises with professional economists and within "professional economics". There prevailed, and still exists, an intellectual tradition denying the relevance of price theory to explain social reality. My personal observations suggest that even professional economists are sometimes shocked by determined application of price theory to observable phenomena *within* the traditional range of "economics". This unease is magnified when economic analysis is applied to sensitive social-political issues bearing on the fundamental aspects of human society. Many economists seem unwilling to recognize that the consequences of different institutions with respect to freedom and the patterns of human life can be subjected to analysis and evidence.

The prevailing attitudes are often revealed in discussions of public policy. Most discussions of "externalities" implicitly refuse to extend the hypothesis used in explanations of market transactions to human behavior occurring under nonmarket institutions. These institutions, it seems, are administered for the "public good" by men or women rarely, if ever, suffering the temptations of "self-realization". All externalities are under the circumstances a natural product of the market sector. Many economists habitually accept models of man derived from political theory or sociology, implicitly denying the vision of Adam Smith whenever they discuss the working of nonmarket institutions. It appears intellectually shocking and thus ideologically motivated to apply an essentially price-theoretical framework to "non-market behavior". A similar frame of mind is frequently observed in discussions of price-wage controls or stabilization policies. The approach to problems of stabilization policies seems occasionally influenced by the idea that agencies and bureaus of "government" will generally use financial policies essentially for purposes of economic stabilization. This idea is a natural expression of the sociological model of man. The alternative model, derived from the Scottish philosophers, emphasizes that financial policies essentially result as responses of politicians, bureaucrats, and blocs of voters to incentives built into the political institutions or political process. The association between financial policies and economic stabilization will remain somewhat haphazard under the circumstances.

These scholarly habits deny that economic theory is in a specific sense "institution free". Optimizing self-interest occurs pervasively, however, and does not depend on a particular set of institutions. Our historical knowledge offers little support for political and sociological views more or less implicitly denying the persistent occurrence of "optimizing self-realization" under any set of institutions. Smith's vision of a social science capable of analyzing the consequences of different institutional arrangements effectively guides us to use the principles of economics to predict the empirical patterns that will be observed under different arrangements.

The two sources of the ideological accusation, described above, share an implicit metaphysical restriction on analysis and social inquiry. The Marxian position follows from a view that truth is reached "on our way to Damascus". History touches you and "you understand". Once you understand that you "understand", you will understand that you understand with certainty, and there is no need for critical assessment. The very request for such an assessment is proof that the request emanates from a mind that fails to comprehend the inherent and self-revealing Truth. The notion of our cognitive adventure as a permanent struggle for assessable knowledge involving fallible views is alien to the Marxian position.

The perception of man that carries the superstructure of

Marxian views cannot be reconciled with two central themes in our reach for knowledge. It cannot accept that knowledge results from groping search by individuals pursuing *their* interests and evaluating options according to *their* views irrespective of social entities and the "historical laws of social motion". Knowledge remains essentially human and is not the consequence of Society or History mediated via an amorphous human vehicle shaped by Society. Neither can this perception accept the inherent fallibility of knowledge, a fallibility ineradicably embedded in our human endeavor irrespective of social categories and historical entities. The Marxian world establishment clearly recognized the danger threatening the basic architecture of its dogmas from a cognitive view stressing human fallibility and the occurrence of optimizing self-interest independent of specific social conditions. Such recognition is revealed by the violent attention devoted to "critical rationalism" in philosophy or by sociobiology in the social sciences.

An "ontological decision" defying critical assessment also enters the academic theme. The decision legislates forever the appropriate fields and guilds of the social sciences. Statements violating such "ontological legislation" are naturally suspect and liable to indictment as "ideological". It follows that the cognitive pretension of any "ideological curse" depends on a metaphysical judgment bearing on the nature of knowledge and the world.

The rejection of more or less implicit metaphysical regulations opens avenues for exploration in the social sciences. A forceful attention to social and political conditions, or a searching examination of broad institutions, is not, per se, an ideological endeavor. An imaginative examination of social issues violating the accustomed attitudes of a profession or the consensus of major groups does not convey, per se, an "ideological stance". Neither is the determined and skillful use of price theory in explanations of social (or "sociological") problems an ideological experience. The substantive merits of the statements advanced in all these cases do not depend on the "ideological curse". The branding of such statements as ideologically suspect, and therefore intellectually obnoxious, on grounds of their content can only be justified in terms of an insupportable but ultimately religious commitment.

The ideological character is determined neither by the relation of specific views, beliefs, hypotheses, or theories to the Marxian vision nor by the proper relation between subject matter and professional guilds. The ideological character does not attach to views and beliefs; it attaches to attitudes associated with views and beliefs. An ideological attitude refuses to reconsider or to reexamine. It refuses to admit potential fallibility and refuses to bow eventually to evidence. An ideological attitude is indulged whenever one refuses to specify any conditions or any observations that could cast doubt on the views advanced. Ideological attitudes may also be revealed by a determined "goropizing"—that is, by systematic efforts to adjust initial beliefs, after the fact, to new observations. Ideological lapses can be suffered by any man and are suffered by all men. Intellectual activities do not proceed in a social vacuum. We are enmeshed in a political context and experience temptations and incentives of various sorts. Since every man holds unexamined beliefs and is therefore prone to ideological lapses, the crucial issue becomes, How frequently do we fail and how serious are the occasions of failure? And a social scientist may also ponder the social arrangements that influence the frequency and weight of lapses.

The occurrence of ideological lapses offers no support for the media fallacy whereby all conflicts between views bearing on social-political matters are interpreted as reflections of clashing ideological positions. My comments on this delicate issue should not be misunderstood. They do not deny the relevant occurrence of value judgments. But I do wish to warn that reliance on the media fallacy occurs more frequently with bad analysis or the unwillingness to recognize the role of searching cognitive efforts. The retreat to differences between value judgments justifies an incomplete or failing analytical examination. Value judgments are indeed important, and I urge careful attention to their nature and role and most particularly to the *appropriate level* at which they enter the argument. But I also caution, emphatically, against the temptation pervading the intelligentsia to substitute value judgments for potential analysis and evidence.

Numerous examples could be adduced to demonstrate the misconstrual of substantive conflict implicitly involving alternative empirical hypotheses as simple matters of differences in value judgments. Subtle incentives encourage such dispositions among the media, but the custom also intrudes into professional discussions. Many arguments present the choice between inflation and unemployment as a clash between "Republican values" and "Democratic values" attaching different weights to inflation and unemployment. This characterization only makes sense relative to a specific class of empirical hypotheses—primarily, a traditional Phillips-relation. It makes no sense relative to an alternative class of hypotheses emphasizing the role of learning and adjustments of expectations to policy experiences. The relevant value judgments assume, under the alternative case, a very different form. The value judgments cannot be confined to trade-offs between contemporaneous unemployment and inflation. They include trade-offs between unemployment and inflation over time. The alternative analysis implies, in particular, that current trade-offs favoring lower unemployment produce both larger unemployment and inflation in the future. The appropriate value judgments must consider the trade-off between current and subsequent unemployment and inflation rates. The value judgments are also affected by the proper analysis of the cost of inflationary and anti-inflationary policies. My remarks are not concerned with the relative status of the alternative substantive views. They intend to emphasize that substantive issues of considerable importance are frequently obfuscated in public discussion by inappropriate value judgments.

Another illustration of a serious misconstrual can be found in discussions of Friedman's essay on methodology. This essay examined a well-established procedure generally used in the literature. The procedure evaluates the acceptability of statements on the basis of the "realism of their assumptions". It should be recognized here that Friedman's intuition, independent of the nature of the argument developed, was quite correct in this matter. Any careful logical analysis of the structure of sentences occurring as "assumptions" or composing theories or hypotheses conclusively establishes that it is logically impossible to derive truth values of hypotheses or theories from truth values of "assumptions". But the required logical analysis of sentences was usually omitted. In the absence of any appropriate analysis, the road was open to misconstruing Friedman's correct logical intuition as an ideological ploy.

The last illustration refers to the dispute about fine tuning and activism in policy. The problem is usually described in ideological terms and interpreted as a conflict between ideological positions. This description again reflects an intellectual failure to penetrate beyond the characterizations dominating the intelligentsia market. The conflict about activist policies primarily expresses contrasting substantive views that bear on the state of our knowledge and the working of policy institutions. Proponents of activism argue more or less implicitly that we (or they) possess sufficiently reliable knowledge about quantitative details of the economic structure, invariant under shifting policies, to justify comparatively fine adjustments in financial policies. They also maintain that policy institutions operate, at least on a first approximation, to maximize social welfare. These claims involve matters of fact about the world, and both are rejected as false by the critics of activist proposals. It would be difficult to deny that value judgments do not enter the argument at some level, but the ideological characterization of the discussion seriously distorts the substantive nature of the underlying issue.

The controversies swirling around Milton Friedman reflect the significance of the issues. They also reflect the state of economics and the social sciences as represented by the prevalent attitudes of practitioners. But controversy is a social transaction with at least two participants. Its occurrence, even when stirred by a single source, does not establish the ideological character of this source. I have no intention of claiming that Milton Friedman never has or never will fall from "cognitive grace". My assurance would be irrelevant and beside the point. But I do maintain that Milton Friedman has powerfully contributed to a broad vision of economics and a sharper appreciation that economics is not about contrived problems but about the world we live in. We should understand that his intellectual thrust is directed toward the very center of contemporary confrontation. This thrust is, moreover, guided by scientific criteria that submit his ideas and the work of all others to searching examination in a competitive struggle for assessable knowledge. Friedman's work addresses fundamentally the institutions of an open society and the survival of freedom and human dignity. So we do encounter ultimate values. And our queries, encouraged by Friedman's example, probe the nature of the institutions protecting these values. Some rationally inspired crusading in this matter seems not quite inappropriate in our time and in this place.

P.T. Bauer

Development Economics: Intellectual Barbarism*

Ortega y Gasset once defined barbarism as "the absence of standards to which appeal can be made."[1] Barbarism in the sense of an absence of intellectual standards characterizes much of contemporary development economics and, to a lesser extent, other branches of economics. Economists holding senior academic positions confuse free goods and scarce resources, systematically ignore the price-dependence of supply and demand, or neglect patent and pertinent evidence. Many of these transgressions exhibit a disregard of elementary canons of logic or an inconsistency with basic tenets of economics.

I shall examine these shortcomings primarily with reference to development economics. Influences at work in other branches of economics are thrown into relief in this field, which makes it useful to focus on it, by analogy with Tocqueville's observation that the defects of the old French monarchy could be best discerned in French Canada, where they stood out most clearly.

---

* Presented at the First Annual Interlaken Seminar on Analysis and Ideology, Switzerland, June, 1974. A similar paper appears in *Schweizerische Zeitschrift für Volkswirtschaft und Statistik*, III 1975: 297–316.

1 José Ortega y Gasset, *The Revolt of the Masses* (London: George Allen and Unwin, 1932), p. 79.

The Vicious Circle, the Widening Gap, and Related Notions

In the 1950s when contemporary development economics got under way, the notion of the vicious circle of poverty was prominent in discussions of the position and prospects of less-developed countries (ldc's). Indeed, in both academic and popular publications this was among the most widely canvassed ideas; mention of underdeveloped or less-developed countries was sufficient to evoke the idea of the vicious circle.

According to the notion of the vicious circle of poverty and stagnation, poverty itself sets up almost insurmountable obstacles to its own conquest. Thus Professor Samuelson wrote in an early edition of his celebrated textbook:

> They [the backward nations] cannot get their head above water because their production is so low that they can spare nothing for capital formation by which their standard of living could be raised.[2]

Another convenient example comes from MIT's Center for International Studies.

> ...the general scarcity relative to population of nearly all resources creates a self-perpetuating vicious circle of poverty. Additional capital is necessary to increase output, but poverty itself makes it impossible to carry out the required saving and investment by a voluntary reduction in consumption.[3]

The reference to a voluntary reduction in consumption in this passage is notable because the distinction between voluntary and compulsory conduct is irrelevant if it is the general scarcity of resources that is the operative obstacle to the increase in output.

If the notion of a generally operative vicious circle of poverty were valid, no individual group, community, or society could have risen from poverty to prosperity. The world began in a very primitive state and has received no resources from outside; the development that has taken place, one way or the other, would have been impossible if poverty necessarily implied stagnation.

---

2 Paul A. Samuelson, *Economics: An Introductory Analysis*, 2d ed. (New York: McGraw-Hill, 1951), p. 49.

3 *Study Submitted by the Center for International Studies of the Massachusetts Institute of Technology to the State Committee Investigating the Operation of Foreign Aid* (Washington, D.C.: Government Printing Office, 1957), p. 37.

The vicious circle is still encountered in discussions on development. But since the mid-1960s it has come to be overshadowed by assertions about the wide and widening gap between the West and the ldc's. Thus, according to the celebrated Pearson Report,

> The widening gap between the developed and developing countries has become a central issue of our time.[4]

Again, according to the 1974 UN Declaration on the Establishment of a New Economic Order,

> The gap between the developed and the developing countries continues to widen in a system which was established at a time when most of the developing countries did not even exist as independent States and which perpetuates inequality.

The notions of the vicious circle and the widening gap are related. If the thesis of a generally operative vicious circle of poverty and stagnation were valid, both the absolute and the proportionate differences in incomes between rich and poor countries would necessarily widen. But no such simple inference is possible once it is seen that the notion of the vicious circle is invalid. Although the shortcomings of the idea of the gap as a worthwhile basis for discussion or policy are not so immediately obvious as are those of the vicious circle, they are nevertheless radical, as is evident from an examination of the idea.

The size of the much-canvassed gap between rich and poor countries depends on where one places the line dividing the two global categories. Because there is no discontinuity in international incomes, the line of distinction, and therefore the size of the gap, is arbitrary. The latter can be changed arbitrarily by moving the place of the line dividing rich and poor countries.

It is often obscure whether the gap refers to the ratio of average income in the West to average income in the Third World or whether it refers to the absolute magnitude of the difference between the two averages. The term *gap* would suggest the latter. On the other hand, the general context and tenor of the discussions often suggest that it is the ratio

---

4 *Partners in Development: Report of the (Pearson) Commission on International Development* (New York: Frederick Praeger, 1969), p. 3. The signatories of the report included full professors of economics from the United States, Japan, and Germany and the vice-chancellor of a major British university.

that is being considered. The distinction is important because the two measures change at different rates and often move in opposite directions. This elementary but fundamental point is often neglected.

The relative economic position of countries changes in the course of history. It has changed even in relatively recent history, as is evidenced, for instance, by Germany, Japan, and Britain. Countries have been promoted from the less-developed to the developed category (for example, Japan and Italy). Reclassification affects both the composition of the two categories of countries and the size of the gap.

It is inappropriate to lump together and average the incomes, living standards, and rates of growth of the countries of the Third World. Though most Third World countries are poor, this does not make them the same. The Third World is a huge and diverse aggregate that covers most of the globe and encompasses societies ranging from many millions of aborigines to many millions of inhabitants of huge cities. The aggregation and averaging of such a huge and profoundly diverse collectivity is of little meaning. There are pronounced differences in incomes and rates of material progress among Third World countries; indeed, these differences may be wider than they are in the West. Many Third World countries have in recent decades grown much faster than many Western countries, including the United States and Britain, so that the ratio between per capita incomes in these Western countries and in the faster-growing Third World countries has declined.

These basic weaknesses in the concept of the gap between the West and the Third World are compounded by major conceptual errors involved in income comparisons between widely different societies. For instance, although national income statistics and comparisons are staples of the advocacy of international wealth transfers, they are not adjusted for differences in age composition. The proportion of children is much larger in the Third World than in the West. The incomes of children are usually lower than those of adults. The conventional comparisons confuse differences in income and differences in age, and this obscures the interpretation of the evidence.

The biases and errors in international income comparisons involving ldc's are far wider than is usually recognized. Professor Dan Usher has shown that they often amount to several hundred percent.[5] Yet academic and official publications purport to estimate per capita incomes for Third World countries, or even for the entire Third World, to the nearest dollar. The errors and biases do not remain constant over time, for such reasons as changes in age composition or in the relative importance of subsistence agriculture.

Discussions of the gap and, generally, of international income differences usually ignore the implications of changes in mortality. In recent decades mortality in the Third World has declined much faster than in the West. Over the last 25 years or so, both the absolute and the relative differences in life expectation between the two aggregates have narrowed substantially. Thus this gap, which is relatively unambiguous, has not widened but narrowed. At the same time, the higher survival rate in the Third World has adversely affected conventionally measured per capita incomes by increasing the proportion of children and of old people in the Third World. This change reflects an improvement and not a deterioration: most people like to survive and see their children do so.

International income differences and changes such as those encapsulated in the gap cannot be discussed sensibly on the basis of statistics without examining the background. Thus, in many ldc's, government policies have reduced incomes in their own countries and thereby widened the income differences between prosperous countries and their own countries. For instance, the explusion of ethnic minorities has directly reduced per capita incomes in many ldc's and thereby promptly widened the income differences between the West and these countries.

This is an incomplete list of reasons why the familiar references to the wide and widening gap cannot serve as a basis for sensible discussion, much less as a worthwhile basis for policy.

Another major theme of the current development literature is the alleged damage inflicted on ldc's by international economic intercourse, especially by commercial relations with the West. According to this literature, a declining ldc

5 Dan Usher, *The Price Mechanism and the Meaning of National Income Statistics* (Oxford: Oxford University Press, 1968).

share in world trade and unfavorable and persistently deteriorating terms of trade of ldc's are evidence of the unfavorable or even damaging character of the international economic relations of ldc's.

In fact, external economic contacts do not harm but benefit the peoples of ldc's by widening their range of opportunities—notably, by opening up markets for their products and by providing a large and varied volume of imports. They also act as channels for skills and capital, as well as for new ideas, methods, and crops. The most advanced groups and sectors in ldc's are those with the most extensive external contacts, and the most backward are those with the fewest or no such contacts.

Some of the transgressions in this general area of discussion are extremely crude. Thus, ostensibly serious publications instance the decline of the volume of exports from one country as evidence of a decline in the world demand for that product, thereby confusing the quantity supplied from one source with the total demand for the product. Similarly, it is often suggested that particular ldc's are harmed by a low price elasticity of demand for their exports, as this is supposed to make it difficult to expand their export earnings. But since exports from one country are usually a small proportion of world supplies (especially long-term supplies, after allowing for changes in capacity), the price elasticity of demand for these exports is unlikely to be low. Even if this price elasticity *were* low for the exports from a country or group of countries, this could benefit rather than damage the exporters, since they could then both increase their earnings and save resources by imposing or raising export duties. These self-contradictions are often compounded in publications that complain simultaneously about the damage to ldc's from the development of substitutes for their exports and the damage from a low price elasticity of demand for them. The contradiction should be evident: the presence of substitutes increases the price elasticity of demand.

Many of the statistics in support of allegations of unfavorable external developments are plainly manipulated by such devices as omission of countries, commodities, or commodity groups or by changing the base period of the comparisons, always to emphasize alleged externally caused problems of the less-developed world. Thus, petroleum and petroleum products are often excluded from these discussions, even though these are by far the most important exports of ldc's, many times more important than any other commodity.

The concepts of unfavorable or deteriorating terms of trade are meaningless except in relation to a base period. In discussions on the terms of trade, the base periods are often readily shifted to omit those periods over which the terms of trade of ldc's have improved greatly—for instance, by substituting the early 1950s, the years of the Korean or post-Korean boom, for certain earlier periods. All this is apart from the senselessness of aggregating large numbers of countries, whose external trade differs radically, whose terms of trade move very differently, and in whose economic life the importance of foreign trade differs greatly. It is just worth noting, however, that insofar as such exercises have any meaning, the commodity terms of trade of most ldc's have been much more favorable since the Second World War than in earlier times, and that the factoral terms of trade are almost certainly much more favorable than ever before. Moreover, the volume of their external trade has expanded vastly in recent decades. Thus the familiar allegations about the unfavorable terms of trade of the Third World are at best misleading and more often the opposite of the truth.

A variant of the notion of external responsibility for Third World poverty is the familiar idea in academic, official, or popular discussion that the development of poor countries necessarily entails unfavorable balance-of-payments problems. This is a recurrent theme of Professor Myrdal's writings. In one of his major books he wrote that "there must be something wrong with an underdeveloped country which does not have foreign exchange difficulties."[6] This is not so. No balance-of-payments difficulties were experienced in the early history of the advanced countries or during the rapid progress of many ldc's in the last hundred years. Conversely, many rich countries frequently experience such difficulties. Persistent balance-of-payments problems have nothing to do either with poverty or with material progress. They are inevitable if the government of a country, whether

6 Gunnar Myrdal, *An International Economy* (London: Routledge and Kegan Paul, 1956), p. 270.

rich or poor, advancing or stagnating, pursues an inflationary policy while attempting to maintain overvalued exchange rates.

The insubstantial arguments and notions reviewed in this section are also misleading on a less obvious level in that they divert attention from the personal, cultural, social, and political determinants of economic achievement and development.

Economics without Prices and Costs

Lay discussions of economic matters habitually treat an activity or its output as if it were an equivalent addition to total output, income, or welfare, regardless of the alternative use of resources—that is, of cost. This practice has in recent years crept into apparently technical literature with increasing frequency, especially in development economics, where it is almost standard in publications on state-sponsored industries or trading corporations.

In the development and planning literature, the activities of state-sponsored industries, trading corporations, or so-called development banks are commonly regarded, without examination of the provenance of the resources, as somehow representing a net contribution to activity and development. Development expenditure or investment expenditure is also frequently treated without considering either the alternative use of resources or the social and political repercussions of the collection of the funds. Some years ago several full professors of economics at a leading American university seriously proposed that the United States should undertake to supply all the money capital that could be used productively, in the sense of increasing money incomes, in any ldc.[7] This is perhaps a limiting case of the treatment of a scarce resource as a free good.

---

7 Max F. Millikan and Walt W. Rostow, *A Proposal* (New York: Harper 1957), where the authors seriously propose that, if per capita incomes in an ldc rise by between 1 and 2 percent per annum for five years, that country can be assumed to be on the point of takeoff (whatever that means) and should receive as much foreign aid as it can absorb—that is, in practice, unlimited amounts. This proposal thus treats a scarce resource as if it were a free good. Moreover, it advocates most far-reaching policies on the basis of estimates of changes in per capita incomes in ldc's of 1 or 2 percent when in fact such statistics are subject to margins of errors of several hundred percent. The notion that changes in per capita incomes in these countries can be assessed within 1 percent reveals total unfamiliarity with conditions there.

Recognition of supply and demand as functions of prices, costs, and incomes rather than as fixed physical quantities should be the hallmark of the economist. Yet ostensibly technical publications often ignore this simple consideration, in contexts in which this is inadmissible. Neglect of opportunity cost and disregard of supply and demand as functional relationships obliterate the difference between technical and lay discussions.

Such unwarranted disregard of the effects of prices was conspicuous in the protracted discussions in the 1950s and '60s, in the *Economic Journal* and elsewhere, on the operations of the state export monopolies of British West Africa. Since the Second World War, all major export crops of British West Africa have been in the hands of state buying monopolies that have withheld from producers a large part of market prices. The effects of this underpayment on output and exports were ignored or even denied by supporters of these monopolies, both in journal articles and in such apparently authoritative publications as the World Bank report on Nigeria.[8] (Similarly, the effects of consumption taxes on demand have often been ignored in the literature, which often implicitly assumes a zero elasticity of demand

---

It is of some interest that Professor Paul Rosenstein-Rodan, who endorsed the Millikan-Rostow proposal (with which, indeed, he was closely associated), wrote in a widely publicized paper that one of the many vicious circles afflicting ldc's was a lack of qualified economists in development planning. "Programming in Theory and in National Practice," mimeographed (Cambridge, Massachusetts: MIT, Center for International Studies, 1955).

8 International Bank for Reconstruction and Development, *The Economic Development of Nigeria* (Baltimore: Johns Hopkins Press, 1955). The prospects of Nigerian agriculture were a main theme of the report, which reviewed a long list of factors affecting production—including, for instance, agricultural services, water supply, and plant diseases. The price received by farmers was not mentioned in the report's list of determinants of agricultural output even though this was especially pertinent in the context, both because in Nigeria producer prices were prescribed by the official export monopolies and because the substantial costs of production and transport of export crops ensured that supply must be affected by producer prices.

The report of the Bank mission comprised a main report and 21 technical reports, including one on the operation of the state export monopolies. The personnel of the mission included several economists; the chief economist of the mission subsequently became director of the World Bank's Economic Development Institute, established for the training of economists from ldc's.

There are many such instances in reports commissioned by governments and international organizations. A set of specific examples will be found in an exchange between Dr. John H. Adler and myself in the *Journal of Political Economy*, October 1956.

without making this clear. The World Bank report on Nigeria is again one of many examples.)

These various lapses are sometimes rationalized, usually ex post, by reference to alleged rigidities or absence of economic motivations or such evident irrelevancies as the absence of perfect competition. All these rationalizations usually disregard costs and the fact that incomes are limited; they are also inconsistent with easily available evidence, including evidence of the common practice of subsidizing commodities, the production of which governments wish to encourage.

While the lapses noted in this section may be most frequent in development economics, they can be found also in other branches of economics, especially Soviet economics, labor economics, and even in mainstream economics. A conspicuous example is provided by discussions of the balance of payments without reference to domestic prices, incomes, exchange rates, or monetary and fiscal policies, such as the discussion in the 1940s and '50s of the dollar shortage and of the likelihood or even inevitability of its persistence. Many economists, including leading price theorists, treated this matter without reference to these variables. And it was the discussion of the alleged dollar scarcity that initiated the notion of a persistent shortage of foreign exchange allegedly afflicting ldc's.[9]

Ideas and Policies

The ideas examined so far are often found in contexts that appear to be analytical or descriptive; so the political thrust of the ideas, though often evident, is only implicit. In certain other widely publicized notions, the policy proposals are explicit.

One major theme of contemporary development literature is that comprehensive planning or central planning, in the sense of close state control of economic activity outside of subsistence production, is indispensable for development. For instance, Professor Myrdal wrote:

> Now, what amounts to a sort of superplanning *has* to be staged by underdeveloped countries with weak political and ad-

9 See P. T. Bauer and A. A. Walters, "Economists and the Dollar Problem," *Lloyds Bank Review*, April 1975.

> ministrative apparatuses and a largely illiterate and apathetic citizenry. But *the alternative to making the heroic attempt is continued acquiescence in economic and cultural stagnation or regression which is politically impossible in the world today;* and this is, of course, the explanation why grand scale national is at present the goal in underdeveloped countries all over the globe and why this policy line is unanimously endorsed by governments and experts in the advanced countries.[10]

Central planning is unquestionably *not* indispensable for development, however, and no amount of italicization will justify Myrdal's statement.

Professor Kitamura of Tokyo University expressed the same opinion more briefly, but just as emphatically.

> Only planned economic development can hope to achieve a rate of growth that is politically acceptable and capable of commanding popular enthusiasm and support.[11]

Professor Kitamura's assertion is especially paradoxical since his country made rapid progress *without* this policy. Evidence is irrelevant, however, to an article of faith. The same article of faith underlies the many academic publications, especially in the United States, which urge that formal comprehensive planning by aid-recipient governments should be a condition of foreign aid.

There is no empirical or logical basis for the assertion that comprehensive planning is necessary for material progress. It played no part either in the development of the now highly developed countries or in the substantial progress of many ldc's that have advanced rapidly since the end of the nineteenth century. Nor is this surprising. Central or comprehensive planning does not augment resources. It only concentrates power, and by doing so it creates power. In a decentralized system of decision making there are no such positions of power as are created by comprehensive planning. The resources employed by the planners come from other public or private uses. It is certainly not clear why the overriding of the decisions of private producers and consumers should increase the flow of income, much less the

10 Gunnar Myrdal, *Development and Underdevelopment* (Cairo: National Bank of Egypt, 1956), pp. 63, 65 (italics in the original).

11 H. Kitamura, "Foreign Trade Problems in Planned Economic Development," in *Economic Development with Special Reference to East Asia,* ed. Kenneth Berril (London: Macmillan and Co., 1964), p. 202.

flow of goods and services desired by consumers, which make up the standard of living.

The axiom that comprehensive planning is indispensable for development has often been adduced as a basis or a rationalization of economic policy in many ldc's, usually in support of the imposition of close state controls, which have become the rule rather than the exception in ldc's since the 1950s.

Many of the formal plans were modeled on the Soviet Five-Year Plan. Its principal architect, the late Professor P. C. Mahalanobis, wrote in the keynote document that preceded the Second Five-Year Plan:

> In the long run, the rate of industrialisation and the growth of national economy would depend on the increasing production of coal, electricity, iron and steel, heavy machinery, heavy chemicals, and the heavy industries generally which would increase the capacity for capital formation. . . . The heavy industries must, therefore, be expanded with all possible speed.[12]

These became the priorities of Indian planning.

> The expansion of the iron and steel industry has obviously the highest priority since, more than any other industrial product, the levels of production in these materials determine the tempo of progress of the economy as a whole. . . . Heavy engineering industries are a natural corollary of iron and steel works. The high priority accorded to them arises both on this account and from the fact that they will provide from within the country a wide range of industrial machinery and capital equipment, such as locomotives for railways and power plants for the generation of electricity. . . . In this context the creation of basic facilities such as the establishment of heavy foundries, forges and structural shops is absolutely necessary.[13]

The Soviet inspiration is evident. It is not true that economic development or the growth of industry or the rate of capital formation depends in any way on the prior development of specific types of heavy industry. These passages do not pay even lip service to living standards, consumer demand, or cost of production.

---

12 P. C. Mahalanobis, "Draft Plan Frame for the Second Five-Year Plan." In *Papers Relating to the Second Five-Year Plan* (Delhi: Government of India Planning Commission, 1955), p. 43.

13 *Second Five-Year Plan* (Delhi: Government of India Planning Commission, 1956), p. 394.

Professor John P. Lewis—former director of the United States Agency for International Development in India, for 15 years distinguished service professor of economics at Indiana University, and subsequently dean of the Woodrow Wilson School at Princeton—wrote in a book on Indian development policy:

> It has been decided in India that it is the duty of government —and it cannot be delegated—to create and maintain that "growth perspective" which, Albert Hirschman has rightly insisted, is the one sine qua non for successful economic development.
>
> Outside supporters of the Indian development process who refuse to accept this proposition well-nigh disqualify themselves from the outset.[14]

The first part of this statement is obviously invalid. The maintenance by the government of a growth perspective (whatever that means) cannot possibly be the only condition of successful economic development. The second part simply recognizes that those who wish to participate in political decisions may have to accept nonsensical statements.

Marxist-Leninist Influences

Marxist or Marxist-Leninist influence is discernible in some of the ideas and arguments noted in the preceding sections. This influence is pronounced and perhaps even pervasive in contemporary development economics. It is evident in many specific notions, proposals, and simple transgressions in the literature, including publications by authors who are not Marxists or who disclaim any influence by Marxism-Leninism. I shall quote two prominent Marxist Leninist authors whose remarks throw into sharp relief widely expressed interdevelopment literature, but usually in more muted form.[15]

14 *Quiet Crisis in India* (Washington, D.C.: Brookings Institution, 1962), p. 28.

15 I shall quote from academic authors rather than from politicians or political writers, since my primary concern in this essay is with the state of development economics. It is notable, however, that many Marxist-Leninist Third World politicians are widely respected by Western academics and often quoted by them. For instance, the late Dr. Nkrumah was widely respected and often quoted in the West. At least one of his books was published by Heinemann Educational Books. Some characteristic passages from the books of this respected thinker are reproduced in my *Dissent on Development* (Cambridge, Mass.: Harvard University Press, 1972), pp. 151, 157, 162.

Paul A. Baran, a prominent Marxist-Leninist, was full professor of economics at Stanford University. He contributed the article on economic development to the American Economic Association's *Survey of Contemporary Economics*. His book *The Political Economy of Growth*, from which I shall quote some representative passages, is a widely used university textbook. According to Baran, the backwardness of ldc's is due to capitalism.

> It is in the underdeveloped world that the central, overriding fact of our epoch becomes manifest to the naked eye: the capitalist system, once a mighty engine of economic development, has turned into a no less formidable hurdle to human advancement....[In the underdeveloped world] the difference is between abysmal squalor and decent existence, between the misery of hopelessness and the exhilaration of progress, between life and death for hundreds of millions of people. ...socialist transformation of the advanced west would not only open to its own peoples the road to unprecedented economic, social and cultural progress, it would at the same time enable the peoples of the underdeveloped countries to overcome rapidly their present condition of poverty and stagnation.
>
> To the deadweight of stagnation characteristic of pre-industrial society was added the entire restrictive impact of monopoly capitalism. The economic surplus appropriated in lavish amounts by monopolistic concerns in backward countries is not employed for productive purposes. It is neither plowed back into their own enterprises, nor does it serve to develop others.[16]

These observations are refuted by the rapid progress of many ldc's, especially in Southeast Asia, West Africa, and Latin America, where over large areas the conditions of existence have been transformed in the last hundred years. The progress was initiated by contacts established by the West; the most advanced and advancing sectors are those in contact with the market economies of the West, and the most backward are those without such contacts, the aborigines or the desert peoples being the limiting cases. Over the last hundred years, huge agricultural, mining, commercial, and industrial complexes—such as the oil, copper, tin, rubber,

16 Baran, *The Political Economy of Growth* (New York: Monthly Review Press, 1957), pp. 249–50; 177.

and tea industries, to mention only the most obvious—have been built up in many ldc's with reinvested profits.

The late Soviet academician I. Potekhin was a prominent Soviet authority on ldc's, especially Africa. He wrote:

> The economic essence of colonialism, whatever form it takes, consists in exporting a part of a colony's national income to the metropolitan country without return imports of an equivalent value. This explains why metropolitan countries made such big strides in their economic development during the last century while colonies lagged behind. . . . Why is there little capital in Africa? The reply is evident. A considerable part of the national income which is supposed to make up the accumulation fund and to serve as the material basis of progress is exported outside Africa without any equivalent.[17]

These remarks are again simply untrue. There are no remittances abroad from much of Africa, and none from the poorest parts; thus they cannot explain the low level of capital. Such remittances as there are represent a return on resources supplied. Again, the West was far more advanced than Africa when it established its colonies, and its material prosperity was generated by its own peoples. Finally, many of the richest countries have few or no contacts with Africa.

In many Western universities, Soviet economic writings have come to be taken seriously as works of scholarship. This adds interest to Potekhin's observations. Both authors quoted in this section are explicit Marxist-Leninists. Closely similar ideas can be found in the writings of other development economists, including non-Marxists.[18]

Background to Barbarism

Many of the transgressions in development economics, such as those noted here, are both so crude and ubiquitous that—in this branch of economics, at any rate—one can speak appropriately of a decline of standards or even of their disappearance. Books published a generation or two ago, such as those by Vera Anstey, Alan MacPhee, and W. K. Hancock, are much more informative and often of greater pre-

17 I. Potekhin, *Problemsof Economic Independence of African Countries* (Moscow: Academy of Sciences, 1962), pp. 14–15.

18 See my *Dissent on Development*, especially essays 3, 4, 5, 16, 18, and 24.

dictive value than much of the current development literature.

Such a situation invites the question of how it has come about. It is indeed tempting to consider the reasons behind the sorry state of affairs in development economics and, to some extent, in other branches of economics. I have no space for adequate treatment of the background of the present state of development economics, and however detailed such a discussion would be it would still be necessarily somewhat conjectural. This is so because, while the validity of an argument can be examined and criticized conclusively by reference to evidence and logic, observations on the reasons why people accept or canvass arguments cannot be conclusive. They are also irrelevant to the validity of a critique. For these reasons, any discussion of what might underlie expressions of opinion and arguments necessarily is on a different logical plane from that of an examination of the validity of the argument.[19]

Yet some remarks on the background of this situation of barbarism might be appropriate. Critical examination of bizarre but widely espoused arguments and opinions is more effective if plausible reasons can be advanced for how these opinions came to be canvassed and accepted. I shall therefore suggest broadly what seem to me to be the main reasons, often interrelated, behind the ubiquity of these egregious transgressions in development economics. But I repeat that these reflections must be conjectural, and their acceptance or rejection does not affect the validity of the critique in the earlier section of this article.

The paramountcy of politics, the subordination of knowledge to political purpose, is a major factor behind some of the crudest transgressions in development economics. It is often reinforced by the pursuit of narrower personal and group interests, including financial, status, and emotional interests. Since the Second World War the rapid expansion of much of economics—notably, development economics—

19 In recent years the curious state of much of contemporary economics has drawn serious comment from prominent economists—including Professors Leontiff and Phelps Brown and Mr. G. D. N. Worswick—whose arguments add no specific political thrust. Some of their observations are noted in an article by Professor A. A. Walters and myself, "The State of Economics," *Journal of Law and Economics*, April 1975.

has been powered largely by a belief, mostly greatly exaggerated, in the practical possibilities of economics for purposes of policy.

The rapid expansion of the social sciences in recent decades has presented familiar problems for the maintenance of standards. In development economics this difficulty has been much exacerbated by the closeness of the subject to the political arena; by its prominence in public discussion; and by the links between the practical concerns of politicians, civil servants, businessmen, and foundation executives and the interests and concerns of academic economists. Many academic development economists have been drawn into international organizations or into various other kinds of official activities. This has often made it easy to define or rationalize quite simple transgressions by suggesting that they were necessitated by political and practical considerations, including, on occasion, the need for unanimity. Effective exposure of lapses then becomes very difficult.

The role of the politicization of knowledge and of the operation of group and personal interests in these transgressions is suggested by their systematic bias. The direction of most of the crudest lapses is not random. They consistently suggest conclusions or inferences that lend spurious plausibility to demands for pervasive or even drastic state economic controls and for large-scale forcible wealth transfers.

The influence of Marxism-Leninism has exacerbated the problem of the maintenance of minimum standards. In Marxism-Leninism the paramountcy of politics is evident; indeed, objective truth is apt to be identified with promotion of the political purposes of Marxism-Leninism.[20]

Perhaps paradoxically, the spread of mathematical economics, including econometric techniques, has not protected

20 I cannot examine in detail the reasons for the wide acceptance of this Marxism-Leninism in development economics. Briefly, I think that its appeal derives from its threefold features. It is, first, an intellectual structure comprising method, analysis, and observation, which claims to explain the operation and prospects of society. Second, it is an all-embracing messianic creed promising salvation on earth but in the indefinite future—that is, here but not now. Third, it is a program for political action. That Marxism, and Marxism-Leninism, is an intellectual structure, a messianic creed, and a political program should always be remembered in assessing its appeal. In the context of development economics and in the external relations of ldc's, it is the second and third elements of Marxism-Leninism that largely explain its appeal. The socialist influence in certain key activities—notably, the media and the international organizations—has helped to spread the appeal.

economics from the effects of politization. Indeed, the adoption of these methods has at times made it more difficult to resist the paramountcy of politics, notably, by providing a facade protecting crude lapses of analysis, neglect of evidence, and imprecision and vagueness in the use of underlying concepts.[21]

The significance of the paramountcy of politics is ignored by those of our colleagues, including some of the most distinguished, who argue that differences among economists reflect primary differences in analysis and observation—that is, in positive economics. If this were so, it would be hard to explain the frequency of elementary transgressions of logic and of fact by leading practitioners. For the sake of worthwhile academic discussion, we may often have to act as if these lapses reflected inadequacies in positive economics only, rather than the pursuit of political objectives or of self-interest. But the belief that this is really so produces an inadequate view of the academic scene—and is an insult to the intelligence of prominent economists.

21 It has often been claimed (by Pigou, among others) that mathematical methods can at any rate serve as a barrier to charlatans. This claim overlooks the possibility that these methods could act as a protective facade for them.

James M. Buchanan**

A Hobbesian Interpretation of the Rawlsian Difference Principle*

In this paper I shall consider Prof. John Rawls's principle of distributive justice and offer an interpretation that has not, to my knowledge, been previously developed, despite the lengthening bibliography of Rawlsian-inspired criticism and analysis.[1] Critics of this principle have concentrated attention almost exclusively on the extreme risk averseness that is implied, and indeed, the term *maximin principle* has been widely substituted for Rawls's own preferred term, *difference principle*. In an earlier review article, I expressed mis-

*Reprinted, with some changes, by permission of the author and from *Kyklos* 29 (1976): 5–25. The paper was initially presented at the Second Annual Interlaken Seminar on Analysis and Ideology, Switzerland, May 1975, and later at the Western Economic Association meetings, San Diego, June 1975. It also appears in *Freedom in Constitutional Contract*, James Buchanan, Texas A&M University Press, 1977.

** I am indebted to my colleagues, Gordon Tullock, Victor Goldberg, and Arthur Denzau, and especially to John Rawls, Harvard University, for helpful suggestions.

1 Inspired, of course, by *A Theory of Justice* (Cambridge, Mass.: Harvard University Press, 1971). The argument of the present paper was stimulated directly by Robert Cooter's discussion in "What Is the Public Interest?" mimeographed (Cambridge, Mass.: Harvard University, 1974). Cooter interprets Rawls to say that all persons have rights to equal lots in a just society. From this premise, Cooter is able to derive the difference principle contractually, and without relating it to risk preference. Cooter does not, however, fully integrate this interpretation with the importance that Rawls himself attaches to the original position. At one point in his paper, Cooter argues that the assumption of equal strengths in the original position implies rights to equal lots, but he does not fully explain why this follows.

givings about this principle similar to those of other critics.[2] My own emphasis was, however, on what I considered to be Rawls's unsatisfactory reconciliation of the two parts of his analysis: "(1) the interpretation of the initial situation and of the problem of choice posed there, and (2) the set of principles which. . .would be agreed to."[3] I argued that Rawls's fundamental contribution lay in his elaboration of the contractarian approach or method, essentially (1) above, and I suggested that both Rawls and his critics should abandon their utilitarian-like search for uniqueness in the outcomes of idealized agreement. As later discussion in this paper will indicate, this remains my own position, but under the interpretation to be advanced here, Rawls's insistence that both parts of his analysis remain essential and complementary can be readily understood. Rawls does not, however, properly describe the assumptions that are required to make his model internally consistent. These assumptions can appropriately be classified as Hobbesian in tone.[4] Some of these assumptions have been drawn more fully by Robert Cooter,[5] but neither he nor Rawls seems to have fully recognized the implications. When these assumptions are carefully presented, the whole Rawlsian construction takes on quite different characteristics from those normally attributed to it.

The interpretation in this paper allows the analysis of Rawls to be related closely with the analysis of Hobbesian anarchy that has been recently developed.[6] In particular, it allows me to relate Rawls's usage of the original position to my own use of the equilibrium position in Hobbesian anarchy as the basis for a hypothetical social contract. The interpretation also places Rawls's construction in a somewhat more positivistic setting than has appeared to be the case.

2 "Rawls on Justice as Fairness," *Public Choice* 13 (1972): 123–28.

3 Rawls, *Theory of Justice*, p. 15.

4 Rawls does say explicitly that his original position corresponds to the state of nature in traditional contract theory (*Theory of Justice*, p. 12), but he does not go beyond this.

5 Cooter, "Public Interest."

6 See Gordon Tullock, ed., *Explorations in the Theory of Anarchy* (Blacksburg: Virginia Polytechnic Institute, Center for the Study of Public Choice, 1972), and my own book *The Limits of Liberty: Between Anarchy and Leviathan* (Chicago: University of Chicago Press, 1975).

A Crusoe-Friday Model

It will be helpful to present the analysis in a highly simplified two-person model in which the dimensionality of agreement is limited to the minimum. This model is familiar to economists, and it allows most of the relevant points to be developed. The more complex dimensions of agreement required in full-fledged, even if hypothetical, social contract can be readily appended to this basic "economic" model. I should emphasize, however, that the analysis is intended, as is that of Rawls, to be applicable to the conceptual agreement on the basic structural arrangements of society.

Consider Crusoe and Friday alone on the island. They live in Hobbesian anarchy; no law exists, and each person acts on his own to produce and to defend stocks of a single all-purpose consumable commodity, which we may call fish. Let us assume that, in this setting, the net income of each person amounts only to one or two units per day. Under our interpretation, this is the "original position" from which any idealized contractual agreement emerges.[7] This is not made fully explicit by Rawls, and his discussion does not fully describe the characteristics of the position that would be maintained in the absence of agreement.[8]

Note that I have not assumed that Crusoe and Friday are "natural equals" in the sense that their net incomes in the state of nature are equivalent. This may or may not be the case, and the model should allow for either equal or unequal incomes. I postulate only that a "natural distribution" will come to be established, implying that each person has the strength-ability to maintain whatever position comes to be defined in this equilibrium.[9] In this rude setting, both Crusoe

7 Strictly speaking, the "original position" need not be the equilibrium of Hobbesian anarchy. As the discussion below will indicate, the initial position conceptually may be different. However, the knowledge that this Hobbesian equilibrium will be the social state in the absence of agreement must inform the choices of parties, whatever the characteristics of the initial position. Hence, for clarity in discussion it is best to treat the Hobbesian equilibrium as the initial position.

8 However, see Rawls, *Theory of Justice*, p. 103, where he states that in the absence of agreement "no one could have a satisfactory life." In a 1974 response to critics, Rawls says that "being in the original position is always to be contrasted with being in society." "Reply to Alexander and Musgrave," *Quarterly Journal of Economics* 88 (1974): 638. See also Cooter, "Public Interest," pp. 27-28.

9 For a formal analysis of the equilibrium natural distribution in Hobbesian anarchy, see the paper by Winston Bush in *Theory of Anarchy*, ed. Tullock.

and Friday should recognize the advantages of cooperation, of joint action, of contractual agreement. The critical questions involve the degree of information about the results of cooperative action that the parties may possess in the initial position and the basic technology that cooperative action embodies. As the analysis in this paper will demonstrate, in the Rawlsian framework as here interpreted there must be rather full information about alternative production-distributional alternatives available under cooperation, while remaining within the restriction that individualized positions cannot be fully identified. Also, the interpretation is more readily understood if we assume that cooperative action necessarily introduces a dramatic shift in the technology of producing income or product. The jointness aspects of the basic structure of social arrangements become predominant. By way of a simplified economic illustration, we might say that the Rawlsian model allows Crusoe and Friday to commence fishing with a boat once agreement is reached, whereas in anarchy this degree of cooperation is not possible, and each man has to fish without a boat. The cooperative arrangement involves participation in the provision and use of a genuinely public good. In this framework, it becomes impossible to impute separate income shares to the two parties, Crusoe and Friday, since the whole production is clearly a joint product.

Crusoe and Friday agree to act jointly, to become partners in social arrangements; gross production increases dramatically, but there is no means of imputing separate shares. Furthermore, in the original position and before agreement is reached, although both persons can predict with accuracy the vector of production and distributive shares, neither person can predict what his role in joint production will be. Once joint action is taken, there is one quantity of the good that could be produced under a simultaneous agreement to share equally in income or product. This represents one point on a "production-distribution" possibility frontier. And this equal-sharing regime involves a higher net income for each party than the income attainable in anarchy.[10] There may exist, however, different and

10 This is not a logical consequence of joint action. It is possible that the increase in total product consequent on joint production can be realized only in regimes of

larger quantities that could be produced under regimes of unequal sharing. The increase in total output is presumably possible because of the response to income incentives. Agreement could be reached on one of these unequal-share imputations only if the income total of the least-advantaged is thereby increased over the income total attainable under equal sharing. This is the much-discussed "difference principle," and we must try to see precisely why the results indicated by this principle will emerge in the setting postulated.

Each of the two persons can, by withdrawing his cooperation, plunge the system back into Hobbesian anarchy. And this is predicted to be possible by both parties at the time of the initial agreement. The "marginal product" of each man is extremely large, and payment in terms of "marginal productivity" would far more than exhaust the total product. For illustration, think of the situation in which Crusoe secures an income of one unit and Friday secures an income of two units in genuine Hobbesian equilibrium. Cooperation promises to yield a total income of twelve units, provided that these are shared equally between the two parties, with each person getting a net income of six units. The "marginal product" of each man is nine units, since this represents the difference in total product between the cooperative outcome and the Hobbesian outcome. Each person can, therefore, enforce the equal-sharing version of the cooperative outcome.

At this point, the veil of ignorance, stressed by Rawls, becomes relevant. In the original position, in Hobbesian anarchy, the persons do not know their respective abilities within the cooperative technology, nor do they know how each will respond to income incentives in participating in joint production. They know only that each of them can, by unilateral action, shift the whole system back into anarchy by the simple expedient of withdrawing cooperation. Conceptually, therefore, it is plausible that an initial stage of agreement will be some common acceptance of the symmetrical sharing outcome. Having reached provisional agreement on this stage, however, the actors may, on further

unequal shares. In terms of figure 1, there may be no point C on the 45° line that is Pareto-superior to A. This result would, however, seem sufficiently bizarre to rule out its serious consideration.

consideration, find that the income positions of *both* persons can be improved by the specific introduction of distributional inequality. Work incentives may be such that unequal sharing will increase total product. This step in the agreement may, but need not, involve the identification of the recipient of the high income. Even if the two persons are are identical in their work-effort responses to rewards, an unequal-sharing outcome may still be Pareto-superior to an equal-sharing outcome.[11] Or, perhaps more plausibly, there may arise some mutual recognition as to the potential responses to work incentives that allows the person who will secure the high-income share to be identified. In either case, to the extent that envy is absent, there should be contractual unanimity on a shift from Hobbesian anarchy to a set of social arrangements that will maximize the income of the least-advantaged.

This scenario places a somewhat different light on the concept of justice inherent in the predicted final outcome. In the original position, acting behind the veil of ignorance, individuals agree on the difference principle of income distribution because they mutually recognize the threat potential possessed by the relatively disadvantaged in any sharing outcome that fails to meet the requirement of Pareto superiority over the equal-sharing solution.[12] The latter position or solution becomes, in effect, a necessary way station, at least in terms of the agreement, between Hobbesian anarchy and the final position. The existence of many possible unequal-sharing outcomes that are Pareto-superior to the original position but that may not be Pareto-superior to the equal-sharing position under social cooperation becomes irrelevant. Behind the veil of ignorance, neither person would accept unequal-sharing arrangements that do not dominate, in the Pareto sense, the equal sharing regime.

---

11 Consider a situation in which the two persons are basically similar but in which efficiency requires that one of the two take the role of residual claimant who monitors the performance of the other. On problems of organization raised by the recognition that monitoring must take place, see Armen A. Alchian and Harold Demsetz, "Production, Information Costs, and Economic Organization," *American Economic Review* 62 (1972): 777–95.

12 At one point in his argument, Rawls comes very close to making this the basis for his whole construction. *Theory of Justice,* p. 15. See also Rawls, "Reply," pp. 647 ff.

Note that this argument does not, at any point, rely on risk averseness, and indeed, in this argument it seems wrong to substitute the term *maximin principle* for *difference principle*. The parties in the original position are not considering alternative production-distribution arrangements in the sense conceived by most of Rawls's critics. They are considering alternative social structures, all of which require the cooperation of *all* parties for continued viability. The arrangement chosen must satisfy minimal requirements of justice if it is expected to be maintained. For this reason, the arrangement that qualifies may, but need not, maximize *expected* utility for a person who remains behind the "veil of ignorance" in the "original position." There may be general agreement that the arrangement dictated by the expected-utility criterion would not be maintainable as a system of social cooperation, as a joint contractual venture, for the simple reason that the least-advantaged, whoever this might be, would not stand for it. And this potential behavior might well be predicted at the time of the initial agreement.[13]

We may illustrate the analysis arithmetically in our simplified Crusoe-Friday model. Four situations may be specified: (*a*) Hobbesian anarchy; (*b*) equal sharing under joint production; (*c*) unequal sharing advantageous to the least-advantaged under joint production—a Rawlsian solution; and (*d*) the utilitarian solution in which total product or income is maximized. These situations are exemplified in table 1 below. In this illustration, expected income is higher under *d* (10.5) than under *c* (9), on the equiprobability assumption that seems plausible enough in this setting. But rational choice makers in the initial position, in *a*, will eschew the selection of those institutions required for *d* because of their shared prediction that these institutions will not be viable. The person who finds himself on the short end in *d*, with an income of only five units, will be predicted to act to force the system back to that of equal shares, where his income moves up to six units. He can enforce this threat here, since his continued cooperation is required in what is essentially a joint venture.

13 See Rawls, *Theory of Justice*, pp. 175 ff., and "Reply," pp. 652–53.

Table 1

Setting	Technology	Total Product	Shares of Crusoe-Friday
(*a*) Hobbesian anarchy (the original position)	Independent production	3	1:2
(*b*) Equal sharing	Joint production	12	6:6
(*c*) Unequal sharing, Rawlsian	Joint production	18	11:7
(*d*) Unequal sharing, utilitarian	Joint production	21	16:5

Geometrical Analysis

We can remain within the two-person model and present these results geometrically, using a construction that is an emendation of that introduced by Rawls.[14] This allows us to clarify the distinction between the Rawlsian solution, as here interpreted, and the utilitarian solution. In figure 1, the incomes of the two persons are measured on the two axes. The initial situation is the equilibrium natural distinction in Hobbesian anarchy, shown at point *A*, where Friday secures the higher income of two units. The equal-sharing outcome when joint action is undertaken, upon contractual agreement to engage in a cooperative venture, is shown at *C*.[15] Note that, as illustrated, this represents a dramatic increase in total product and hence in the income of each party. This position becomes, in the process of agreement, a way station toward agreement on a more complex arrangement that might involve unequal shares. Both parties can improve their income positions by northeastward moves from *C*. The Rawlsian solution is shown at *R* or *R′*, each of which might be considered equally likely if there is genuine ignorance as to roles in the original position. The shift from *C* to *R* (or *R′*) is a Pareto-superior move and hence one upon which agreement should be forthcoming at the time of the initial agreement. Considered as a discrete and lumpy set of alternatives, any point along the curve northeast of *C* (on either curve)

14 *Theory of Justice*, pp. 76–77.

15 See n. 10 above.

can qualify on Rawlsian precepts. But if the whole set of possibilities is examined, the single point for step-wise agreement would seem to be that shown at *R* (or *R*′).

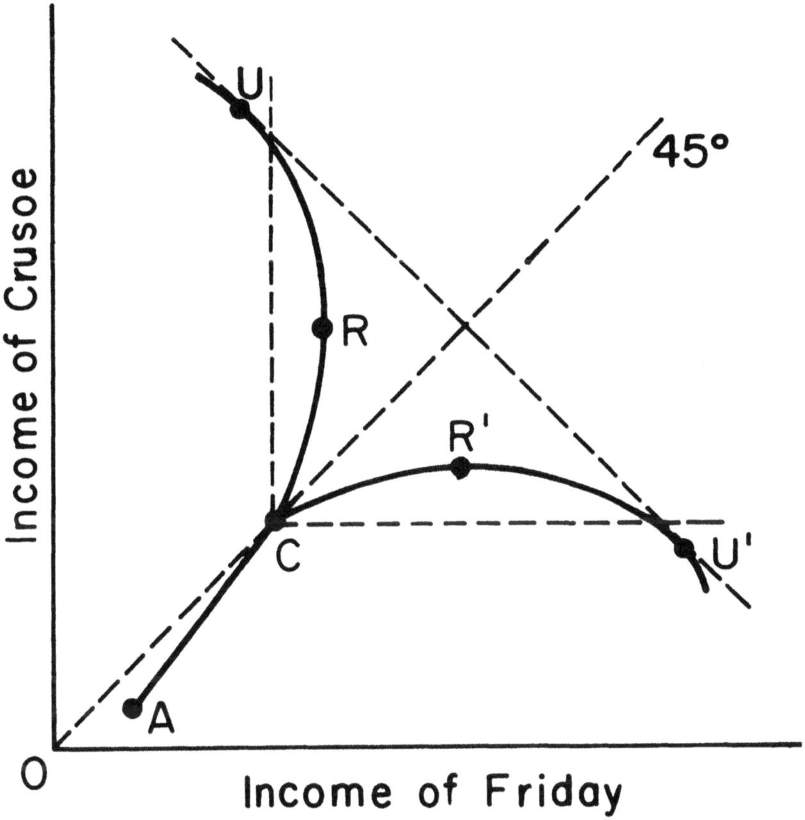

Figure 1

The total income of the two-person community is maximized at *U* (or *U*′), the utilitarian outcome. And, under an equiprobability assumption (with the outcome at *U* equally likely with that at *U*′), expected utility for each person is maximized by the selection of the institutional regime that will generate this result. Note, however, that in *U* (or *U*′) the low-income partner in the cooperative enterprise secures less than in the much *less* productive equal-sharing regime. In the original position, each party must surely ask himself something about the viability-enforceability of any contractual agreement that might be reached. In particular, he must ask whether or not the "least-advantaged" person, himself or the other, will readily acquiesce in a regime that generates an outcome such as that shown at U (or U'). Will a person not predict that, finding himself in the low-income role at U (or U'), he might threaten, directly or indirectly, to plunge the whole system of social cooperation back into anarchy unless he secures at least that which he can guarantee in the equal-shares regime? Hence, rejection of the utilitarian regime in the initial position emerges from the rational choices of participants who recognize the extreme vulnerability of such a regime to the threat potential held by the low-income party, whoever this might be.[16]

From Two to Many Persons

As we shift from a two-person to a many-person setting, the limitations of the difference principle of distribution become somewhat more evident. In the two-person example discussed, the dependence of the cooperative gains on the continuing acquiescence of each of the two parties is reasonable, especially when the technological shift from noncooperative to cooperative behavior is assumed to produce relatively large increases in total product. Consider, however, a society of n persons. As before, the original or initial position is one of Hobbesian anarchy, where the life of each person is "poor, nasty, brutish, and short." There is no requirement that the net incomes of all persons be substantially equal in this setting; all that is required is that each person secures a sustainable income that is dramatically lower than that which he might expect to secure under a regime of social cooperation. Why should the rational choice of a distributional rule be represented by agreement on a position analogous to R or R' in the two-person case, depicted in figure 1?

To generate this result, it is necessary to assume that *any* person who might find himself in the role of least-advantaged can, by withdrawing his cooperation, plunge *all* of

16 Objection may be raised here to suggest that the threat potential is symmetrical over all parties. A return to Hobbesian anarchy will harm both persons; hence, why should the threat potential of the least-advantaged person be especially considered? My argument, as well as that of Rawls, presupposes that persons do act from other than purely utilitarian motives, that "justice," as perceived, does matter.

the other persons back into Hobbesian anarchy, back to the setting in which all incomes are dramatically reduced. That is to say, the whole structure of the society, as a society generating real income for its members, must be vulnerable to almost total disruption by the defection of any one member. In a sense, this is the extreme converse of the idealized competitive equilibrium. In the latter, the withdrawal of effort by any one person has, in the limit, no effect on the welfare, the income levels, of other persons. The total product of the group falls by precisely the amount of the previous marginal contribution of the person who withdraws. The income receipts of persons remaining in the game are not modified by marginal changes in the number of players. In the limiting case at the other extreme considered here, the withdrawal of any one member of the team essentially reduces the whole product of cooperative endeavor to zero.[17] In in-between cases, in which there are increasing returns to numbers, the withdrawal of a person will reduce the amount available to others (there will be externalities), and this effect may be small or large depending on the shape of the total-returns function. The marginal product of each person may exceed the average product, in which case the threat potential of any one person will vary depending on the size of the divergence.

A model of increasing returns may be plausible if there are extreme advantages of joint action, if the structural arrangements of society require the cooperation of all members for their productivity in generating net incomes or product. An assumption to this effect may be an inference of Rawls's analysis, as here interpreted. But additional argument may be adduced in favor of its relevance for the objectives that Rawls set for himself. Ask the question: Under what conditions can a social group, a community, insure against its vulnerability to disruption by a tiny minority, or even by a single person? The immediate answer is that it

17 Consider the utilitarian solution, a non-Rawlsian production-distribution that may be in the core of the game, in that *no* coalition can secure gains by defecting from the cooperative arrangements. *Any* coalition, however, including one-person coalitions, may impose major damages on *all* others in the group by defection. In this case, the stability properties often attributed to the core may be absent. A distribution satisfying Rawlsian norms may not meet the requirements for the core, but it possesses the additional feature that the threat of defection, even if wholly successful, probably cannot secure an improvement in the position of *any* coalition.

can do so by adopting, establishing, and enforcing laws, legal rights, which limit—sometimes severely—the ability of noncooperative persons to disrupt the functioning of the basic structural order of the society. In a system without laws, without punishment for violation, without a police force, it is not at all implausible to suggest that a single dissident can indeed wreak havoc on all of his fellows.

In this context, Rawls may be implying that he is not principally interested in a society with policemen.[18] In a meaningful, if overly restricted sense, such a society cannot meet reasonable criteria for justice. In this sense, Rawls may be trying to lay down distributional rules or principles that will insure against defection in the absence of law and law enforcement. The Rawlsian world that satisfies the norms of justice can remain an anarchy, an ideal one that is ordered by the willing acquiescence of all persons, including those who are least-advantaged. Interpreted in this light, we can give the whole Rawlsian construction more obvious relevance to the events of the modern world.

This relevance is, of course, enhanced when we extend the difference principle from the level of the single person to that of groups. This possible extension is related to the implicit assumptions made about the potential enforceability of law in the community. For example, in the original position, a person may rationally choose on the basis of an assumption that potentially dissident isolated persons, or even very small organized groups, will not be able to disrupt the orderly functioning of society, will not be able to reduce its productivity dramatically, in which case there would be no Hobbesian argument for applying the difference principle within these limits. On the other hand, rational choice in an original position might well incorporate the assumption that a potentially dissident large minority, or a majority, of persons, finding themselves in disadvantaged positions relative to those of a small minority of high-income persons, would abandon the support without which legal order could not survive. Indeed, in such a setting, the majority may simply enforce a distribution akin to that sug-

18 See, for example, Rawls, *Theory of Justice*, pp. 261, 576–77. However, when he discusses the free rider problem in connection with the provision of public goods, Rawls seems to accept the necessity of an enforcing agent (pp. 266 ff).

gested by the difference principle, quite independently of what should be chosen in the original position.[19]

There is, of course, no need to adopt this large-group model for applying the difference principle. The point to be stressed is that there is a specific relationship between the presumption made about the enforceability of law and the range over which the distributional principle adopted is to be extended. Realistically, dissidence of a relatively large minority may promise social chaos, in which case care must be taken lest a group of this size should emerge in postconstitutional sequence with income less than it might expect to secure under an equal-sharing regime.

Informational Requirements and Outcomes Under Alternative Contractual Settings

The informational requirements for rational choice in the original position are severe in the interpretation placed on the Rawlsian analysis here. Individuals must be fully informed as to the alternative positions available to the society under cooperative action, positions described by a vector of total production and distributive shares. They cannot, however, know anything at all about their own roles or situations relative to those of others in the community. As Cooter suggests, an individual must know everything in general and nothing in particular.[20] If these requirements are accepted, and if the norms of justice are interpreted as elements of a social order in the absence of enforcement institutions, ra-

19 The argument here concerning predictions about majority behavior turns the earlier position of Buchanan and Bush on its head, so to speak. We had suggested that the Rawlsian distributional principle, even if chosen in the original position, would not be enforced in the postconstitutional stage unless a majority of the community's members secure benefits of transfers. Underneath our analysis, however, was the presumption that, independently of Rawlsian transfers, persons can secure incomes in the private sector that may, if anything, generate a higher total product than with transfers. We did not consider the prospects that, without transfers, the whole social structure might either collapse or be seriously eroded, prospects that emerge explicitly when we interpret Rawls in the Hobbesian framework. James M. Buchanan and Winston C. Bush, "Political Constraints on Contractual Redistribution," *American Economic Review* 44 (1974): 153–61. Note, also, that Sidney Alexander adopts essentially the same view when he suggests that the advantaged would be able to maintain their positions. "Social Evaluation through Notional Choice," *Quarterly Journal of Economics* 88 (1974): 615.

20 "Public Interest," p. 25.

tional agreement on the difference principle of income distribution becomes logically predictable.

We may, however, accept the original position as the meaningful basis for contractual agreement and seek to derive norms for social order without resort to such restrictive requirements for information. It is reasonable to suggest that, in the equilibrium of Hobbesian anarchy, persons are largely ignorant about the gross productivity of cooperative endeavor. Their initial step toward improvement in their status may lie in their recognition that mutual gains will be forthcoming from a simple definition of rights, a drawing of boundaries on allowable behavior concerning both persons and things. Having acknowledged this potentiality for mutual gains, however, the persons may also recognize the necessity for some enforcement of whatever rights are agreed upon. Each man will know that, without some means of enforcement, each person will have a free rider incentive to violate the agreed-upon terms, to defect from the social contract. This will prompt, as a part of the rationally chosen initial agreement, some contractual structure of enforcement that will insure that costs are imposed on those who violate its terms.[21]

Once these steps are taken, the structural arrangements of society are complete, and persons can produce income and product independently or jointly, as efficiency considerations dictate. They may, however, also recognize distributional considerations at the time of the original agreement. They may seek to insure that broad bounds or limits be placed on the degree of distributional disparities that might emerge under the operation of the social institutions chosen. These limits may be drawn without knowledge of the production-distribution feasibility set.

This is illustrated, again for the two-person model, in figure 2. Crusoe and Friday commence, in Hobbesian anarchy, the same original position as that described for figure 1. In this different framework for analysis, however, the two parties cannot predict the locus of possibilities as in the Rawlsian setting for figure 1. Instead, the parties know only that substantial gains can be secured from an agreed-upon

21 This summarizes the analysis of the hypothetical contractual process that is developed in detail in my *Limits of Liberty*.

structure of rights. But they also seek to insure that final outcomes fall within certain distributional limits. For purposes of discussion, let us say that the two persons agree that one shall not receive a net income more than two times that of the other. The allowable range of income distribution is then bounded by the rays *T* and *P* in figure 2.

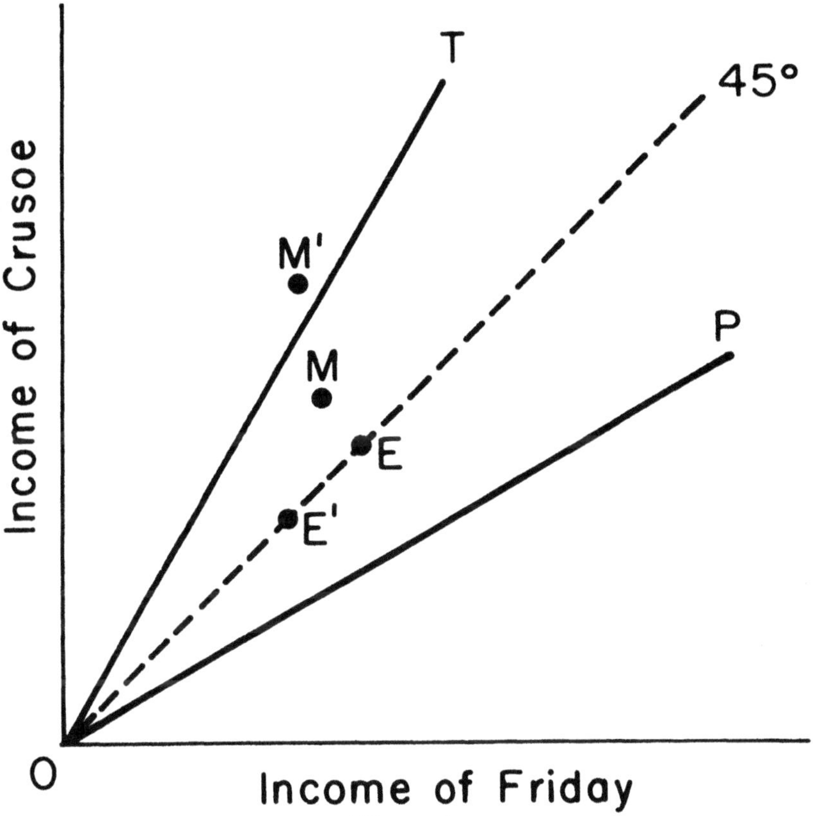

Figure 2

Suppose, now, that a position such as *M* is attained under the set of institutions chosen in the original position. There is no way of knowing how this position stands with respect to the Rawlsian criterion for distributive justice. If, in fact, point *E* should be an alternative possibility, *M* would not qualify as just under Rawlsian precepts. If, however, *E'* should be the equal-shares outcome that lies on the feasibility locus, then point *M* would in fact meet the requirements of the difference principle. Note also that the distributional boundaries emergent from an agreement of this sort may involve either more or less ultimate income inequality than that implicit in a Rawlsian contract. For example, if the distribution M' should emerge, it might qualify as acceptable under Rawlsian precepts if E' is the equal-shares prospect, but M' would not qualify under the insurance criterion offered here as an alternative set of terms in the original contract.

The Fragility of Social Order

The consideration of an alternative contractual framework in the preceding section was, in one sense, a digression from the main argument of this paper, the Hobbesian interpretation of the difference principle. Economists in particular have been unwilling to look behind their benign assumptions, so to speak, and to examine the vulnerability of the social-economic-political structure to disruption. Economists, intellectuals, and politicians alike have tended to concentrate their attention on flaws in the social process that seem amenable to easy correction, on the implicit and almost unrecognized assumption that remaining elements in society are indubitably fixed. It is, for example, relatively straightforward for economists to call attention to the external diseconomies generated by industrial discharges in our streams or by internal-combustion-engine discharges in the air and for politicians to enact legislation imposing regulation or, on occasion, penalty taxes.[22] It must surely be recognized, however, that the reduction in real income, meaningfully measured, produced by the increase in crime probably far exceeds the damage caused by, say, water pollution. The quality of life in major American cities since World War II has been affected more by crime in the streets than by smog. And where are the economists who bring into their simplistic welfare analytics the potential for social damage wrought by industry-wide strikes, notably those in public utility and public service enterprises?

22 For a public-choice explanation for the political dominance of direct regulation rather than taxes, see James M. Buchanan and Gordon Tullock, "Polluters' Profits and Political Response: Direct Controls versus Taxes," *American Economic Review* 65 (1975): 139–47.

Honest assessment of life about us should suggest that there has been an erosion in the structure of legal order, in the acknowledged rights of persons, and that, indeed, modern society has come to be more and more vulnerable to disruption and the threat of disruption. Increasing interdependence is acknowledged, but the increasing vulnerability that this interdependence brings with it has not yet been properly incorporated into our thinking.

It is at this point that the contribution of Rawls, as here interpreted, can be extremely valuable. In this view, Rawls is not, as many of his critics have charged, providing a philosophical-ideological basis for egalitarian income-wealth transfers superimposed on a market order.[23] Rawls warns repeatedly that this is not what he is about and that he is trying to derive principles for the establishment of the basic structure of society itself. The assumption natural to the thinking of economists, to the effect that a market-determined distribution would emerge *de novo* and that this distribution would always be available for use as a benchmark from which transfer policy might be discussed, is inappropriate in the Rawlsian analysis. This point is clarified under the interpretation advanced in this paper, where the benchmark, the position that is the effective alternative in the absence of agreement, is defined as the equilibrium in Hobbesian anarchy. Instead of presenting a sophisticated rationalization for egalitarian transfers in a sociopolitical order that, in its basic structure, is implicitly assumed to be invariant, Rawls may be viewed as attempting to call attention to the increasing vulnerability of this structure to disruption.

I should emphasize that this interpretation represents an attempt to bring Rawls's efforts more closely in line with my own. We share a set of quasi-Kantian, contractarian presuppositions as opposed to a Benthamite utilitarian conception. In the latter respect, the various attempts that have been made to treat Rawls's whole effort as little more than the derivation of a "social welfare function" reflect misunderstanding of his basic construction.[24] To a contrac-

23 This view of Rawls's work is shared both by those who welcome the implied argument for egalitarian transfers and by those who oppose it. For one of the most severely negative reactions, see Robert Nisbet, "The Pursuit of Equality," *Public Interest* 35 (1974): 103–20.

24 For a recent example of this nature, see Alexander, "Social Evaluation."

tarian, there exists no means of evaluating alternative positions of society external to the conceptual agreement among actual or potential participants. In the utilitarian calculus, no matter how sophisticated its mathematics, the original position is a redundancy. To the contractarian, the original position provides the basis from which the social structure must be derived, the starting point for analysis. The veil of ignorance becomes the device that allows agreement to become possible since, behind this veil, individuals cannot predict their own narrowly defined self-interests. As Rawls clearly suggests, his construction does *not* depend on persons acting on the basis of other motives than self-interest. The original position forces them, in effect, to choose on the basis of precepts of fairness because these precepts, in that setting, are consistent with self-interest.

My earlier criticism of Rawls's book was based on the notion that the presentation and elaboration of the idealized contractarian process was his important contribution and that his complementary argument concerning just what precepts of justice might emerge from this process was both narrow and distracting. In the alternative interpretation that I have tried to develop in this paper, the tie-in between the two parts of Rawls's construction becomes logically consistent. The specification of the particular norms of justice emerges from a recognition of the difficulties in and even the necessity for enforcement.

Empirical questions become important in assessing the significance of Rawls's construction for possible institutional reforms. How interdependent have persons become in a complex social order? How vulnerable is the system to disruption? These questions are tied together by the efficacy of legal institutions. One cannot begin to answer these questions without making predictions about the willingness and ability of decision makers to enforce nominally defined rights and to punish violators of these rights. If attitudes in the society of the 1970s are such as to make individuals in positions of authority unwilling to punish defection, continued drift toward the chaos of anarchy must be predicted.[25]

---

25 For a general discussion of the problem here, see my paper "The Samaritan's Dilemma," in *Morality, Altruism, and Economic Theory*, ed. E. S. Phelps (New York: Russell Sage Foundation, 1975), pp. 71–86.

How might this drift be arrested? My own efforts have been directed toward the prospects that general attitudes might be shifted so that all persons and groups come to recognize the mutual advantages to be secured from a renewed consensual agreement on rights and from effective enforcement of these rights. Rawls may be, in one sense, more pessimistic about the prospects for social stability. Enforcement may not be possible unless the prevailing distribution meets norms of justice—notably, those summarized in the difference principle. Whereas I might look upon the breakdown of legal enforcement institutions in terms of a loss of political will, Rawls might look on the same set of facts as a demonstration that the precepts of a just society are not observed.

As noted earlier, the interpretation that this paper places on Rawls's analysis and construction is more positive than may seem warranted. Parts of his argument may be read to suggest that individuals *should not* abide by the distribution of rights assigned in the existing legal order unless this distribution conforms to the norms of justice. And persons in the original position *should not* agree on a set of social arrangements that are predicted to place strains on individual norms of adherence and support. This more normative setting is consistent with Rawls's ambiguity and ambivalence on enforcement and punishment. But this leaves open the definition of the norms themselves. The difference principle can be identified as emerging from contractual agreement in the initial position only if the participants make the positive prediction that least-advantaged persons or groups will, in fact, withdraw their cooperation in certain situations and that the threat of this withdrawal will be effective.

Gérard Gäfgen

Galbraithian Economics*

The Methodology and Political Economy of Neoinstitutionalism or a New Vulgar Economics?

Modern economic analysis with its sophisticated techniques has severe shortcomings in explanation and as a contribution to policy making, especially where we have new phenomena, for example, the multinational firm, or new kinds of policy problems, for example, the fight against stagflation. This gives rise to dissenting currents ranging from Marxist thinkers to such lonely figures as Clarence A. Ayres, John Kenneth Galbraith, or Gunnar Myrdal, viewed by A. G. Gruchy as a sort of leaders of neoinstitutionalism in the post-World War II period.[1] One can easily discern characteristics common to the whole group of dissenting economists; they all emphasize the sociocultural background of the economy, social change, and qualitative modes of analysis. Yet, not only do the neo-Marxists differ from the neoinstitutionalists proper, above all in their self-justifying methodology and in their ideology of radical social change, but there are also wide differences among the individual thinkers in their remedies for the deficiencies of conventional economics and their cures for the pressing problems of contemporary industrial socie-

* Reprinted, with some changes, by permission of the author and from *Kyklos* 27 (1974): 705–31. An earlier version of the paper was presented at the First Annual Interlaken Seminar on Analysis and Ideology, Switzerland, June 1974.

1 A. G. Gruchy, *Contemporary Economic Thought: The Contribution of Neo-Institutional Economics* (Clifton, N.J.: 1972).

ties. So if one wants to demonstrate problems inherent in the dissenting mode of socioeconomic thinking, the best one can do is to choose one of the leading figures as an example.

One of the big problems of institutionalism has always been that it lends itself to an easy popularization or that it may even become identical with popular storytelling. The extraordinary success of the writings of John Kenneth Galbraith and the resonance his ideas have found among economic laymen have led us to choose as a most relevant example of popular institutionalism the Galbraithian system as it now stands. The other reason is Galbraith's claim that he has now built up a complete system of explanation.

Galbraith's new book, *Economics and the Public Purpose,* is intended to form a sort of *summa theologica* of his thinking as developed in *American Capitalism, The Affluent Society,* and *The New Industrial State.*[2] He himself speaks about putting it all together or giving "the whole system" (p. ix). Although his critics already saw the emerging close of the Galbraithian system in his *New Industrial State,*[3] Galbraith has now corrected this view and is claiming to have built up a complete and consistent system eliminating errors, filling in lacunae, and adjusting contradictions in his former writings. Since in the introduction to his new book he himself describes the relations between the old and the new ingredients of his mix of ideas, we can dispense with giving an outline of the history of his thinking and may concentrate on analyzing the new-old system as such.

Why do we choose the problem of vulgarization as a sort of point of attack? Of course, there is nothing bad *per se* in a popular philosophy of the social economy of so-called organized capitalism, but if it becomes politically influential and if it gets adopted by some schools or disciplines of the social sciences as *the* right new view of the economic system, a critique of the methods employed and of the contents of the propositions becomes, socially, a highly important affair.

---

2 J. K. Galbraith, *Economics and the Public Purpose* (Boston: Houghton Mifflin, 1973); *American Capitalism; The Concept of Countervailing Power* (Boston: Houghton Mifflin, 1952); *The Affluent Society* (Boston: Houghton Mifflin, 1958); *The New Industrial State* (Boston: Houghton Mifflin, 1967). All page and chapter references in the text are to *Economics and the Public Purpose.*

3 S. Gordon, "The Close of the Galbraithian System," *Journal of Political Economy* 76 (1968): 1-11.

Karl Marx knew very well the importance of popular writings on economics, when he denounced the writings of Frédéric Bastiat and other late followers of the classics as "vulgar economies" furthering only the interests of the ruling class and performing only ideological functions. Although neo-Marxists hold that contemporary economics, too, shows important traits of bourgeois vulgar economics, we have to examine this point only for Galbraithian economics. Galbraith's ideas certainly do not serve class interests directly (although they may serve the interests of the author himself and some of his fellow intellectuals or politicians); only the Marxist radical will reproach him for a reformistic apology for "late capitalism."[4] Nevertheless, his ideas may be profoundly misleading in theory and, being influential by vulgarization, in practice. Should this be the case, we are not entitled to ascribe this to the popularization as such—though a point could be made that any popular author in the social sciences must be a *terrible simplificateur*—nor to the particular nonmathematical qualitative mode of analysis that Sharpe has christened the "lower economics" and identified with institutionalism.[5] Any approach describing the functioning of and changes in the major economic institutions of a society has some problems in common with Galbraithianism but does not necessarily share all his potential deficiencies. Even if some deficiencies should prove to result from the simultaneous description of the whole institutional framework, this would be no argument against a sociocultural view of economics or against an analysis of the interdependence between some bundle of important social regulations and the working of parts of the economy—for example, between "property rights" and market processes.

So far, we have demonstrated the importance of a critical appraisal of the Galbraithian system. One difficulty we have met is that this critique overlaps with an appraisal of qualitative thinking as such in economics. Unfortunately, the language of qualitative reasoning also explains the far-reaching diffusion of Galbraith's ideas among the general public

4 See, e.g., A. Böhnisch, "Neue Formen der Apologetik der Spätkapitalismus: Der Theoretiker J. K. Galbraith," *Deutsche Aussenpolitik* (East Berlin) 14 (1969): 341–50.

5 M. E. Sharpe, *John Kenneth Galbraith and the Lower Economics* (White Plains, N.Y.: International Arts and Sciences Press, Inc., 1973 and 1974).

—which is furthered even more by the quasirhetorical techniques he employs. Needless to say, it is just this style that makes it difficult to extract from his work clear-cut propositions and hypotheses on which to base argumentation. What serves the vulgarization of his ideas seems to serve at the same time to protect them against direct forms of criticism. In spite of this difficulty, we want to analyze his system just like any other system of institutionalist economics. Even if some of the points to be made will appear rather obvious to the professional economist, they were not always easy to extract from the metaphorical, satirical, paradoxical, aphoristic, in any case suggestive, phrasing of J. K. Galbraith. The reader should also remind himself that even the trivial parts of the norms of scientific discourse are a valuable aid for discovering untenable propositions—though they may not prevent the use of these propositions in everyday politics or in small-talk pseudoliterary conversations. No critic can hope to convince Galbraith, who wants to stand as a lonely thinker against the whole economics profession and who does not share Keynes's view about "what foolish things one can temporarily believe if one thinks too long alone, particularly in economics."[6] But a critique may perhaps contribute to a distinction between what in Galbraith's work deserves attention and further investigation by the social scientist and what should be dismissed or even combatted as misleading social thinking and public opinion.

Some Characteristics of Galbraithian Thinking

Concept Formation and Structure of Theories

Galbraith's work rests heavily upon a mixture of holistic reasoning, intuitive and impressionistic demonstration, and reference to common sense. There are occasional remarks intended to justify this procedure or to refute what he thinks is the core of established economic theory. But in general, the methods and contents of his analysis mutually support each other—as in radical economics: the correct view of economic society induces the initiate to accept the underlying methods of analysis and to reject other approaches as mere

6 J. M. Keynes, *The General Theory of Employment, Interest, and Money* (London: Macmillan, 1936), p. vii.

expressions of the real social forces discovered by the true doctrine. So one has to extract typical modes of reasoning from Galbraith's intricate ideas and sustain these assertions by citing examples from his work. Proceeding in this way, one may state as the principal characteristic that Galbraith pretends to have an implicit knowledge of the whole social system—without giving a definition of the concepts employed or a statement of the epistemological presuppositions. So his diagnosis is that the defects of the American economy "are part of the system as they are part of the reality.... They are deeply systemic" (p. 211). This systemic approach permits him to postulate the system itself as a cause after having built this system upon a chosen aspect of society.

With Galbraith—as with Marx—this aspect is the power "exercised in unequal measure by producers" (p. 211). Nobody would deny that this is an aspect of utmost importance, and Marxist critics have praised Galbraith for recognizing this; but they have rightly objected that he arbitrarily locates the center of power rather exclusively with the technostructure of the industrial corporation without basing this on a theory of fundamental social processes—in a Marxian view, for instance, on a theory of class struggle.[7] Therefore, Galbraithianism is not acceptable even for the adherents of a total and simultaneous analysis of society as such. Rather than any thorough discussion of this problem in Galbraith's writings, we find only a laconic rejection of the socialism of Eastern Europe and a plea for a necessary tendency toward his very personal version of "socialism" (chap. 27). In his *New Industrial State* this version took the form of a convergence of all modern economic systems toward a planning system centered around the big industrial firm, but in his new book, partial and total socialization is part of his political program for remedying inequalities and disproportions. Neither this assertion of convergence nor the idea of the death of the market as the main institution of the capitalist system nor the systemic approach as such can claim originality; each has many predecessors that were philosophically better supported. This is true of Karl Marx, but in relation to Galbraith, Thorstein Veblen has been stressed more often

7 See A. Bohnisch, "Die theoretischen Anschauungen von J. K. Galbraith und ihr Einfluss auf die gegenwärtige Wirschaftspolitik der USA," *Wirtschaftswissenschaft* (East Berlin) 10 (1962): 434–46; idem, "Apologetik des Spätkapitalismus."

as an antecedent whose vision of the present and future role of the engineer in modern industrial society rested upon considerations of human instincts—considerations that were completely at fault but at least constituted a claim to a fundamental theory.[8]

Beyond these considerations of a badly founded systemic view, there are the well-known arguments of Karl Popper against "holism" as an attempt to grasp at once the very essence of a whole culture or historical period. To meet the usual criteria of the philosophy of science, scientific propositions should lead to universal hypotheses subject to the possibility of falsification by empirical observation; in the social sciences, as a rule, this is so only for theories of the middle range. This renders difficult the analysis of complex social phenomena, but it does not restrict us to small problems because we can put together particular theories or hypotheses to form tentative models of larger dependencies—models which then must be subjected to further tests, for instance, by way of political experiments. But this is just the contrary of the Galbraithian approach, which presupposes, as the French would put it, *la science infuse*; the reader of Galbraith, if a bit skeptical, always wonders how he comes to know all this.

To prevent this last objection Galbraith employs certain techniques of suggestion and pseudovalidation that are intended to make his assertions look like carefully derived and empirically well-established hypotheses. The aims of these techniques seem to contrast with his principal aim of originality, which he seeks to attain by formulating even relatively trivial sentences in a provocative manner. But this contrast disappears or diminishes when one sees that many of his assertions are rather weak and others are supported only by an interpretation of reality working through one-sided abstraction, exaggeration, false generalization—that is, what Gordon calls the simplism of Galbraith.[9] Thus, Galbraith concedes that there exists a continuum of very different types of economic units in the United States, but he pretends that "little is lost and much is clarified by dividing business

8 For example, H. Demsetz, "The Technostructure, Forty-Six Years Later," *Yale Law Journal* 77 (1968): 802–17.

9 Gordon, "Close of the Galbraithian System," p. 636.

organizations between two classes, those that deploy the full range of the instruments of power...and those that do not" (p. 10). Now, one can clarify many logical and conceptual problems by constructing extreme types of behavioral units, but this is only a heuristic device and not a means to construct a big system from parts that have otherwise stood the test. With Galbraith, his whole system *consists* in this dichotomy between two classes of economic units; it is nothing but a classification elevated to the dignity of a system.

Galbraith himself knows this fundamental weakness of his approach very well. Therefore he builds in some precautionary measures against the reproach of overstatement, which he expects to be advanced against him by a "person who is resisting truth" (*sic*, p. 87). His anticipative response to such a reproach consists in restricting the scope and content of previously advanced propositions but continuing to deduce the working of the system from the stronger form of the propositions. So he concedes that his assertions about the power of the managing technostructure are fully valid only for the largest corporations and that even there we observe some reactions of the stockholders (pp. 87–89), but he then returns to the predominance of the technostructure over the capitalists and to the fictitious omnipresence of the mature corporation in the industrial sector of the economy, provoking the attack of the conservatives as well as the Marxists and adding thereby to the impression of being the only person in possession of the truth. After having made some concessions in descriptive details, he maintains the big vision and simplifies it to such a degree that even the international monetary crises can be attributed to unintended cumulative effects of the machinations of the technostructure (p. 322). Let this last example serve at the same time as an instance of Galbraith's simplistic view of causation whereby he prefers to see monocausal relations instead of complex sets of conditions that neither his stereotyping conceptual apparatus nor his propagandistic intentions permit him to describe or to handle adequately.

"Simplistic" and "holistic" conceptualizations are well suited to deducing at will propositions about dysfunctions of a system. The same purpose is served by theories of behavior that put no limits on the type of behavior producing the negative effects one wants to criticize. This is particularly true for the behavior of social units that alone are claimed to possess power, for this, then, means power without limitation. Repeatedly, critics have charged Galbraith with advancing a theory of behavior of the big firm which just states that the firm will impose its will on its environment, on consumers, on stockholders, on the government, etc. Although he sketches some primitive mechanisms like advertising, channels of political influence, complacency with the nominal wage demands advanced by labor unions, he acknowledges no clear restrictions on managerial behavior, that is, no costs to incur for the advantages brought about by a certain behavior. Galbraith has never reacted to this criticism; indeed, his conception of behavior seems essential for the conclusions to be derived. He thereby neglects all the results of long debates in the social sciences about behaviorism and motivation theories as well as economic theories of behavior, for which he has nothing but disdain. As a rule, in the behavioral sciences, behavior is derived from the interplay of at least two factors: motives or preferences of the actor, on the one hand, and the situation perceived or the restrictions, on the other hand. The social environment constitutes an important part of these restrictions, and in his *American Capitalism* Galbraith identified even countervailing institutions like labor unions and government that constrain the behavior of the firm. Since his *New Industrial State*, however, these institutions have become auxiliaries of the corporate enterprise, helping it to dominate its environment. Perhaps there really has been a process by which the 2,000 largest enterprises have gained more power over the market and more influence over some institutions of the state; but why not describe such a process by using an operationally meaningful index of power and by specifying the restrictions that have been removed or weakened? There are some traces of such an approach in Galbraith's description of the inside evolution of the modern corporation: the weakening of stockholder control, the emergence of a managerial bureaucracy, the self-supply of large portions of capital requirements. But externally, the firm completely controls all important elements of its environment, and nobody knows why General Electric has not yet taken over all of the United States.

Galbraith believes that when the technostructure of the corporate firm is no longer subject to the market and no longer guided to maximize profits for others, it not only can pursue its own goals and transcend the market in its influence on the attitudes of society and the actions of the state but can do so without encountering any obstacle—for instance, without acting upon other markets with other competitors or without rivalry in political influence (chap. 9). Any contrary influence by stockholders, creditors, consumers, government, and unions can easily be overcome (chap. 10). Perhaps it should be stressed that Galbraith refuses to give a unified theory of the behavior of the technostructure, pretending that in each industry or firm the compromise between the different inconsistent purposes pursued will be different (pp. 108–9). How this fits with the idea of pervasive power remains an open question, for a compromise presupposes restraints on the possibilities of goal attainment. The main area of power seems to be the control over prices, with price competition completely excluded; other forms of competition that persist are regarded as usually furthering the purposes of all competing firms (chap. 11). Apparently, this must be so only to get rid of still-persisting restrictions of market power.

A striking example of the Galbraithian theory of unrestricted power is the apparently costless manipulation of consumer wants by advertising. Nobody would deny that advertising plays an important role in the creation of wants; but advertising resources are not unlimited, and its effects are heavily diminished by actions of rival firms. Alfred Marshall knew this very well, as he knew also the cultural character of want formation, in which actual influence by advertising is only a small part. There are, at best, but a few "natural" or "original" wants, and in a civilization in which the production of material wealth has grown to a high level, economic activity—for example, by specifying a person's place and kind of work—possibly determines more and more the character of our wants. This poses serious problems for the meaning of economic welfare and for the "right" direction of production. Mere prejudice against material production, which Galbraith seems to share with some nineteenth-century romantics, does not solve these problems. This prejudice rests upon a theory according to which false and artificial wants are created only by the modern industrial corporation, a theory that neglects the most simple anthropological literature on the subject and obscures the real problem of how to select and articulate the wants that should be satisfied in a modern industrial society.

Validation and Evidence

Galbraith's concepts and theories do not lend themselves to easy testing, nor does he want to formulate them in such a manner that falsification would become possible. But since he wants to present them as a good description of the reality of everyday life under industrial capitalism, he uses such surrogates for empirical validation as are plausible for the common reader. There are several such strategies:

—common sense evidence: the suggestion that "everybody knows";
—practical relevance: reference to political action presupposing the existence of the assertion (there you see it);
—immunization against contrary evidence: conceding exceptions to and unimportant deviations from the essential truth.

Because everybody can see the areas of abundant production in the United States—automobiles, weapons, soaps, etc.—and because Galbraith pretends that abundance is a result of power, "a moment's thought. . . will suggest that the present analysis is not in conflict with common observation and common sense" (p. 145). Everybody also knows the disproportion between the railroads and the road transport industry, which *must*, of course, be a triumph of the powerful technostructure of the automobile industry (p. 317).

There is a whole chapter (chap. 20) devoted to the "ultimate test of a set of economic ideas," namely, "whether it illuminates the anxieties of the time" (p. 198). According to this test, any idea explaining the existence of problems that public opinion regards as politically important or that the reader is persuaded to regard as the main anxieties of our time must be not only a valuable contribution but *the* truth about the issues in question. Galbraith merely has to point to disproportions between the public and the private sector, to the existing structure of public expenditure, to inequalities in the distribution of income, to the pollution of the environment, etc.—all phenomena that he has previously declared be a consequence of properties of a system dominated by a technostructure. So the existence of a women's liberation movement "proves" that Galbraith's analysis of the crypto-servant role of women in our society must be right. Again, we have what he calls "the validating reaction" (p. 233). Even for the appropriateness of policy measures, for example, prohibition of particular types of production and consumption to avoid pollution. Galbraith's most important argument is that they correspond to "what is already being done" (p. 289). This must be seen in the context of his attitude toward existing tendencies, which he confounds with the normative and the recommendable (see the Galbraithian policy implications stated below). His "new socialism," which consists in the socialization of the underdeveloped sectors, is also founded on the "most reliable of tendencies —and the best of tests of the validity of social diagnosis—which is that circumstance is forcing the pace" (p. 279); this means that governments are already taking action in this direction. In this way, Galbraith's diagnosis becomes an apologetic justification for any political tendency that he declares progressive—and, over and above this, is even declared an empirical test. This is really an exercise in the art of persuasion, creating for the lay reader an experience of self-evidence and easy understanding.

Analogous effects are attained by Galbraith's strategies of immunization. By employing a nonoperational concept of power, which is not defined by reference to specific dimensions (pecuniary, physical, etc.) nor by its scope or its limits, he can attribute any evil to the power of the technostructure. In scientific explanation, the use of unexplained terms or entities is inevitable for any theories of higher degrees of refinement or abstraction, but then the propositions containing these terms must impose clear restrictions on the hypotheses to be deduced from them. This is not the structure of Galbraithian theorizing, which uses the undefined terms in a way that fills them with intuitive content *while* deducing from them other propositions. There are other, related forms of immunization. Galbraith rather often gives a seemingly strong or even extreme description of a case and then slowly adds a lot of qualifications, until the previous assertion is weakened to such a degree that no observation could contradict it. So the purposes pursued by the technostructure—like growth of the firm or minimum profits—imply certain types of behavior, but finally these are declared compatible with any behavior observed in different firms or industries (chaps. 10, 11). The same pattern of reasoning is applied to price-setting behavior (chap. 12). In chapter 14 the assertion that firms have power over the consumer is attenuated by alluding to the costs and difficulties of the task of controlling consumer reactions, but if such obvious limitations of power must be conceded, Galbraith quickly finds other ways in which firms are profiting by advertising: advertising of all firms together serves the whole industry and encourages the false belief in happiness-through-consumption. The thesis of the mutually neutralizing effects of oligopolistic advertising must be false, because, were it true, "steps would long ago have been taken to limit advertising outlays by common agreement" (p. 141). This is a typical Galbraithian argument because it presupposes what has to be proved: the power of the technostructure to take not only individual action but also collective action, be this even illegal or yet-to-be legalized. Further, must we take for granted that advertising affects also the average propensity to consume out of total income? There is economic and econometric research on this subject, but still no conclusive results. In a very intricate manner, arguments are supporting one another, though the one is only a new form of the other disguised as new evidence. Multinational firms are another example: according to Galbraith they form a transnational system, and it is the technostructure as such, not the foreign firm, that menaces the sovereignty of national governments. This proposition is not in full accord with the predominance of American firms in this field; therefore, the true evidence must lie in the future, when the technostructure of the other countries will have developed to the same degree as is already the case in the United States (see chap. 7).

If there is a sort of law asserted by Galbraith and reality does not conform to it, he simply adds exceptions to the law —a technique that, if completed, is well known in the philosophy of science as the principle of "exhaustion." At the end of a chapter treating of the pervading political influence of the technostructure, Galbraith hastens to add that this power is not plenary and occasionally even breaks down (p. 163). Nobody should say that Galbraith has set up untenable propositions or that he has not seen important aspects of reality. Unfortunately, he cannot exhaust all exceptions to his laws; for instance, some developments in capital markets and in management techniques are contrary to his idea of a centralized and powerful technostructure: tendencies of decentralization in modern management organization, the rise of the conglomerate type of corporation, the appearance of big institutional lenders in the capital markets.[10] Even a great many exceptions of this sort do not discourage Galbraith, who seems to think that his own truth "has winged feet as compared with a qualification in pursuit of a bold proposition."[11] Anything that does not fit the grand vision is declared to be a minor qualification. Thus, the mass media are subject to the interests of the technostructure, but they show a certain degree of nonconformity because, to be successful, they must satisfy their customers (chap. 16). If the technostructure does not use direct repressive techniques, this is no sign of a limitation of power but must be attributed to the ineffectiveness of such techniques, because otherwise the technostructure would have made use of them (chap. 22). So limitations, qualifications, and exceptions serve only to reaffirm the "bold propositions" forming the core of Galbraithian system construction.

Critique of Economic Theory and Related Ideologies

Galbraith exposes his own ideas by contrasting them with established economics or what he thinks or pretends established economics to be. For him, it consists of extreme neoclassical propositions and—for purposes of macroeconomic stabilization—a bit of neo-Keynesianism, and it performs only ideological functions in favor of the ruling technostructure by removing from the image of the economy any evidence of power.[12] To support this suspicion he must present economics as built upon the profit-maximizing firm, subordinate to the instruction of the autonomous consumer, and upon the state, subordinate to the interest of the citizen (chaps. 2, 3). Such an economics does not serve the understanding of the system but guides attention away from inconvenient

10 The last was already raised as an objection to *The New Industrial State*. Ibid., pp. 638–39.

11 Galbraith, *Affluent Society*, p. 30.

12 J. K. Galbraith, "Power and the Useful Economist," Presidential Address to the American Economics Association, *American Economic Review* 63 (1973): 1–11.

facts and ensures economists a quiet life (pp. 26–27). Obviously, Galbraith's sketch of modern economics does not take into account many developments of the last 40 years, for example, with respect to the theory of the firm, the micro- and macroeconomics of disequilibria, and elements of power in the theory of distribution. It does not acknowledge the existence of Cambridge (England) nor of a monetarist counterrevolution nor of European thinkers like Myrdal or Preiser. This is not to defend the shortcomings of economics, which Galbraith is quite right to stress—its failure to take full account of the growth of the large firm, of phenomena of unequal distribution, of permanent inflation and stagflation. But contemporary economics has made many efforts in these directions and cannot be treated simply as a mere assemblage of "vulgar" neoclassical ideas. To justify his own vulgar economics Galbraith apparently needs a dummy of economics representing the same level of popular understanding.

Just as ideas serve to conceal the reality of power relations, so must some institutional arrangements. The power of management is elaborately disguised by "elderly boards of directors, . . . the solemnity of corporate liturgy, . . . board chairmen or presidents" (pp. 86–87), none of which has any real competence or information. Policies of the state like antitrust measures serve the same purpose of disguise because they pretend—assisted by neoclassical economics—that monopoly is the only problem of power, whereas the real power is exercised by the whole managerial class. This resembles neo-Marxist ideas according to which policies to enforce competition are ineffective, and even if they hit single capitalist firms they serve the interest of Capital (as an ideal entity). The separation of micro- and macroeconomics and the ensuing Keynesian policy are interpreted in an analogous way. Because stabilization policy is shaped in a way that leads to a permanently high level of government expenditures and to adjustments of taxes (but in a way that does not hurt the pecuniary and other revenues of the technostructure), it is proved thereby that Keynesians are servants of the technostructure. This is strengthened by a consequence of the separation of macro- and microeconomics—economists' neglect of entrepreneurial influence upon the state. Economists pretend to combat underemployment by Keynesian policies and they deny the necessity of governments' purchases of weapons in execution of this policy; this renders their political propositions all the more suspicious.

To insinuate ideological purposes is a very easy way to discredit ideas and theories; we do not want to apply this device to Galbraith himself, who has important interests, as a bestseller writer and as a spiritual leader of American Democrats, to write as he does. Moreover, an ideological background of ideas is no proof of their invalidity in the empirical sense. Galbraith is firmly convinced that only others are ideologues; therefore, he even takes the fact that his ideas are criticized by most professional economists as a proof of having hit on the important points and thereby having discovered the truth. This denies in advance any value to what we could still propose in favor of other efforts to overcome the traditional bias of conventional economics.

GALBRAITHIANISM AS AN APPROACH TO POLITICAL ECONOMY

The Galbraithian State

Galbraith believes that the value of his thinking lies in the rediscovery of power in economic and political life, which, according to the idea of power introduced, become inseparable. Established economics and even political science have to be overcome by this new approach, for political science "is also the captive of its stereotypes—including that of citizen control of the state"[13]—a phrase that shows a complete neglect of recent developments in political science, too. For politics to "become a part of economics"[14] Galbraith offers an eclectic description of possible channels of contact and influence between the technostructure of the corporations and the institutions of the state and of society, all of which may take actions that in a sense serve the interest of the technostructure. This should replace the false image of the state underlying neoclassical reasoning (we would prefer to speak of an inadequate image of the state in most of neoclassical theory, a deficiency that the new political economics has long begun to remove).

13 Ibid., p. 6.

14 Ibid.

The building blocks of the system whereby political influences are partners of the technostructure are: the bureaucracy of the state, the legislature, the mass media, and the intellectual establishment. The agencies and bureaus of the state live in a bureaucratic symbiosis with the technostructure, interchanging persons with it, intervening with policy measures to maintain favorable market conditions, purchasing the goods that technologically advanced corporations are particularly able to produce, exercising state power in a way that produces a need for these goods (for instance, fostering an aggressive foreign policy that leads to large expenditures on weapons). Via the dependence of the legislature, above all of its committees and their chairmen, on the bureaucratic institutions of the state, the influential parts of the legislature also further the interests of the technostructure. All this is not based on a theory of the functions of the "capitalistate," as is the case in neo-Marxian theories, but constitutes a simple collection of assertions and occasional observations. Where is the worldwide environment that imposes restrictions on the foreign policy? Where are the new demands addressed to the state from different parts of society? How to avoid empirically empty reasoning that attributes to every action of redistribution, health policy, etc., the aim solely of maintaining the essential parts of the system and thereby serving the interests of the technostructure? We saw already the danger of such arguments in the case of mass media, which depend for part of their revenues on the advertising expenditures of the firm (chap. 12). If public opinion under the influence of the media, but also of opinion leaders, is often critical when it comes to product quality, pollution, etc., then for Galbraith this is only to divert attention from the true center of power; if it is favorable to the purposes of the technostructure, the same point is proven. (For these functions of public opinion—for instance, disguising the decreasing marginal utility of further goods—see chap. 16.)

What Galbraith regards as the most important influence on subjective beliefs is the establishment, which consists of allies and acolytes of the technostructure and also belongs to the wealthy classes (because its qualifications are defined according to the needs of the technostructure). This too has been better described by Karl Marx, who also knew better the difficulties of this view: there must be intellectuals of the left who do not exercise their profession as producers of ideologies in the interest of the ruling class; how does this division of opinions and beliefs take place? The educational system must be viewed as a subsystem performing, as Talcott Parsons would put it, the function of pattern maintenance (of beliefs and qualifications) needed for the purpose of the total system and thereby for the purposes of the industrial corporation. The educational system and every institution contributing to the formation of values and attitudes must therefore be dominated by docile servants of the technostructure. Galbraith acknowledges some degree of freedom left over in this subsystem because he needs this as a point of departure for his strategy of reform. This is no new idea, but it "explains" progressive and leftist tendencies in the universities and elsewhere; it gives, again, an impression of deep understanding to the reader; and it secures new acolytes of Galbraithianism from among progressive-minded intellectuals lacking economic and social perspicacity.

Other phenomena of our time are also explained by the conspiracy of the technostructure with other groups or institutions. Not only the form of stabilization policy by demand management but also the permanent inflation that does not respond to a policy of demand contraction is an outflow of such a symbiosis. It cannot respond because it is necessary to the functioning of the system, for the technostructure is allied with the industrial labor unions to whom it concedes periodic increases of nominal wages that it has the power to pass on in product prices. The prices administered in this way do not respond to variations in demand; any attempt to fight inflation by demand management must lead to stagflation. Neither inflation nor restrictive policies are dangerous for the big industrial firm, since such policies hurt only other parts of the economy. Therefore, we observe permanent inflation and inefficient anti-inflationary actions. Because of the social consequences of inflation as well as of politically induced underemployment, this must eventually lead to wage and price controls, the beginnings of which we can already observe. Here too, Galbraith seems to see the initial abolition of the system; he does not ask whether there are alternative anti-inflationary policies that perhaps include wage and price controls as a transitory component. It seems that he wants to maintain his predilection for direct controls (stemming, perhaps, from his successful practice as a price controller), although the system dominated by the technostructure could perhaps be changed in many other ways. All these ways presuppose a change of the subsystem of political power and influence; it is difficult to see how this can take place if the system is really as closed as Galbraith views it. We shall see that his own strategy of reform is not compatible with the strength of the system as previously described.

Dualism in the Galbraithian System: Inequality and Asymmetry of Power

Theories identifying only one center of power in society must view the rest of society as dominated by this center; they construct a dualistic system with asymmetric power relations. They are thus in sharp contrast to theories of pluralism that presuppose at least two sectors of equal power or the always renewed formation of countervailing power, as did Galbraith in his *American Capitalism* of 1952. By describing now only the relations of the dominant technostructure to other parts of the economy, Galbraith can no longer explain what happens *between* the technostructures of different firms; if in their external relations to the rest of the economy the market has disappeared and has been replaced by the dictatorship of the technostructure vis-à-vis the consumer and the state, the terms of exchange between the firms themselves must be determined by a market relationship, be it oligopolistic or to a certain degree bilaterally monopolistic. Galbraith is unable to say anything about this; he only knows that the firms make "contracts." If one abstracts from this inner problem of the dominant sector, the other sectors can safely be described as groups that are exploited by the technostructure. They are the rest of the producing private sector, called the market system in contrast to the planning system of the large industrial firms; the households of the consumers; the state institutions; in part, foreign countries in which the sector of large industrial firms is not yet sufficiently developed. Curiously enough, the workers' class does not belong to the exploited groups because of the strange alliance between the technostructure and the labor unions. This is difficult to understand, for the technostructure lowers the real wages every time it raises prices in response to a wage increase. So it *must* exercise exploiting power vis-à-vis the workers too, as is always the case if we have only *one* privileged economic class, be this the class of Ricardo's landlords or that of Marx's capitalists.

On the other hand, Galbraith has added an exploited group whose relation to the functioning of the system is a bit farfetched: the crypto-servant class of women. As he views it, there must be someone accepting the charge of administering the growing consumption of material goods, which demands much time and labor; this is a *conditio sine qua non* for the growth of consumption and thereby for the power of the technostructure. The activities of the housewife are regarded as a high social virtue, which constitutes at the same time the nonpecuniary reward for women's labor. Galbraith tries to show the persisting dominant role of the husband in household matters and to unveil the related ideological attitudes, but he cannot explain why the system requires that a pecuniary salary be refused to housewives (chap. 4). So there are two groups, forming the overwhelming part of the population, whose role in the system dominated by the industrial corporation remains analytically obscure.

As for the people occupied in the services industry, in construction, and in agriculture—the domain of the small firm—they form the logical counterpart to the mighty managerial class, for they are subject to the fate of the market and to the adversities of restrictive stabilization policy. Galbraith gives a sometimes striking description of the characteristics of these economic sectors, including his favorite activities—the arts. His contention is that these are sectors of sharp competition, of relatively low prices, of great efforts by the small independent entrepreneur leading to self-exploitation, of low wages expressing exploitation, and of insufficient power of the labor unions (chaps. 6–8). Of course, he knows exceptions in the form of well-organized markets, as in the medical profession, or in the form of state aid, as in agriculture. It would be easy to cite still other exceptions, until there are left some marginal groups that can no longer represent one half of a dual system. This is not to deny the existence of many underprivileged groups but only to question the usefulness of Galbraith's classifications. Exploitation of the consumer and the citizen is a genuine consequence of his system; so dubious innovations are forced upon the manipulated consumer by the technostructure, just as they are introduced in the provision of public goods even if they do not serve the citizen (e.g., new weapons systems; see chap. 15); but the exploitation of the other groups mentioned is no necessary factor for the working of the system.

That the market sector is a heterogeneous group weakens the arguments for the existence of terms of trade that work against the underdeveloped countries as part of the market system. There remain some forms of "imperialism" by single firms that are interested in vertical integration and long-range contracts to ensure the supply of raw materials at stable prices (chap. 13), and there remains the abolition of the old international market system by the multinational firms exploiting those countries that have not yet developed giant industrial organizations. But even there, strong forces may work against the highly developed industrial sector, as demonstrated by the rising prices of goods of the primary sector during the last years and by the organizational possibilities of monopolizing the market for raw materials. Since according to Galbraith incomes are not related to functions but result from an arbitrary exercise of power, income differences within the technostructure between positions and levels are arbitrary too. Again, we have an observed inequality that remains nearly unexplained and is not necessary for the functioning of the system (see chap. 24). As regards dualism and inequality, there is not much left of the systemic character of Galbraith's analysis.

The Dubious Policy Implications of Galbraith's Analysis

Values and Facts

The man of letters—as opposed to the man of science—sketching a grand diagnosis of our time is exposed not only to the dangers of uncontrolled holism but also to the confusion of values and facts—be it wishful thinking interpreting reality so that it can be condemned or praised or be it its inverse: fatalism that takes for recommendable what is viewed as existing or evolving. As Gordon has put it in his comparison of Galbraith and Veblen, "There is no practical (and perhaps no philosophical) difference between asserting that something is inevitable and considering it to be desirable."[15]

15 Gordon, "Close of the Galbraithian System," p. 638.

What Galbraith describes as the planning system is viewed by him as an inevitable tendency of contemporary history to which all measures of policy must be adapted: since overall coordination in the system is not assured—with exception of the "contracts" concluded by the technostructure with its partner suppliers or the state—coordination by the state must be introduced (in *The New Industrial State,* even this seemed to be implied automatically in the planning system of the technostructure). Since the planning system is conducive to stagflation, it must be supplemented by new ways of price control. What, then, is inevitable and what can be changed depends on what is regarded as constituting the essential characteristics of the system. Of course, in any policy problem, there is a previous decision about what are to be viewed as the constraints and what as the political parameters. This is partly a constitutional question about the norms and institutions to be conserved, but the rest is a question of feasibility: What do theory and observation predict to be the consequence of different policy actions? Are there empirically founded theoretical beliefs far-reaching enough to remove even some of the restrictions?

In Galbraith there are no such distinctions to be found, and there remains a fundamental contradiction between his determinism relating to the main tendencies of contemporary society and his "general theory of reform," constituting the last third of his new book (chaps. 21–31). No wonder his strategy of reform and his measures to correct the evils of the planning system lack theoretical foundations and leave the reader unconvinced as to their efficacy. Again, a comparison with neo-Marxian thinking shows that Galbraith is not successful in trying to establish his standpoint beyond the alternative positions of a "bourgeois" objectivism with an open society and Marxist partiality with a largely deterministic view of evolution: if there are inevitable tendencies in the main traits of capitalistic societies, the only option can be passive description or revolutionary action to precipitate evolution. But Galbraith does not want to be a mere radical; he applauds radical critiques of economics only when this fits his intentions.[16]

16 See the citation of J. G. Gurley, "The State of Political Economics," *American Economic Review* 61 (1971): 53–62, in Galbraith, *Economics and the Public Purpose,* p. 27.

Disregarding the problem of giving direct normative content to propositions about "discovered facts," we still have the problem of choosing the fundamental values governing the choice of relevant aspects of reality and of the policies to be derived. In a very suggestive manner Galbraith tries to convince the reader that he *has* discovered the relevant problems because his propositions relate to the very needs of our time as everybody perceives them. But in this respect, too, the radicals would be more consistent by showing their own position in the social context they analyze; this must be the standpoint of someone who wants to treat analysis and valuation with the same method. In the valuations of Galbraith there is a marked predilection for aesthetic values combined with a vague egalitarianism. But he does not tell how we can reconcile a disdain for mere goods, above all private goods, with a better standard of living for the average man. This is the attitude of an intellectual leader who, residing in one of the highest percentiles of the income pyramid, can easily give way to his preferences for the fine arts and for public goods, above all for those of aesthetic character whose distributive effects are known to be largely in favor of the rich. But let us not make out of this critique a study in prejudice; it suffices to restate that the value foundations of Galbraithian policies are not well laid open and lack consistency.

Deficiencies of Underlying Analysis

While Galbraith declares other lines of economic analysis totally irrelevant and even misleading, he does not offer an alternative analysis of social phenomena that would enable him to construct feasible and efficient policy measures. The study of market processes can be employed, according to Galbraith, only for part of the whole system, and even there his program would demand that account be taken of the power relations to the other parts of the system. The functioning of the planning system itself is seemingly explained by the contracts to be concluded between the giant firms themselves and between them and the government agencies, but there is no mechanism of bargaining, arbitrage, or competition to fix the terms of these contracts. From the lack of coordination between the market and the planning sector, which is conducive to structural crises, Galbraith concludes that coordinating activities must be introduced on the national and even the international level. But since he is not able to analyze the existing organization of the economy as a whole—and by just this deficiency cannot claim to use a really systemic approach—he also cannot derive propositions enabling him to organize his new economy into a coherent system. There are neither institutions analogous to those of the French *planification* nor any criteria for guiding intersectoral investment decisions or incentives and norms of behavior that would make such a planning machinery work. He does not even touch upon experiences that have been had with planning institutions and mechanisms of coordination under different circumstances; so his last chapter, which ought to describe the mechanisms of a better regime, only vindicates the possibility of such an order.

The same has to be said about his proposals for a combination of monetary and fiscal policy with direct controls, which looks rather sophisticated at a first view and even contains indicators for stabilization measures (see chap. 30). His mix of policies rests upon the dichotomy between the market and the planning sector, the ineffectiveness of antitrust policy and even of all conceivable measures to strengthen competition, ineffectual monetary policy, an unalterable pattern of behavior in the domain of collective bargaining, etc. There are some realistic traits in this picture, but it definitely lacks a solid theoretical base at the micro level as well as at the macro level. For instance, his program of stabilization consists of permanent price and wage controls in the planning sector, low interest rates, minimal wage legislation, and some demand management that tolerates a certain degree of unemployment but tries to avoid at the same time a shortage of qualified workers in the planning sector and upward price pressures in the market sector—or the inverse in case of a recession. There are no reflections on adverse effects of minimum wages, because for Galbraith redistribution makes obsolete the goal of high employment; there are no rules governing the optimal supply of money; there are no possibilities to compensate an excess supply in the planning sector combined with inflation in the market sector.

Galbraith's policies to equalize power and income contain massive protection, state aid, and weakening of competition in the market sector; he has, however, no theoretical framework to analyze the far-reaching consequences of this for providing the population with a sufficient, secure, and cheap supply of services from this sector. Galbraith completely ignores recent research on the economics of discrimination, on minimum wages, on collective monopolistic practices in the liberal professions, etc., and takes into account only the immediate effects of protection and control, whereas it has always been regarded a virtue of the economist to consider the whole set of consequences in a systematic framework (see his superficial treatment, "Policy for the Market Sector," chap. 25). One of the surest signs of policy without theoretical refinement seems to us to be the recommendation of purely compulsory measures; Galbraith sees no other way to combat the male privilege in the technostructure than to order compulsory quotas for women at all levels of management and a compulsory overrepresentation of women in the educational institutions. As regards the protection of the environment, he is right in stressing that we lack above all an appropriate system of information, but here too he could recommend really more than restrictions, prohibitions, and pollution norms. To propose an expansion of the supply of public goods, particularly of the publicly subsidized arts, means to lift the planners to the role of guardians of the well-being of others; in this respect, there are no mechanisms recommended for the articulation of preferences by the citizen—a main problem in the expansion of the public sector. So a deficit of theories is supplemented by presupposing a benevolent and omnipotent policymaker (or one who relies on the inspiration of wise intellectual leaders).

In a work pretending to analyze the hitherto neglected power relations in society, a strategy of reform has to demonstrate how to change the distribution of power that till now has prevented the realization of these reforms. For this purpose an empirically valid economic theory of political processes would be necessary. In spite of his claims to have constructed such a political economy, Galbraith cannot make use of his own analysis to derive a political strategy that in practice would render feasible the realization of his policy proposals. Apart from the rather pleonastic insight that the reformers must get influence over the legislative and administrative institutions of the state—which then would have to execute the whole program of reforms—Galbraith proposes a campaign for the "emancipation of belief" (chap. 22). A changing conscience—which, according to his reflections on the anxieties of our time, is already under way—should lead to a changing composition and behavior of the political bodies. One may agree with his view of the pivotal role of the state machinery, although according to his analysis the state is not the true source of power; one may also concede the importance of agitprop emanating from the campus and other centers to which the technostructure was obliged to leave a certain degree of freedom. But if the network of power is really so intricate and firmly established as Galbraith asserts, then his proposals for reform have a background of voluntarism and subjectivism that prevents the construction of a truly realistic strategy: Where are the social strata serving as a sociostructural base supporting the propagation of the reforms? Where are the political allies of Galbraith if he weakens the power of the industrial labor unions? How can different pressure groups be motivated as supporters of his program?

These questions are asked, not only by those who would conclude that only revolutionary conspiracy can break up the existing power system, but also by political analysts who have observed the mechanisms of reform mongering. For instance, by propagating a moderately reformistic platform one may bring about an alliance of reformers with members of "ruling classes," who must fear that in the absence of reforms revolutionary forces would eventually take over. Galbraith's neglect also of advances in the political sciences prevents him from considering strategy choice as a problem of applied social sciences. What he has written in this respect must be regarded more as a left-wing pamphlet intended for party politics within the U.S. Democratic Party. Though there exist quite different concepts about what belongs to a modern conception of political economy, Galbraith's political program is difficult to reconcile with any of these conceptions as long as we want to regard them as belonging to the social sciences.

Whereas from a standpoint of social theorizing a critique must advance many objections against the last version of the Galbraithian system, it cannot deny the stimulating and provoking effect of Galbraith's writings. He reminds us of the need for putting together our usual piecemeal theorizing and for developing an all-embracing view that includes the problems of power and political feasibility and is conducive to a consistent program of reforms. So economic theorists like Meade have been inspired by Galbraith to sketch a program of social and economic policy evolving from a critique of *The New Industrial State*.[17] If the relevance of the problems raised is a criterion by which to judge the writings of a social scientist, then Galbraith surely has won a point. If we add realism and the usefulness of the propositions for policy purposes, then the direct judgment may be rather negative, but as with any important piece of literature we must not forget the indirect effects emanating from the reception or rejection of the ideas produced. In this latter respect, there remain a lot of enlightening responses to be hoped for, preventing too strong an influence of the new vulgar economics.

17 J. E. Meade, "Is 'the New Industrial State' Inevitable?" *Economic Journal* 78 (1968): 372–92; also published as "Ist die moderne Industriegesellschaft von J. K. Galbraith unvermeidlich?" *Hamburger Jahrbuch für Wirtschafts- und Gesellschaftsgestaltung* 14 (1969): 226–47.

Hans G. Monissen

"Economics and the Public Purpose"

Some Discussion Points Related to Chapter Three of John K. Galbraith's Homonymous Book*

When Harold Demsetz reviewed Galbraith's *New Industrial State,* he stressed the author's remarkable talent "to rally popular support for ideas not now popular."[1] Without questioning this view by entering into a detailed analysis of the characteristic features of the demand and supply conditions of the competitive market for ideas and beliefs, we suspect that Demsetz laid too much stress on Galbraith's powers of persuasion and thereby strongly underrated Galbraith's superior ability to know the market conditions for his products and to react to the demand functions of his consumers. We think it is not too far-fetched to classify both *The New Industrial State* and Galbraith's two prior popular writings[2] as major historical reference books that articulate, support,

* Reprinted, with some changes, by permission of the author and from *Schweizerische Zeitschrift für Volkswirtschaft und Statistik,* III 1975: 317–35. The paper was presented at the First Annual Interlaken Seminar on Analysis and Ideology, Switzerland, June 1974.

1 Harold Demsetz, "The Technostructure, Forty-Six Years Later," *Yale Law Journal* 77 (1968): 802.

2 John Kenneth Galbraith, *The New Industrial State* (Boston: Houghton Mifflin, 1967; 2d ed., rev., 1971); *American Capitalism: The Concept of Countervailing Power* (Boston: Houghton Mifflin, 1952); *The Affluent Society* (Boston: Houghton Mifflin, 1958).

and manifest the otherwise unstructured cultural uneasiness of his typical reader.

The book under discussion, *Economics and the Public Purpose,* is Galbraith's latest treatise on problems of our mature capitalistic societies.[3] As usual, the master's literary sphere of activity spans too large a collection of contemporary economic and social issues to allow for an adequate and responsible treatment of all the problems raised. Thus, a discussant is necessarily forced to comply with his intellectual idiosyncrasy by being selective. In our opinion, the most important part of *Economics and the Public Purpose* is the section entitled "The Planning System" (pp. 81–175) and covering almost one third of the whole book. On this part of the book we will concentrate our discussion. "The Planning System," by referring directly to Galbraith's prior work in *The New Industrial State,* is the focal point leading toward a visualized final close of the Galbraithian system. Furthermore, understanding the workings of the planning system is a proper starting point for a more general assessment of his broader vision of the workings of capitalistic industrial society and his proposals for socioeconomic reform.[4]

Our discussion, related almost exclusively to this particular part of *Economics and the Public Purpose,* follows Galbraith's thematic structure; however, we have chosen headings that are more suited to a general summing up and that also provide a comparison to mainstream economic reasoning. Even at the risk of being repetitive, we thought it worthwhile to summarize somewhat broadly Galbraith's major ideas before taking up specific points.

The Structure of the Industrial Economy: An Overview (Part Three, IX)

As Galbraith diagnoses it, our modern economy is shaped and structured according to the interests of a small group of giant corporations—"the world of the few hundred technically dynamic, massively capitalized and highly organized cor-

3 John Kenneth Galbraith, *Economics and the Public Purpose* (Boston: Houghton Mifflin, 1973). All page and chapter references in the text are to this work.

4 For further discussion of these and related issues, see Gérard Gäfgen, "On the Methodology and Political Economy of Galbraithian Economics," *Kyklos* 27 (1974); 705–31, reprinted in this volume, pp. 79–104.

porations" that perform society's planning functions.[5] For obvious reasons, Galbraith calls this sector the planning system, which should be contrasted with the market system[6] —a minor subdivision of the whole economy with some performance characteristics as described by neoclassical economic theory. This state of affairs may be regrettable, but Galbraith reminds us not to forget that it is by no means a mere historical accident. Technological imperatives dictate increasing plant and firm size and industrial concentration. In addition to the "Eigendynamik" of modern technology, organizational advantages push the firm size over the level determined by least-cost considerations because ever-increasing firm size allows an almost complete control of all environmental variables, which include the firm's costs conditions, technology, output prices, the response of consumers, and the possible interventions of central government agencies. "When the task lends itself to organization, there is no upper limit to the size of the market" (p. 82).

Borrowing from the work of Berle and Means and of Veblen,[7] Galbraith states that the owners of the modern firm—for all practical purposes, the stockholders—have lost control over the activities of the management. Group decision making has replaced the classical Schumpeterian entrepreneur. The effective power is transferred to the whole anonymous body of the executive salaried planning staff—the technostructure, as Galbraith christened this group in *The New Industrial State* by constructing an odd but suggestive neologism. It is interesting to note that top management is completely adjusted to the interest of the lower levels of the hierarchical control pyramid and has confined itself to a mere ritualistic approval of the decisions of the lower-ranking specialists.

Galbraith follows his previous efforts in *The New Industrial State* when he starts by constructing a model describing the development of "the corporate sector" of the economy.

5 Galbraith, *New Industrial State* (1971), p. 28.

6 The world of smaller-sized firms acting mainly as price takers. Galbraith's definition lacks operational meaning because, at the same time, he admits some monopoly elements guiding these firms' behavior.

7 Adolph Berle and Gardiner C. Means, *The Modern Corporation and Private Property* (New York: Macmillan, 1932); Thorstein B. Veblen, *The Engineers and the Price System* (New York: Viking Press, 1921).

The corporate sector is the focal point for a visualized larger model—the dual economy—elucidating the characteristic features of our mature capitalistic societies. As a pure descriptive starting point, it is certainly appropriate to remind the reader that the bulk of our gross national product originates in a few hundred giant corporations. But to "infer" from this a quasi-deterministic tendency toward "Brobdingnagian size," as one critic aptly has described it,[8] and large firm size as a prerequisite for technical progress and efficient production is much too superficial, for it fails to show both analytically and empirically the relevance of the described linkage and, in addition, ignores the favorable policy climate created by permissive and accommodating government behavior in the past. Criticism along this line was especially raised by Walter Adams,[9] and there is no reason to cover these issues once more. But it is interesting to note that Galbraith modifies this historicistic approach somewhat when he includes in *Economics and the Public Purpose* a chapter on socioeconomic reform.[10]

When Solow charged Galbraith with "big-thinking," he certainly had in mind Galbraith's preference for casting his arguments in extremely simple forms by neglecting all structural and institutional details.[11] The actors in Galbraith's economic scene are either aggregated sectors or monolithic management groups tied together in stable intra- and inter-industry relations to pursue what he calls their "common protective and affirmative purposes." The reader very often gets the impression that the "planning system" consists of a single, giant, completely vertically and horizontally integrated firm with a homogeneous executive body. This ap-

8 Walter J. Adams, "Another View of the New Industrial State," ed. Edwin Mansfield, *Principles of Microeconomics—Readings, Issues and Cases* (New York: Norton & Company, 1974), pp. 101–104; first published in *Hearings before Subcommittees of the Select Committee on Small Business* (Washington, D.C.: Government Printing Office, 1967).

9 Walter J. Adams, "The Military-Industrial Complex and the New Industrial State," *American Economic Review* 58 (May 1968): 652–65.

10 For purposes of the history of economic ideas, we should note that *Economics and the Public Purpose* is not only Galbraith's "summa theologica" but also the direct intellectual linkage to his first major work, his monograph *A Theory of Price Control* (Cambridge, Mass: Harvard University Press, 1951).

11 Robert M. Solow, "The New Industrial State or Son of Affluence," *Public Interest* 9 (1967): 1.

proach is very convenient, for it allows a complete discarding of the intricacies of the modern theory of relative prices. In both *The New Industrial State* and *Economics and the Public Purpose* Galbraith contests the coordinate function of the market and rejects the working of the price mechanism.[12] In his prior work he failed to develop a theoretical model explaining the organization of the economic system.[13] He tries to fill this gap in his latest book by referring to a "deus ex machina," the interfirm contract. Lacking any price-theoretical foundation, this device, as we will see, is nothing more than an ad hoc description.

Similar price-theoretical difficulties arise with regard to the behavior of the "technostructure." Aggregating the executive body of the corporate firm into a monolithic group is the major ingredient of the Berle-Means theme of separation of stockholders from corporate control. But we should note that neither economic theory nor empirical evidence validates such a procedure.[14] In Galbraith's analysis, the members of the technostructure play a role dictated by their common interests, which derive from "their common protective and affirmative purposes." But there is no mechanism defined that could account for deviating (individual?) behavior, which from a strict methodological point of view means that their behavior remains largely unexplained.

The discussion of the technostructure demonstrates in a striking way that Galbraith adheres to a methodological collectivism—popular, for instance, in contemporary sociology —which should be contrasted with the methodological individualism practiced by the majority of the economics profession. Our aim is certainly not to degrade methodological collectivism by drawing a sample of possibly atypical ex-

12 It is certainly correct to observe that the institutional framework included in our standard textbooks on price theory—the narrow private-property budget constraint —is inadequate for dealing with problems of our mixed economy. But it is certainly strange to conclude from this, as Galbraith does, that price theory per se is useless.

13 Scott Gordon, "The Close of the Galbraithian System," *Journal of Political Economy* 76 (1968): 635–44; James E. Meade, "Is 'the New Industrial State' Inevitable?" *Economic Journal* 78 (1968): 372–92; Myron E. Sharpe, *John Kenneth Galbraith and the Lower Economics* (New York: Macmillan, 1973), p. 45.

14 See especially Armen A. Alchian, "Corporate Management and Property Rights," in *Economic Policy and the Regulation of Corporate Securities*, ed. Henry G. Manne (Washington, D.C.: American Enterprise Institute, 1969).

amples from one single written source but to point at an inherent danger of this approach, namely, its neglect of structural details and slighting of individual behavior differences. The issue under discussion is not that technostructures pursue their own interests but that they do this in different ways and in varying degrees. Recent work in economics has taught us that different modes and degrees of discretionary managerial behavior can be systematically and coherently explained by reference to different socioeconomic penalty-reward structures or different assignments of property rights or entitlement rights structures.[15] Whatever may be the consequences of different institutional arrangements on the allocative efficiency of the economy, there is little or at least inconclusive empirical evidence that separation of management from control (whatever this catch phrase may mean) implies that the market value of the total compensation in terms of pecuniary *plus* nonpecuniary rewards of management in technostructure-oriented firms with large stock ownership dispersion is comparatively higher or that the wealth of the stockholder is less guarded.[16] This conclusion could be modified if we considered so-called regulated industries, and it may well be that Galbraith's analysis is strongly influenced by observation of these industries. The above-mentioned result is the implication we derive from economic theory if we assume a competitive market for labor (management) inside and outside the firm and a competitive market for corporate control.[17] We exclude the market conditions of the product market from this list because product market competition is neither a necessary nor a sufficient condition. It is not necessary, because the issue is the optimal exploitation of a given market position on which both management and stockholders may capitalize. It is not sufficient, because a given degree of managerial discretion may be typical for a whole industry.

As a marginal note, we should emphasize that Galbraith excludes top management from the actual decision process.

15 Armen A. Alchian and Harold Demsetz, "Production, Information Costs and Economic Organization," *American Economic Review* 62 (1972): 777–95.

16 Compare Alchian, "Corporate Management."

17 The latter control mechanism is discussed in Henry G. Manne, "Mergers and the Market for Corporate Control," *Journal of Political Economy* 73 (1965): 110–21.

The function of the directors is confined to a mere ritualistic ratification of the decisions of subordinate staff members. Taken to its logical consequence, the argumentation could be applied to any position in the organizational decision pyramid, with the surprising result that the lowest level of the hierarchical order has the actual power and any higher level has only a ritualistic function. Similar arguments were submitted in Galbraith's earlier book *The New Industrial State.* But in the same context—and there is no textual evidence that he changed his position in his later writings—he assigns to the top management group a very crucial and decisive role that cannot be reconciled with the above-mentioned mere ceremonial function: "It selects the men who comprise the group that make decisions, and it *constitutes* and *reconstitutes* these groups in accordance with changing needs."[18] Sharpe is correct when he sets forth the inherent contradiction of the dual management role.[19] The very fact of selecting the decision-making body means selecting one's own preferred decisions, which means that Galbraith's position is reduced to a mere camouflage for an otherwise untenable hypothesis. With regard to the empirical foundation, there is now overwhelming evidence for industries in different countries that a change in top management positions may have a decisive effect on the behavior of the corporation.[20]

Managerial Discretion
(Part Three, X and XI)

According to Galbraith, modern corporate management pursues its own pecuniary and nonpecuniary interests and not those of its legitimatizing owners. Given the near omnipotence of the technostructure, it is not difficult to fulfill its major protective interest, namely, to secure its own existence. The main possible sources of intervention—owners and creditors—are excluded from any discretionary activity by the provision of an uninterrupted flow of earnings. A plurality

18 Galbraith, *New Industrial State* (1971), p. 83, italics added.

19 Sharpe, *Galbraith and the Lower Economics*, p. 50.

20 For a short sample of more dramatic examples for the United States, see ibid., pp. 51–53.

of other instruments is available to exclude also the other major groups challenging the autonomy of the incumbent management. This we will discuss below. Given the guarantee of its protective purposes, the corporate firm can be directed toward the fulfillment of the intrinsic interest of the technostructure, which is the realization of a growth rate as large as possible. Growth serves directly the nonpecuniary and indirectly also the pecuniary purposes of all members of the technostructure. The first strategy for growth is the largest possible expansion of production and sales given the existing plant and firm size; the second strategy is the quite obvious effort to take over existing smaller-sized firms.

In Galbraith's theory of the firm, corporate management seeks to pursue a "panoply of organizational interests."[21] But these pecuniary and nonpecuniary interests can all be subsumed under the most important goal, which is to obtain the greatest possible rate of growth of the firm. Galbraith borrows from the work of Baumol and others when he maintains that after earning a minimum rate of profit the firm proceeds to trade off higher profit rates for the prospect of increasing the growth rate of the firm. Galbraith—like Baumol—is mistaken when he thinks that growth rate maximization is the dynamic counterpart of the static model of sales revenue maximization. It is the latter model to which he refers several times when comparing his analysis with the "old-fashioned" model of profit maximization. The following discussion is addressed to the evaluation of some analytical aspects of the two models referred to by Galbraith: growth rate maximization and sales revenue maximization.

Given any initial state of the firm, growth rate maximization—and this may be, at least at first sight, surprising—requires intraperiod profit maximization, that is, profit maximization in every current and future period *given* the inherited stock of capital. Contrasted with a firm maximizing profit, a firm striving for growth rate maximization will permanently overinvest—at least under steady-state conditions, for which almost all models are constructed. There is a straightforward analogy to the neoclassical growth model, in which the firm might deviate from the golden rule path

21 John Kenneth Galbraith, "Economics as a System of Belief," *American Economic Review* 60 (May 1970): 473.

because the investment rate is too high. For his own hypothesis Galbraith states an important proviso, namely, that a necessary minimum rate of profits must be secured. Without any further information about the workings of the capital market, it may well happen that the desired rate is exactly equal to the rate that maximizes the present value of the firm. Galbraith does not specify the mechanism determining the required minimum rate, which means that the reader has to invent his own discriminating test implications.

Recently, Harold Demsetz has designed such a test. The result was unambiguous: there is no empirical evidence of any relationship between any of several indices of a firm's technostructure orientation and a measure of the trade-off between the average annual growth rate of sales and the average annual rate of return on equity over the analyzed period 1958–70. Perhaps Demsetz's analysis includes the wrong test variables. But in this case the real Galbraith should stand up and formulate the adequate test environment.[22]

Almost all models emphasizing growth rate maximization are formulated under steady-state conditions, which means that there is no ambiguity with regard to the maximand variable. Under non-steady-state conditions there is a whole range of variables offering a choice for the best target. Non-steady-state conditions raise another familiar problem. We recall from capital theory that maximizing the internal rate of return on investment leaves the scale of the operation completely unspecified. The same is valid for Galbraith's proposal to maximize "the" growth rate of the firm.

More important, growth rate maximization has no static counterpart. Or, if we state it otherwise, the dynamic counterpart of the static model of sales revenue maximization is not maximization of the growth rate of the firm but maximization of the present value of discounted future sales revenue.[23] The applied discount rate is a subjective mag-

22 Harold Demsetz, "Where Is the New Industrial State?" *Economic Inquiry* 12 (1974): 1–12. There is a theoretical ambiguity in Demsetz's procedure, for he thinks incorrectly that growth rate maximization is the dynamic counterpart of sales revenue maximization. And it may well be that the latter model performs better.

23 See John H. Williamson, "Profit, Growth, and Sales Maximization," *Economica* 32 (1966): 1–16.

nitude and not market-determined. This fact does not offer a direct and simple operational test implication. But without entering into the particulars of this model, it is sufficient to note that it has nothing in common with a model emphasizing maximization of a growth rate. For the most general case, static sales revenue maximization—usually stated under the proviso of a given minimum profit restraint[24]—yields a revenue level and therefore an output level larger than the one forthcoming under conditions of pure profit maximization. And it should be obvious that a model leading to overproduction must be based on different behavior assumptions from those of a model leading to overcapitalization. It is now up to Galbraith to resolve the contradictions caused by the use of two different models of the behavior of the capitalistic firm.

Sales revenue maximization tries to evade the index number problems associated with defining the output of a multiproduct firm, and if we judge from the underlying behavioral motivation of the somewhat technically specified hypothesis of the sales revenue model—that is, maximizing sales revenue will enhance the power of the technostructure and enlarge the spectrum of pecuniary and nonpecuniary advantages given by an increased capital basis, increased firm size, extended market share, etc.—we are inclined to assume that the inventors of such models are virtually interested in maximizing "output" subject to a given minimum profit level. We know from introductory price theory that sales revenue and production are usually positively related only up to a certain output level. An output maximizer subject to a minimum profit constraint may push production over the maximum value of sales revenue. But then we have to admit that management relies basically on two different utility functions, one for each branch of the total revenue curve.

Sellers' Pricing Behavior
(Part Three, XII)

In order to avoid the risks and hazards of the market, which is the prerequisite for rational and efficient planning, the

24 An economically somewhat strange hypothesis, because in fact it implies that management is not willing to trade off a small amount of sales revenue for whatever large amount of current profits offered as a compensation.

Galbraithian firm must be able to control at least the prices of its final products. To fulfill this is not difficult because the size of the corporate firm in its given industry allows monopolistic price fixing. Given the controllability of product prices, "their safest recourse is to exercise the initial control not over production with its uncertain effect on price but to fix the price. Production is then accommodated to what can be sold at that price" (p. 114). It follows from the affirmative purposes of the technostructure that the prices set to foster growth are necessarily lower than the prices set by a wealth- or profit-maximizing firm. The oligopolistic structure of the typical capitalistic industry requires price leadership by a dominant firm, for otherwise the uncoordinated activities would be self-destructive. Once more the common protective purposes of all technostructures involved guarantee a quasi-automatic coordination of all major firms to their mutual advantage.

The actors in the Galbraithian world are all price searchers. Of course, Galbraith does not use this term, which has some implicit connotations referring to information and adjustment costs. A systematic analysis of these cost items is completely lacking in his writings.[25] Recognition of the existence of these costs would prevent him from reproducing the familiar but definitely wrong clichés derivable from standard static price theory, namely, attributing to the activities of so-called imperfect competitors the undesirable consequences of too small an output level at too high prices with the result of excessive profit rates and inefficient allocation of the social product. According to Galbraith, technostructure-oriented firms modify somewhat this "neoclassical" result because they strive for sales revenue maximization.

Whatever the goal function may be, the decisive factor is that these imperfect competitors control prices. Here Galbraith's position is most confusing, for setting prices says nothing about the underlying search process. Changing prices has the consequence of a corresponding change in the quantity sold. This could be called the power to administer prices. But we should note that, from a negatively sloped

25 Arbitrary implicit assumptions about the magnitude of information and adjustment costs, either zero or infinite, are to a large degree responsible for a faithful adherence to the market classification scheme of standard neoclassical price theory.

demand curve per se, nothing can be inferred with regard to market power or ability to earn "excessive" profits. "A modern myth has grown up around the 'facts of life' in price-searchers' markets—the facts that their prices fluctuate less than those of price-takers' markets, the prices of the individual firms change at about the same time, and the largest firm usually is a price leader."[26] The first phenomenon disappears simply by referring to a lack of any factual evidence supporting the conjecture that price searchers administer prices regardless of demand and supply conditions, disregarding for the moment the errors in interpreting the underlying statistical data.[27] The phenomenon that the prices change at about the same time is the result of an adaptive search process conditioned by the same environmental variables. Finally, from the fact that the largest firm usually initiates this process, it does not follow that it has the power to dictate the prices for the remaining firms in the industry.

The Effects of a Wage Increase—Some Formal Extensions (Part Three, XII)

Of utmost importance is the controllability of prices because some major cost items, especially labor costs, are not fully within the control of the firm. But the firm has the compensating option that any conflict with organized labor can be resolved at the expense of the buyers of the final products in form of higher output prices. He maintains: "In the planning system. . . increased wage costs can readily be passed on to the public." "Usually the price increase will be more than sufficient to offset the cost of the wage increase; this is because the occasion of the price increase following the wage increase is used also to rectify the level of earnings in favor of the firm. . . . That price increases usually follow wage negotiations shows, more than incidentally, that profit maximization is not a purpose of the technostructure. If revenues can be increased just after a wage increase, they could, obviously,

26 Armen A. Alchian and William R. Allen, *University Economics: Elements of Inquiry*, 3d ed. (Belmont, Calif.: Wadsworth, 1972), pp. 343–44.

27 For a recent test of this position with regard to technostructure-oriented firms, see Demsetz, "Where Is the New Industrial State?" *Economic Inquiry* 12 (1974): 1–12.

have been increased well before" (p. 118). It is usually a dominant firm, knowing both market and industry conditions best, that acts as a price leader and initiates this adjustment process. We should expect that the strong ostracism of price competition within a specific industry should open the door for different modes of nonprice competition, especially advertising efforts. But somehow, a mechanism that Galbraith does not explain is effectively working so that the individual selling efforts will be coordinated to the mutual benefit of all firms in the industry.

The discussion in *Economics and the Public Purpose* repeats some ideas presented previously in *The New Industrial State.* There Galbraith argued that a firm maximizing profits would have no incentive to pass on a wage increase because the wealth-maximizing price is already determined. The fact that the modern corporation does pass on wage increases thus disproves—according to Galbraith—the profit-maximizing hypothesis. Solow, in his review of the book, charged Galbraith with committing a sophomore error: "The ideal textbook firm will indeed pass along a wage increase, to a calculable extent."[28] To locate the essence of the dispute between Solow and Galbraith: Both agree about the qualitative aspects of the adjustment but disagree, apparently, about the quantitative magnitude, because according to Galbraith the price increase will be more than sufficient to offset the wage increase, a result that is hardly accommodated by any of the familiar models of the firm.[29]

When Galbraith discusses the management goals, he relies on the growth rate maximization model. When he discusses pricing behavior and output decisions, he refers to sales revenue maximization. But even here—as is clear from the quotations above—Galbraith's analysis is blurred by inconsistencies and mistakes. It is therefore worthwhile to set forth in a brief summary the characteristic adjustment responses of some more familiar models of individual firm behavior, both of the entrepreneurial and managerial type, related to a general change in one of the environmental con-

28 Solow, "New Industrial State," p. 107.

29 It may be that Galbraith intends to discuss the parallel development of wages and prices during a period of inflationary growth. Given this interpretation, the description will simply beg the question.

ditions, a change in the wage rate (see tables 1 and 2). As mentioned, we reject Galbraith's model of the price-setting firm for explaining the price structure of a specific industry. But it is possible to generalize the analysis to the case of price leadership by an appropriate reinterpretation of the revenue function and to use the results as a simple test of logical consistency.

Our sample of representative firm models includes three entrepreneurial models (the familiar profit maximization model; a model emphasizing sales revenue maximization, which could reflect Galbraith's static theory of the firm; and a model focusing on output maximization). The managerial models, (4)–(6), are modified versions of some of the proposals found in the literature on managerial economics. We omit a further discussion of the first-order conditions and concentrate our interest directly on the derived comparative static responses of a change in the money wage rate on some key economic variables, which is the subject matter of the quoted Galbraithian conjectures. Ignoring for a mo-

Table 1
Some Simple Models of the Individual Firm

Entrepreneurial Models

Profit Maximization:*

1. $\pi = R(q, A) - C(q, \bar{w}) - A$
   $R_q > 0,\ R_A > 0,\ C_q > 0,\ C_{\bar{w}} > 0;$
   $R_{qq} < 0,\ R_{AA} < 0,\ C_{qq} > 0;$
   $R_{qA} > 0,\ C_{q\bar{w}} > 0.$

Sales Revenue Maximization Subject to a Minimum Profit Constraint (Galbraith's Model):

2. $\underset{q,\,A}{\text{Max}}\ R(q, A)$ subject to $-R(q, A) + C(q, \bar{w}) + A \leq -\pi^0$

Output Maximization Subject to a Minimum Profit Constraint:

3. $\underset{q,\,A}{\text{Max}}\ q$ subject to $-R(q, A) + C(q, \bar{w}) + A \leq -\pi^0$

Managerial Models

Two Modified Versions of the Williamson Model:†

4. $\underset{q,\,S,\,A}{\text{Max}}\ U(S)$ subject to
   $$-R\,(q),\,S,\,A) + C\,(q,\,\bar{w}) + S + A \leq -\pi^0$$
   $$U_S>0,\ R_S>0.$$

5. $\underset{q,\,S,\,M,\,D,\,A}{\text{Max}}\ U\,(S,\,M,\,D)$ subject to
   $$-R\,(q,\,A) + C\,(q,\,\bar{w}) + S + M + D + A \leq -\pi^0$$
   $$U_S>0,\ U_M>0,\ U_D>0.$$

A Modified Version of the Ames Model:‡

6. $\underset{q,\,\pi,\,A}{\text{Max}}\ U\,(q,\,\pi)$ subject to $-R\,(q,\,A) + C\,(q,\,\bar{w}) + A + \pi \leq 0$
   $$U_q>0,\ U_\pi>0.$$

NOTE:

A = advertising expenditure
C = total production costs
D = discretionary profit
M = managerial emoluments
p = output price level $[R(.)/q]$
q = output
R = total sales revenue
S = staff expenditure
$\bar{w}$ = given nominal wage rate
π = total profit
π^0 = minimum required profit level

---

*To generalize the analysis to a model of price leadership, we could assume that the revenue function includes the reaction functions of the rival followers in the industry.

†Oliver E. Williamson, *The Economics of Discretionary Behavior: Managerial Objectives in a Theory of the Firm* (Englewood Cliffs, N.J.: Prentice-Hall, 1964). In order to simplify, we have excluded a revenue effect of staff expenditure in model (5).

‡Edward Ames, *Soviet Economic Processes* (New York: Irwin, 1965), p. 50 ff.

Table 2
Comparative Static Responses of a Change in the Money Wage Rate on Selected Endogenous Variables

Model	A	p	q	R	π
1	–	? (+)	– (–)	– (–)	– (–)
2	?	? (+)	– (–)	– (–)	0 (0, –)
3	–	? (+)	– (–)	– (–, +)	0 (0)
4	–	? (+)	– (–)	– (–)	0 (0)
5	–	? (+)	– (–)	– (–)	? (?)
6	?	? (?)	? (?)	? (?)	? (?)

NOTE: Signs in parentheses specify model responses excluding advertising expenditure. The only information used are the signs of the first and second partial derivatives, first- and second-order conditions, and the *Kuhn-Tucker* theorem. The Hoteling-condition was applied in model (2).

ment the last model and abstracting from the signs in parentheses, we observe that the response pattern is quite uniform for the different models. An increase in the wage rate will depress sales revenue and decrease the output level. The effects on advertising expenditure are (with one exception[30]) negative, which implies, because advertising expenditure and prices are both instruments to affect the quantity sold, that the price responses are generally undetermined. If we exclude advertising expenditure, we observe that the price effects become generally determined. But there is no basis for accommodating the Galbraithian conjecture that there is a compensation of the negative cost effect. Only two results are ambivalent. This occurs when the firm is operating either at or to the right of the maximum revenue value. In model (2) this implies that profits will decrease (and not increase, as we conclude from Galbraith's contentions) and in model (3) this means that total revenue will increase.

Until now, we have excluded model (6) from our discussion. We see that none of the response signs can be deter-

30 Contrary to an a priori conjecture, the effects on A and q in model (2) are asymmetric. This follows from the fact that a change in the wage rate has no direct effect on advertising costs but is directly related to production costs, C.

mined without adding a priori, unjustified restrictions.[31] It is a good example of an instance in which even an apparently simple model yields no specific information. If we would base the analysis on a linear cardinal utility function, as Ames did in his original work, the results are clear-cut. Following an increase in the wage rate, profits, revenue, advertising expenditure, and output will decrease and the price level will increase.

In summary, Galbraith's contentions remain unsubstantiated. We could, of course, construct a disequilibrium model and assume that the firms are permanently off their demand curves. This model might yield the Galbraithian results, but only temporarily. Needless to say, such a model would imply an inventory and rationing adjustment process that is not accommodated by the existing empirical information. Which firm model is the correct one? Even if we leave aside this basically empirical question, we should note that the concomitance of the vague notion of a mainly unstructured firm model, of purely specified test implications, and of little, if any, empirical evidence is not an acceptable methodological basis for the complete rejection of the neoclassical model of wealth maximization.[32]

The Organization of the Industrial Economy
(Part Three, XIII)

In Galbraith's diagnosis, ability to control output prices is only one step toward a complete accommodation of major environmental variables and toward a neutralization of all major exogenous control mechanisms. The second step is to control cost items, too. Apart from labor costs, which pose

31 We could, for instance, specify the signs of the second direct and cross partials in order to get more direct information. This is, of course, not valid, because we would assume cardinal properties for the utility function. Something like this happened in the work of Williamson, who sometimes ignores the fact that his procedure is based on ordinal measurement assumptions. See Oliver E. Williamson, *The Economics of Discretionary Behavior: Managerial Objectives in a Theory of the Firm* (Englewood Cliffs, N.J.: Prentice-Hall, 1964).

32 For a new orientation of the traditional theory of production and exchange that avoids some major shortcomings of neoclassical theory, compare the literature of the new theory of property rights. See especially the review article by Eirik G. Furubotn and Svetozar Pejovich, "Property Rights and Economic Theory: A Survey of Recent Literature," *Journal of Economic Literature* 10 (1972): 1137–62.

a special problem, the normal strategy is to try to take over the supply sources of the inputs. Another device, much more important for coordinating the heterogeneous and conflicting interests of the various firms comprising the industrial system, is offered by the technique of the economic contract. The contract between different firms allows the protection of prices, costs, sales, and supplies to the mutual benefit of all firms. "The contract can be thought of as extending the security which the large consumers' good firm has in its own markets or the large weapons firm has in its relation with the government throughout the planning system..." (p. 125). A complex system of interlocking contracts has filled the place of the market and price mechanism that has failed to coordinate the activities of the firms in the planning system. It is, of course, quite obvious that the stronger bargaining power of the larger firms will push the profit rates of the smaller ones to a minimum acceptable level.

We mentioned above that in *The New Industrial State* Galbraith was not able to give a satisfactory explanation of the coordination of the plans of one firm with those of the other firms. It seems that Galbraith himself felt the necessity of inventing a device that should supersede the neoclassical notion of the price and market mechanism. This device is Galbraith's theory of contracts. "The contract is central for the protection of prices and costs and of sales and supplies at these prices and costs" (p. 128). If we understand a contract as a specification and a characterization of the content of a bundle of property rights that are exchanged in a mutually acceptable arrangement, it is quite obvious that Galbraith's theory is nothing more than a pure description of observed economic transactions. Analytically, it is a pure description because he fails to give a proper explanation of the specific *terms* of the specific contracts and the *coordination* of the interlocking contracts in the total planning system. To give an economically meaningful explanation would mean that relative price theory would slip in.[33] But this theory is rejected by Galbraith. Thus, once more Galbraith is left with-

33 If Galbraith intends to base his analysis on a theory of multilateral bargaining processes, we should object that these alone are not sufficient for explaining the workings of the adjustment mechanism of a complex economic structure. See Robert A. Dahl and Charles E. Lindblom, *Politics, Economics, and Welfare* (New York: Harper & Brothers, 1953).

out a theory of the organization of the economic system. It may be the case that our interpretation is mistaken and Galbraith thinks of the existence of an effective collusive agreement by all members of the planning system over all industries, whereby the terms and conditions for the viability of the net of interlocking contracts are stipulated, monitored, and policed by a dominant firm in the planning system. We are reminded of the naïve cartel theory whereby a group of competitors agree to share a market. In Galbraith's theory, the different technostructures, motivated by their "common protective and affirmative purposes," agree to share the whole economy. Effective collusive agreements do exist in different forms and in different markets and professions, but to use such a model as the explanation of the whole Galbraithian "planning system" of our mature capitalistic societies would mean leaving the realm of serious economic reasoning. As a marginal note we should add that Galbraith's "test implication" for his theory—namely, the alleged existence of a specific pattern of profit rates, being highest in technostructure-oriented firms—remains uncorroborated by the result of a broad and heterogeneous body of empirical research work.[34]

The Seller-Buyer Relationship
(Part Three, XIV)

According to Galbraith, controlling market prices is only meaningful if the firm is also successful in controlling the response of its buyers at those prices.[35] Advertising and

34 This follows from a cursory inspection of the literature. For substantiation, the reader should consult the survey by Yale Brozen, "The Antitrust Task Force Deconcentration Recommendation," *Journal of Law and Economics* 13 (1970): 279–290, or the review of published evidence by Harold Demsetz, *The Market Concentration Doctrine—An Examination of Evidence and a Discussion of Policy* (Washington, D.C.: American Enterprise Institute, 1973).

35 The original heading of this section in Galbraith's book is "Persuasion and Power." Galbraith (and other writers, too) tries consistently to convince the reader that mainstream economics disregards the power element in dealing with social processes. This is true as far as it concerns the meta-language, but it is certainly not true if the argumentation implies general neglect of a class of empirical phenomena related to the object language. We cannot imagine that the familiar textbook questions in response to scarcity—what determines how much each person produces and gets of the total, etc.—could be misunderstood as not pertaining to the distribution and the effects of "power" in a social system. And it is certainly wrong to assert that these questions remain completely unanswered.

general product management are the strategies that guarantee this success. Tastes and needs of the buyer fall under the authority of the producer. First impression suggests that the interests of different producers in a single market are in conflict, but second thoughts reveal that the common interest in growth and technical innovation resolves this conflict. If the whole system grows, partitioning of product markets and the related distribution of earnings and profits cease to be a zero-sum game. Needless to say, the close connection and interdependence between the technostructure of the larger corporate firms and the bureaucracies of the central government ensures complementary action in the form of assisting government expenditures flowing uninterruptedly at the required level.

Denying consumers' sovereignty and emphasizing producers' sovereignty, together with the assumption of an omnipotent salesman, are Galbraith's favorite pets. Reviewing briefly the literature on the concept of consumers' sovereignty, we have to admit that the definition and use of the concept is highly misleading, which means that Galbraith is basically right in attacking this notion. Sovereignty in its strict meaning implies that the consumer (or the producer) is able to impose his will on the producer (or the consumer). But exchange of money for goods and goods for money cannot be imposed on the other contracting party without ignoring the elementary principles of demand and supply analysis. "Market survival demands no more from sellers than it does from buyers. Each can spend his way into bankruptcy and each can survive bankruptcy without charity only if he remains within his budget constraint. Neither buyer nor seller is sovereign in the economics of the market place."[36] For example, in what sense can we infer that consumers in price takers' markets are more sovereign than consumers in price searchers' markets? Or, what meaning should we attach to the statement that a negatively sloped demand curve facing a producer will increase his producers' sovereignty? Given the state of affairs, we are best advised altogether to discard the concept of sovereignty from the list of economically meaningful terms.

---

36 Harold Demsetz, "Economics as a System of Belief—Discussion," *American Economic Review* 60 (May1970): 482.

With regard to the effects and consequences of advertising on the current and future allocation of goods and services, on the one hand, and the alleged influence of advertising on the stability of prices, market shares, and the degree of competitiveness of an industry, on the other hand, we most certainly need more detailed information. Telser's much-cited conclusion that "there is little empirical support of an inverse association between advertising and competition despite some plausible theoretical theorizing to the contrary"[37] may be well suited to disappointing a popular folkloristic position but should not induce us to overlook that we still lack the theoretical apparatus that rationalizes this conclusion. Reference to an allegedly very complex process of want creation is a polite way of paraphrasing our ignorance, but at the same moment we could implicitly admit thereby that few of man's wants are of biological or genetic origin. We simply have to face the fact, as Demsetz emphasizes, that social scientists have not yet developed a general theory of want creation.[38] But insufficient knowledge about the allocative, aggregative, and welfare-theoretical consequences of advertising should at least make us aware of jumping to the either wrong or trivial Galbraithian conclusion that "manipulation" is all-pervasive and, in addition, a one-sided market phenomenon. Manipulation is costly, which means that producers are prevented from hypnotizing the consumers into any desired price-quantity combination in the price-quantity orthant.

A few points that seem to characterize Galbraith's position could be summarized as follows: (1) There is a danger of confusing the process of want creation with the formal problem of expanding or contracting the available choice set. (2) There is textual evidence that the normative, empirical, and analytical aspects of the assumption "given the wants of the

37 Lester G. Telser, "Advertising and Competition," *Journal of Political Economy* 72 (1964): 558.

38 Demsetz, "Economics as a System of Belief—Discussion," pp. 482–83. We should warn the reader that this notion, although commonly referred to, is somewhat misleading. Specifying the appropriate utility function is mainly an empirical question. All utility functions with which we are familiar are necessarily subjected to a certain degree of semireduction with respect to the social system involved. But from this it does not follow that the effects of advertising should be analyzed as operating on the preference function. The alternative, which may be more promising, is to rely on a more general, socially bounded budget restraint.

consumers'' are misunderstood. (3) There is no rational basis for falling into precipitate ethical judgment that "inborn" or "natural'' wants are superior to "manipulated" or "socially determined" wants.[39] (4) A clear distinction should be made among the effects of advertising, the ethical basis for advertising per se, and the undesirability of misleading or fraudulent advertising. (5) There is a difference between policies trying to improve the basis for better-informed and more rational decision making, on the one side, and, on the other side, proposals to abolish the freedom of consumers' choice in the marketplace, with its implication of accepting or tolerating the negative consequences of uninformed or risky decisions that are later regretted.

The Role of Technical Innovation
(Part Three, XV)

Given the interests of the technostructure, technical innovation will be organized in such a way as to serve its protective and affirmative purposes. It is interesting to note that the labor-saving effects of innovation will be utilized over and above the margins set by least-cost considerations. Capital-intensive methods enhance the security and power of the technostructure and assist, combined with its senior partner advertising, in stimulating the psychic obsolescence of consumer goods. The highest degree of technical obsolescence is of course realized in the military-industrial complex, where the replacement rates are most dramatic.

A general discussion of Galbraith's "Revised Economics of Technical Innovation" can be subsumed under our previous discussion. Once more, the arguments are blurred by price-theoretical inconsistencies and a lack of a specific characterization of the underlying managerial motivational structure. Concerning the allegedly planned obsolescence, we should urge Galbraith to do serious empirical research so as to corroborate this speculative conjecture.

39 Ignoring for the moment Galbraith's untenable position that there is a systematic causal relationship between the degree of affluence in a society and the relative dominance of "socially determined" wants. But we should mention that the reservation stated in n. 38 applies here, too.

Public Policy in the Industrial Society
(Part Three, XVI)

It is not surprising that public policy is strongly determined by the common interests of the planning system. "The planning system, having prestige as a source of goods and services and thus as a source of public happiness, will have influence as a source of political suggestion" (p. 157). In addition to this, a "bureaucratic symbiosis" makes it possible for the planning system to approach the government directly through its relationship with the public officials. Furthermore, the ability of the planning system to pass on a wage increase in the prices of its final products resolves the basic conflict between capital and labor and, as a consequence, allows an endorsement of corporate needs as public needs.

The "bureaucratic symbiosis" allegedly unifies the interests of the technostructure of the major corporations—and especially those working for the defense department—with the interests of the leaders of the political scene.[40] If Galbraith's analytical description is correct, we should be able to observe a stable and riskless performance environment for the large defense contractors under this symbiosis. Again, this speculation is not substantiated by empirical evidence. As a simple test, Demsetz has analyzed the behavior of a sample of thirteen stocks of prime defense contractors. The results he found are rather plain: "These stocks over the period 1949–64 offered to investors about 21 percent more risk, measured by the mean deviation of the year-to-year rates of return, than did thirteen stock randomly selected portfolios."[41]

There is another strand of more indirect governmental promotion to secure a riskless operation of the modern corporate firm, because fiscal policy is always able to provide the suitable set of instruments for creating a favorable business climate. With regard to stabilization policy, we should

40 The political-economic aspects of this popular theme are extensively discussed in Gäfgen, "Galbraithian Economics," which makes it unnecessary to cover these issues once more. For a further discussion of some of the issues involved, compare the two major interpretive treatises on Galbraithian economics by Charles H. Hession, *John Kenneth Galbraith and His Critics* (New York: New American Library, 1972), and Sharpe, *Galbraith and the Lower Economics*.

41 Demsetz, "Economics as a System of Belief—Discussion," pp. 483–84.

emphasize that Galbraith is a devoted Keynesian and a strict adherent to the 45-degree diagram of aggregate demand analysis. The effects of monetary policy are only unreliable concomitant phenomena impeding an effective strategy for influencing monetary and real target variables based on fiscal policy. We hesitate to draw the obvious conclusion from Galbraith's writings that he actually maintained the definitely wrong assertion that the "bureaucratic symbiosis" in fact provided the adequate environmental climate. Empirically, we have to diagnose that the symbiosis failed, and it failed either because government was not interested in promoting the planning system in an unrestricted way by disregarding all social costs or that the central government, by relying strictly on a fiscal policy apparatus, was not able to do it at all. This latter statement is backed by referring to recent empirical work that has produced impressive evidence that the leading simple Keynesian paradigm is a most unreliable and inadequate guide to explanation and control of the behavior of the real world.

Some International Aspects
(Part Three, XVII)

The accommodation of the major influential groups to the needs of the Galbraithian planning system is not restricted to domestic markets but transcends the national territory. Galbraith claims that a multinational system of mutual interconnectives between the major corporate firms works basically in the same way as the national planning system. Efforts to control the environment, thereby immunizing itself from the influence of all major control mechanisms, are unimpeded both nationally and internationally.

Galbraith's notion of the workings of the multinational system may be thought of as a revised reconstruction of the familiar theme of the conspiracy of international capital or as a bourgeois theory of economic imperialism.[42] This may be the case, but the motivation is different. "The master of

42 We call it a bourgeois theory of imperialism because the conflicting managerial interests are apparently amalgamated into the consonant interests of the team spirit of the technostructure—as contrasted with Marxian theories that allow for divergent and self-destructive behavior of the capitalist actors.

persuasion" cannot be satisfied if he does not succeed in subsuming the interests of all technostructures of all industrial societies under the gigantic Galbraithian vision of an economic process that accommodates their "common protective and affirmative purposes." This is big-thinking par excellence.

Instead of a Summary

The issues under discussion are all taken from chapter 3, "The Planning System." According to Galbraith's own position and according to our assessment, this chapter is the most important one, and judged by standards of modern economic theory, it is one of the better parts of Galbraith's treatise. The skeptical reader may test this statement by reading, for instance, chapter 5, "A General Theory of Reform." At the least, this chapter should make it sufficiently clear that Galbraith's poor technical tools, the continual concomitance of inadequate logic, unstated assumptions, unspecified implications, the theoretical background of an obsolete economic perspective—pieces of the price theory of the early thirties and the Keynesian 45-degree diagram—and the absence of any systematic factual evidence do not provide a reliable intellectual basis for dealing effectively with the problems of our mature industrial societies.

Svetozar Pejovich**

The Capitalist Corporation and the Socialist Firm;

A Study of Comparative Efficiency*

The standard theory of production and exchange has provided fundamental insights into social problems that find their source in scarcity. It has demonstrated that, in a competitive equilibrium, the extent of exchange is consistent with the equimarginal principle. The theory has suggested testable implications for a number of world events and, most significantly, explained the efficiency characteristics of competitive markets.

> Competition for and transferability of the ownership rights in the market place thus perform two main functions for contracting. First, competition conglomerates knowledge from all potential owners—the knowledge of alternative contractual arrangements and uses of the resources; and transferability of property rights ensures (via flexible relative prices) that the most valuable will be utilized. Second, competition among potential contract participants and a resource owner's ability to transfer the right to use his resource reduce the cost of enforcing the stipulated terms in a contract . . . because competing parties will stand by to offer or accept similar terms.[1]

* Reprinted, with some changes, by permission of the author and from *Schweizerische Zeitschrift für Volkswirtschaft und Statistik,* 1976, no. 1, pp. 1–25. An earlier draft of the paper presented at the Second Annual Interlaken Seminar on Analysis and Ideology, Switzerland.

** The writing of this paper was facilitated by grants from the Center for Research in Government Policy and Business, the University of Rochester; the National Science Foundation; and the Earhart Foundation.

1 S. Cheung, "The Structure of a Contract and the Theory of a Non-exclusive Resource," *Journal of Law and Economics* 13 (1970): 64.

The limitations of the traditional theory are, however, real and quite significant. They can be traced to the structure of the standard competitive model, which implies (1) that one specific set of private property rights governs the use of *all* resources, and (2) that the exchange, policing and enforcement costs (i.e., transaction costs) are *zero.* The events that fall outside the scope of traditional theory can then be traced either to high transaction costs or the effects of various types of property rights assignments on the allocation and use of scarce resources. In either case, allocative solutions are inconsistent with the equimarginal principle (i.e., private and social costs and benefits are not identical).

Unfortunately, the inability of theory to explain *all* real world events has been only too frequently interpreted as its inability to explain *any* event. Thus, instead of trying to broaden the scope of validity of the standard competitive model, the inapplicability of theory has been blamed on externalities and imperfect competition. A number of ad hoc theories have been developed to deal with these exceptions.[2]

While it is undoubtedly important to insist on the recognition of the inadequacies of the standard theory, it is equally important to recognize that ad hoc theorizing is always restricted to a limited class of observations and can offer no replacement for a more general theory.[3] In recent years, some significant advances have been made in the direction of expanding the scope of the standard theory of production and exchange. A body of literature has grown up around the notion of property rights structures.[4] The key theoretical concepts underlying the property rights approach to a generalization of the standard theory are that (1) the concept of nonattenuated private property rights is no longer accepted as the only relevant configuration and (2) transaction costs are taken to be positive. By placing emphasis on the interconnectedness of property rights, incentives, and economic

---

2 Examples include division of externalities by types, as well as sales maximization, market share, the dominant ownership, and other hypotheses concerning the behavior of modern corporations.

3 See A. Alchian, "The Basis of Some Recent Advances in the Theory of Management of the Firm," *Journal of Industrial Economics* 14 (1965): 30–41.

4 See E. Furubotn and S. Pejovich, "Property Rights and Economic Theory," *Journal of Economic Literature* 10 (1972): 1137–62.

behavior, the property rights approach extends the ability of the standard theory to explain a wider class of real events. More specifically, it derives the implied behavior of many types of firms from the analysis of the interaction of the legal system and economic behavior.

The major objective of this paper is to use the property rights approach to discuss the question, Can the socialist firm offer allocative solutions that are more consistent with the equimarginal principle than those yielded by the modern capitalist corporation? First, however, the paper will briefly discuss the relationship between the concept of property rights and economic behavior.

Property Rights and Scarce Resources

We shall define property rights as behavioral relations among men that arise from the existence of things and pertain to their use. The property rights assignments specify the norms of behavior, with respect to things, that each and every person must observe in his interaction with other persons or bear the cost of nonobservance—a penalty for parking in a no-parking area. Then, the prevailing system of property rights in the community can be described as the set of economic and social relations defining the position of each individual with respect to the utilization of scarce resources. It follows that the right of ownership, whether by a private individual or the state, is but a category of the general concept of property rights.

The right of ownership in an asset consists of the following rights: (1) the right to use that asset *(usus)*, (2) the right to capture returns from it *(ususfructus)*, (3) the right to change its form and substance *(abusus)*, and (4) the right to transfer that asset to others at a mutually agreed-upon price. The last two rights define the owner's right to bear changes in the value of his assets and represent the fundamental components of the right of ownership.

Of course, it is relatively easy to assert that a relationship exists between property rights assignments, transaction costs, and the allocation and use of scarce resources. The crucial problems are to demonstrate that the development and specification of property rights can be explained as responses to social problems that find their source in scarcity and that the content of property rights, in turn, affects the allocation and use of resources in *specific* and *predictable* ways.

Let us begin our discussion with the following questions: What are the expected effects of the absence of property rights assignments in a resource on both the allocation of the existing supply between competing claimants (i.e., the current rate of utilization) and the long-run supply schedule? Clearly, the nonowned resource is a free good as far as individuals are concerned. It is a scarce good, however, from the point of view of the community as a whole. The allocative criteria are then either first-come-first-serve, or violence, or both. That is, if I fail to capture a nonowned good *now*, someone else will. The private cost of "purchasing" a nonowned good includes my opportunity income from labor but not the value of that good to society. The logic of economics then suggests that the rate of consumption of nonowned resources exceeds the rate that would otherwise prevail if the users had to bear the entire social costs.[5]

The absence of property rights in a resource is also bound to affect its long-run supply schedule.[6] A potential investor in a nonowned good must bear the entire cost of policing and enforcing his claim to the future benefits from investment. The absence of property rights raises transaction costs to the investor and consequently reduces the present value of returns from any given flow of expected future returns. It follows that the rate of investment in a nonowned good must fall short of what it would otherwise be in an environment in which transaction costs are lower. Empirical evidence does not seem to refute this conclusion. One has only to ask what happened (and why) to the American buffalo, the whale, nonowned forests, the age distribution of fish in public lakes compared to private, etc. The old dictum that everybody's property is nobody's property seems quite relevant. From the social point of view, the preservation of a resource, as well as incentives to use it more efficiently, re-

5 S. Gordon, "The Economic Theory and a Common Property Resource: Fishery," *Journal of Political Economy* 62 (1970): 124–42.

6 A. Bottomley, "The Effect of the Common Ownership of Land upon Resource Allocation in Tripolitania," *Land Economics* 39 (1963): 91–95.

quires some specification in property rights over that resource.

It is clear that individuals could capture additional benefits for themselves by excluding or constraining others from uncontrolled access to a nonowned resource. It follows that acting in response to their desire for more utility, individuals or groups will try to exclude others from the exploitation of a good whenever their own expected benefits appear to exceed the costs of defining, negotiating, policing, or enforcing the "claim." Of course, the act of exclusion of others from uncontrolled access to a good *means* a change in the content of the prevailing property rights in that good. New property rights are then created and the existing ones changed because it appears profitable for individuals and groups to bear the cost of bringing about such changes. This point relates the standard economic theory to changes in the content of property rights in scarce resources.

Social implications of the creation and specification of property rights are quite significant. When individuals or groups acquire the right to exclude others from exploiting a good, their own costs of using that good exceed their opportunity income from labor. In other words, as individuals capture more rights in a good, the divergence between private and social costs diminishes. *The fuller the specification of property rights assignments in resources, the smaller the difference between private and social costs.* Given the law of demand and man's desire for more satisfaction, *a predictable consequence of improvements in the content of property rights is that resources will move to higher-valued uses.* As individuals capture more rights in resources, some incremental benefits will then accrue to both the individuals and the community as a whole. It follows that nonattenuated private property rights are a powerful, and possibly necessary, condition for the efficient allocation and use of scarce resources.

For example, in the early days of the Roman Empire a form of communal ownership, *ager gentilicius,* developed. *Agri gentilicii* were pastures and forests owned by Gens (a sort of clan of the same stock in the male line, with the members having a common ancestor) and exploited by all members in accordance with their needs. *Agri gentilicii* had all the major characteristics of communal ownership. Gens took care of their pastures because the clan bore the costs of using the land. Yet, privately borne costs from the exploitation of commonly held pastures differ from total social costs for two reasons: (1) not all costs of a member's activity are borne by himself—his private costs of grazing another steer on a commonly owned pasture are clearly below social costs; and (2) nontransferability of land prevents members of the group from capturing for themselves the value of the expected future benefits from pastures. Thus, pastures and forests owned by Gens in old Rome had to be overutilized relative to the rate of exploitation that would have prevailed if each member of the clan had to bear the entire cost of his activity. Then, as agriculture developed in Rome, the relationship between the prevailing property rights and the cost-benefit considerations changed. The development of agriculture raised the value of crop growing relative to ranching. To accomplish the required transfer of land to a higher-valued use, the content of property rights had to be changed. True enough, *ager gentilicius* was replaced by a form of family ownership, *consortium*—a sort of property arrangement that permitted the family to enjoy exclusively a well-defined tract of land but not to sell it. The effects of this new property rights arrangement were many. The clan broke down into smaller family units; individuals captured more rights in the land; the difference between private and social costs of using the land diminished relative to previous conditions; and the land was put into a higher-valued use. The land was still nontransferable, however, and some gap between private and social costs had to remain.

The development of property relations in post-Roman Europe is a classical example of the opposite phenomenon. The institution of private property was fully developed in the Roman law and enforced by the state. This meant that transaction costs of policing one's property were reduced and the differences between social and private costs of using resources narrowed down. However, the collapse of the Roman Empire and a complete disintegration of its legal structure resulted in the replacement of order by chaos. As the costs of defining, negotiating, policing, and enforcing private property rights rose relative to the benefits, a backward change in the content of property rights took place.

Since violence became the predominant method for resolving conflicts of interests among people in a world in which barbaric customs had replaced Roman law, the cost of excluding outsiders from what one considered to be his property increased; and the outcome was, as our analysis would suggest, a return to a sort of property sharing by a larger group. The survival trait for a weaker man was to turn to a stronger man and give him the nontransferable right of ownership in his land in exchange for protection and a right of tenancy—*the right to hold the land of the lord.* The lord-tenant (vassal) relationship then emerged as the basic social institution in medieval Europe. The land held by the vassal was called *feud.* A lord could—and often did—become the vassal of still another man; that is, he became both the lord of a weaker man and vassal of a stronger man. In time, this chain between the lord at the top and the actual toilers at the bottom lengthened, and there developed a sociopolitical system based on a hierarchical method of holding property rights in the most important resource of the day: land *(feuds).* The system eventually developed a great many rules to regulate the rights of lords, vassals, and serfs.

If our discussion above is correct, the creation and specification of property rights can be traced to changes in the economic situation in the community. A question must then be raised: How are changes in the economic situation translated into the development of new property rights?

The basic purpose of exchange is to help us to endure the fact that we live in a world of scarcity. The point is that a person voluntarily exchanges one good for another—a pair of shoes for ten dollars' worth of other things—or substitutes one activity for another—fishing for hunting—because he *expects* to reach a higher level of satisfaction. The purpose of exchange is then independent of the prevailing property rights assignments in the community, although the *extent* and the *terms* of exchange are not. This is an important point which emphasizes the relationship between the content of property rights and economic value. The relationship is inferred from the fact that exchange exists not so much to accomplish the transfer of goods and services but to permit the exchange of "bundles" of rights to do things with goods that are traded. The value of any good that is exchanged, and the value of any activity that is substituted for others, depends on the bundle of property rights that is conveyed in transactions. For example, the value of a house to an individual will be relatively greater if the bundle of property rights acquired contains the right to exclude gasoline stations, factories, etc., from the immediate vicinity of the house. Also, the value of fishing relative to other activities open to an individual will be relatively greater if fishing grounds are not open to all, that is, if some sort of property rights in fishing grounds is established. It follows that the bundle of various property rights held in goods affects the decision maker's choice. Consequently, the content of property rights assignments affects the allocation of resources, the output mix, and the distribution of income.

A *contractual agreement* is the means by which the bundles of rights to do things with goods are exchanged. Every transaction implies a contract, while every contract transfers some specified bundle of property rights from one contractual party to another. The purpose of contractual activity is, then, to specify the bundles of rights that are being exchanged and, in effect, move resources to their higher-valued uses within the constraints imposed by the prevailing property rights structures.

Legal contracts are expensive to draw up and also costly to enforce. It is therefore safe to suggest that the extent of exchange in the community would be sharply reduced if each and every transaction has to presuppose the actual existence of a legal contract. It is equally safe to predict that in his search for more utility, man has learned to economize on the high cost of negotiating, policing, and enforcing legal contracts. All kinds of standardized contracts, sales contracts containing warranties, return privileges, *as is* purchases, etc., serve the purpose of lowering transaction costs and assigning in advance the losses or gains from unpredictable events.[7]

The prevailing property rights structures determine the content of contractual agreements, that is, the bundles of rights that could be transferred via exchange. In other words, contractual stipulations are constrained in a specific

7 See S. MacCaulay, "Non-contractual Relations in Business: A Preliminary Study," *American Sociological Review* 28 (1963): 56–67.

way by the prevailing property rights structures. Thus, a change in the content of contractual agreements presupposes either a change in existing property rights (e.g., changes in the liability assignments for accidental damages) or the development of new rights (e.g., technological development required contractual agreements based on the right of limited liability).

We can now summarize our discussion as follows: Changes in the cost-benefit consideration create opportunities for individuals or groups to capture benefits by engaging in activities that were not deemed profitable before. To engage in those activities means, of course, to enter into some specific contractual agreements that will permit individuals or groups to capture the potential benefits. If the prevailing property relations are poorly attuned to, and fail to enforce, such contractual agreements, legal arrangements or the constraints of custom must change in order to permit the enforcement of new contractual stipulations. Thus, to capture the potential gains it might be necessary to change the content of contractual agreements, but the acceptance of a change in the contractual forms must then lead to a new or modified property rights assignment. It follows that changes in property rights are triggered by the interaction between the prevailing property rights and man's search for more utility. In other words, the creation and specification of property rights can be deduced theoretically.[8]

Property Rights and Economic Organizations

The analysis of the creation and specification of property rights in scarce resources provides two powerful and possibly necessary conditions for extending the standard theory to a wider class of real-world events. First, the analysis establishes that the content of property rights assignments affects the value of goods, the allocation of resources, and the distribution of income. Second, the analysis shows that the development of legal institutions and norms that control the level and character of economic activity can be deduced theoreti-

8 For detailed discussion, see S. Pejovich, "Towards an Economic Theory of the Creation and Specification of Property Rights," *Review of Social Economy* 30 (1972): 309–25.

cally. That is, instead of taking property rights structures as given from without—as a sort of human discovery that is not necessarily related to the current economic situation—the analysis suggests a strong mutual interconnectedness between the legal system and economic life. It is important to demonstrate that the development of property rights is endogenous to the system, because the analysis is then bound to contribute to the development of a theory of the state predicated on the impact of various property rights on the appropriability of rewards by officials.

The next step in relating property relations to economic behavior is to demonstrate that the content of property rights assignments affects the allocation and use of scarce resources in *specific* and *predictable* ways. For without this assurance, there would be no possibility of developing analytically significant and testable propositions concerning the effects of various property rights structures on the behavior of different types of economic organizations. The purpose of this section of the paper is to relate the effects of property relations to the behavior of both the modern capitalist corporation and the socialist firm.

Instead of postulating objectives of the firm, the property rights analysis focuses its attention on *individual actions within* the firm. The behavior of decision makers *within* the organization is taken to hold the key to understanding the behavior of the organization itself. In other words, the analysis takes into account the ways in which the decision makers capture pecuniary and nonpecuniary benefits for themselves.

A good example of an approach that does not focus on property rights is the much-celebrated Lange model, which is predicated on the proposition that the socialist manager is "instructed" to maximize his firm's profit and, more significantly, on the assumption that he proceeds to do precisely that. While the analysis of the behavior of the socialist firm is then straightforward, it is based on a normative construct that has little predictive power. Quite simply, obedience to rules requires more than "orders." What is missing in the Lange model is the analysis of the manager's penalty-reward system, as well as explicit and formal recognition of the cost to the state of detecting, policing, and enforcing appropriate managerial behavior.

A generalization of the standard theory along the lines discussed above requires that we define the bundle of rights in the firm and identify the sources of positive transaction costs. Then, assuming that the decision makers want to maximize their total compensation, we can proceed to develop the implied behavior of various types of economic organizations and evaluate their implications.

Let us define the bundle of property rights that defines ownership in the economic organization[9] as consisting of:

1. the right to receive the *residual* after all other inputs have been paid contractual amounts,
2. the right to *terminate* or *revise* the membership of the team (i.e., the owner of this right is a central party to a set of bilateral contracts), and
3. the right to sell those rights specified under (1) and (2).

The method of analysis is then simple and straightforward. First, we evaluate the bundle of property rights; next, we proceed to establish the effects of property rights assignments on the behavior of decision makers; finally, we deduce the implied behavior of the organization and examine the analytical propositions yielded by the analysis in relation to the broad facts of business experience. In other words, specification of rights reveals the allocation of costs and rewards within the organization, thus permitting a behavioral analysis of the organization.

The Modern Corporation

To establish a proper perspective for our discussion, let us briefly relate the concept of property rights to the behavior of the classical capitalist firm. The owner-manager of the classical firm is entitled to capture the residual, to fire and hire cooperating inputs, and to sell those rights in an open market. He is the decision maker. Importantly, the classical model assumes that the owner's costs of exercising these rights are zero (i.e., transaction costs are assumed away). Thus, cooperating inputs find the cost of raising their total compensation by shirking or purchasing other nonpecuniary

9 See an excellent paper by A. Alchian and H. Demsetz, "Production, Information Costs, and Economic Organization," *American Economic Review* 62 (1972): 777–95.

goods prohibitively high. At the same time, the standard set of assumptions concerning the environment in which the classical firm operates (perfect information, perfect mobility, open entry) renders the contractual pay of all inputs equal to their highest-valued alternative. By implication, the owner must seek the maximum profit in order to survive. The objective of profit maximization is, then, *not a choice objective*. It is a survival trait externally imposed on the firm's owner. The decision maker must allocate his assets to their highest-valued uses in order to earn the survival income (opportunity income). It follows that at equilibrium the equimarginal principle is satisfied; that is, the full equality of social and private costs and benefits is assured in the standard behavioral model of the classical capitalist firm.

The owner of the modern corporation is also entitled to capture the residual, to fire and hire cooperating inputs, and to sell those rights in an open market. The *legal system* imposes no changes in the bundle of rights that defines ownership of the firm. However, the *economic system* does: the ownership of a modern corporation is dispersed among many stockholders. The dispersion of stockholding means that individual owners face positive costs of detecting and policing managerial decisions and of enforcing a wealth-maximizing (or any other) objective.

What are the expected consequences of positive transaction costs on the allocation and use of resources by the modern corporation? Positive transaction costs enable the manager to substitute away from the firm's potential profits to gain various benefits for himself. Of course, the relevant questions to ask are: Given the "dictatorship of management," how can we explain the fact that millions of individuals are investing their assets in common stocks? Why don't they choose other forms of investment? Why has equity financing not been driven out by investment in fixed claims such as corporate bonds? Obviously, some forces within the system bend to protect the interest of the stockholders in publicly held corporations. The purpose of this section of the paper is to identify at least some of those factors and evaluate their effect on the performance of the modern corporation.

An important consequence of positive transaction costs is that the firm's *potential* and *reported* profits might be different. That is so because the manager can increase his total compensation at the expense of the firm's earnings by consuming a number of different utility-yielding goods, such as expense accounts, impressive offices, large staff, beautiful receptionists, approval from not-necessarily-most-efficient colleagues and subordinates, etc. The consumption of those goods raises the manager's total income over and above his contractual pay and is reported to the stockholders as the cost of doing business.

We must note, however, that the manager's on-the-job consumption depends on the existence of the difference between the firm's potential and survival (opportunity) profits. The firm's potential profits exceed its survival profits when a segment of the demand curve facing the firm lies above its average opportunity cost schedule. The standard competitive model of the firm treats this divergence between the potential and survival profits as a short-run phenomenon. For in a world of open markets and zero transaction costs, new entries tend to eliminate the excess profit via size adjustments of existing firms, lower product prices, and higher cost in inputs.

The difference between the *reported* profits and *survival* profits of existing firms regulates the rate of new entries into industry. But, when transaction costs are positive and the manager raises his total compensation via the consumption of nonpecuniary goods, the *reported* profits fall short of the firm's *potential* profits. The flow of new entries must then be inadequate to bring about the adjustment in resource allocation. Thus, an important consequence of positive transaction costs is that the difference between the firm's potential and survival profits ceases to be a short-run phenomenon. For example, if the firm's demand and average opportunity cost functions are $P = 200-Q$ and $AC = 75+.25Q$, respectively, its potential profit is \$3,125. Assuming that transaction costs are greater than \$3,125, the manager can add to his income \$3,125 worth of nonpecuniary goods and conceal it from the owners by reporting the average cost schedule as $AC = 75+1.5Q$. In this oversimplified example the firm's reported profit is equal to its survival profit, and the adjustment in resource allocation via new entries is discouraged.

Nonpecuniary goods that the manager can purchase for

himself are limited to those activities that could generally be justified as the costs of doing business. They have two common characteristics. First, the consumption of nonpecuniary goods is worth something to the manager; it has its money-income equivalent. The consumption of nonpecuniary goods is inferior, however, to the money income equal to the cost of these goods. Second, the owner's loss is in the form of money income. Thus, the redistribution of income that is associated with positive transaction costs is inefficient. The stockholders' loss of wealth exceeds the manager's gain.[10]

It appears that positive transaction costs tend not only to reduce the stockholders' gain in wealth but also to lower economic efficiency of the modern corporation via two routes: (*a*) lower than socially desirable flow of resources into the industry and (*b*) inefficient redistribution of income within the firm. In other words, positive transaction costs act to retard the flow of resources to their highest-valued uses.

This is but a general conclusion that offers no refutable implications and is consistent with any outcome. A behavioral model of the modern corporation must specify the managers' sets of opportunity choices and their costs of purchasing nonpecuniary goods.

The manager's set of opportunity choices with respect to the acquisition of nonpecuniary goods depends on (1) his *own* estimate of the transaction costs and (2) the difference between the firm's potential and survival profits. The lesser of these two factors determines the maximum the manager can spend on the consumption of nonpecuniary goods. It is shown by N_m in figure 1. The conversion rate between profits and the cost of nonpecuniary goods is assumed to be one. It is a useful assumption that does not affect our general conclusion. The maximum amount of profit that the manager can take away from the stockholders is then π_m, which will be less than the firm's excess profits when (1) < (2).

The OY_n curve in figure 2 relates the cost of nonpecuniary goods as borne by the firm to their money-value equivalent

10 See A. Alchian, "Corporate Management and Property Rights," in *Economic Policy and the Regulation of Corporate Securities,* ed. H. Manne (Washington, D.C.: American Enterprise Institute, 1969). An excellent paper on the subject of the firm's behavior is M. Jensen and W. Meckling, "Theory of the Firm: Managerial Behavior, Agency Costs, and Ownership Structure," *Journal of Financial Economics* 3 (1976): 305–60, reprinted in this volume, pp. 163–231.

as seen by the manager. The slope of this line conforms to our assumptions that the cost of nonpecuniary goods exceeds their money worth to the manager and that the variety of those goods that the manager can enjoy is limited to those that could be reported as business expenditures.

At this point it is tempting to assert that the manager will consume N_m worth of nonpecuniary goods in figure 1. Moreover, it is equally tempting to conjecture that the greater the dispersion of ownership in a corporation, the farther right will be the $\pi_m N_m$ line facing the manager. However, the effects of two sets of factors on the behavior of the manager must be incorporated into the analysis. One set affects the cost to the manager of purchasing nonpecuniary goods. The second tends to shrink his opportunity set.

In most corporations the manager receives a money bonus for reporting higher than survival profits. The exact nature of the relationship between additional profits and money rewards varies from one firm to another. But whatever this relationship happens to be, the manager finds that income derived from the consumption of nonpecuniary goods is not a free good. For simplicity, let us assume that the manager's bonus is a constant fraction of the firm's profits: $B = b\pi$. Then, the manager's decision relative to the purchase of nonpecuniary goods can be explained as a trade-off between the two income-producing activities: higher reported profits and the consumption of nonpecuniary goods.

At equilibrium, the manager's rate of substitution of income from additional profit for the consumption of specific goods is b. Since b is the slope of the $B = b\pi$ line, the managers will choose a bundle of N in figure 1 that corresponds to the point in figure 2 where the slope of OY_n is equal to b, that is, where the money worth obtained from spending \$1 on specific goods equals the manager's income from reporting higher profits by \$1. Now, if b is greater than the increment in income derived from spending the N_m dollars on nonpecuniary goods, the utility-maximizing manager will reduce his consumption of specific goods and move up along the $N_m \pi_m$ opportunity line in figure 1.

Let us now assume that the managers have the same preference for the consumption of nonpecuniary goods and that the relationship $B = b\pi$ is the same in all firms. Then, the rate of consumption of nonpecuniary goods will tend to be about *the same regardless* of the differences in the dispersion of stockholding among the various firms. That is, the dispersion of stockholding does not necessarily lead to greater inefficiencies, other things being the same. Let us consider two firms that are equal in everything but the dispersion of stockholding. $N_1\pi_1$ and $N_2\pi_2$ in figure 3 are opportunity sets facing their managers. As long as the managers' own estimates of transaction costs are less than the difference between the firms' potential and survival profits, their opportunity sets can be different. Now, if b equals the slope of OY_n curve at or before N_1 in figure 3, the cost of managers' expenditures for nonpecuniary goods (and the stockholders' loss of profit) will be the same in both firms. Point A depicts such a situation. If b equals the slope of OY_n curve somewhere between N_1 and N_2, say at C, the managers will spend ON_1 and OC respectively. The difference in the consumption of nonpecuniary goods between the managers will exist, but it will be narrowed down.

Next, the manager's future earnings depend on his present performance. That is, if he reports higher than survival profit today, his pay tomorrow might be affected. The problem can be understood as involving a trade-off between the increment of current income from the consumption of nonpecuniary goods and higher *money* income in the future. The indifference-preference analysis can be used here. At any rate, the cost to the manager of purchasing nonpecuniary goods is further increased.

Finally, we turn to the question, Do forces exist within the capitalist system that tend to shrink the manager's opportunity set? As long as stock prices reflect the present value of the expected future consequences of current managerial decisions, market valuation will tend to protect stockholders from less-diligent concern by management for their wealth. The stockholders' freedom to sell shares in a market that reflects the capitalized value of current managerial decisions reduces the power of managers to pursue their own objectives at the expense of profit. For the more shares relative to their total number are sold, the lower will be the price of the firm's stock relative to that of other firms, and this presents a clear danger to the managers. The lower bid price for

Figure 1

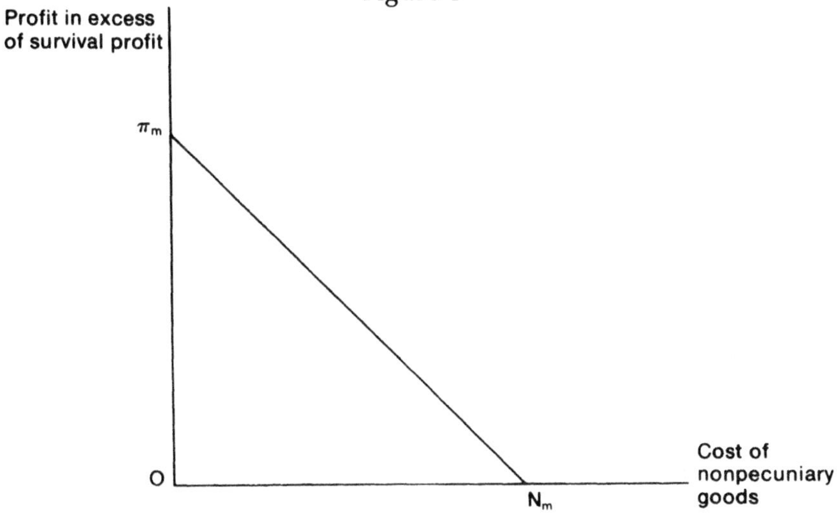

Figure 2

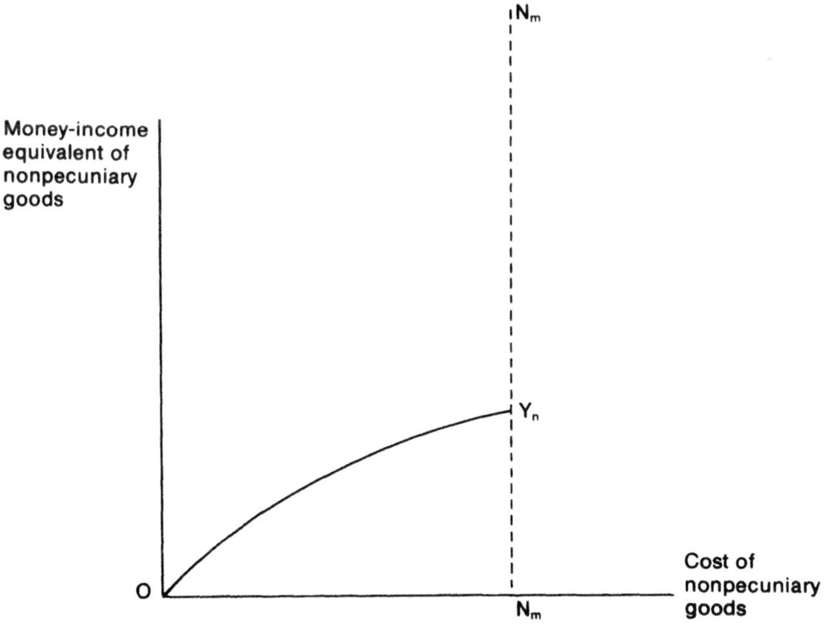

Figure 3

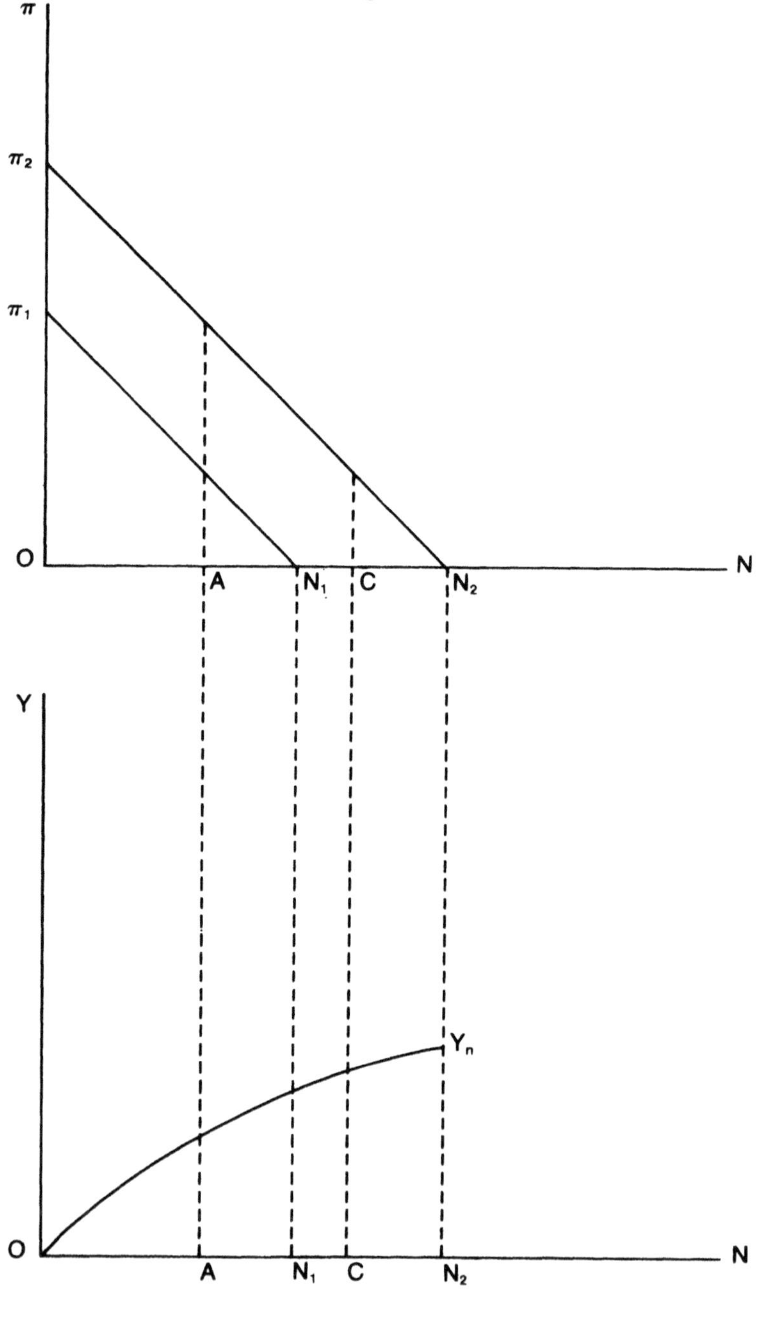

stocks of the corporation with more dispersed ownership would raise the cost to the manager of purchasing nonpecuniary goods. In terms of our discussion, the process reduces the costs to the stockholders of detecting and policing managerial decisions relative to what it would otherwise be. The effect of the capitalization process on transaction costs can be treated as a downward shift in the manager's opportunity line in figure 1. In other words, his opportunity set shrinks.

Market forces tend to reduce the stockholders' costs of detecting and policing managerial decisions. Moreover, they also tend to narrow the differences in the manager's consumption of nonpecuniary goods in corporations with different transaction costs. That is, one should expect to find no significant relationship between the dispersion of stockholding and the owners' gains in wealth (dividends plus capital-value growth). In a recent study, Koshal and Pejovich used the percentage of the firm's stock held by institutions as a proxy for dispersion. It was assumed that institutions are more likely to incur the cost of detecting and policing managerial decisions. Thus, an increase in the percentage of the firm's stock held by institutions was taken to imply a reduction in the dispersion of stockholding. The sample consisted of 38 firms in the chemical industry whose shares are actively traded on the national or regional exchanges. Data were collected for the period 1962–72. The question was then asked, Do dispersed ownership corporations have lower rates of growth of stockholders' wealth (allowing for dividends and capital-value growth) than less-dispersed ownership firms? Regression analysis of both the intrafirm and interfirm data (for each year) showed no evidence of any significant relationship between the dispersion of stockholding and changes in the wealth of stockholders. Several other studies suggested the same results.[11]

Let us now summarize our discussion. The existence of positive transaction costs tends to retard the flow of re-

---

11 R. Koshal and S. Pejovich, "A Note on the Separation of Ownership from Control" (Paper presented at the Western Economic Association, Las Vegas, August 1973). Also see D. Kamerscher, "The Influence of Ownership and Control on Profit Rates," *American Economic Review* 58 (1968): 432–47; J. Elliott, "Control, Size, Growth, and Financial Performance in the Firm," *Journal of Financial and Quantitative Analysis* 7 (1972): 1309–20.

sources to their highest-valued uses. The rise of the modern corporation has then been alleged to impair economic efficiency of the capitalist system. The analysis in this section suggests that a number of factors exist in the capitalist system that tend to reduce transaction costs. Moreover, the analysis suggests that the trend toward more dispersion of stockholding does not necessarily contribute to economic inefficiency of the modern corporation. Market forces act to reduce transaction costs in corporations having different dispersion of stockholding; that is, they reduce the conflict between the manager and the stockholders as well as between the modern corporation and the interests of society.

Yet, transaction costs remain positive and the manager of the publicly owned firm can—indeed, he does—depart from the ideal wealth-maximizing objective. Such divergence should be considered as a cost that stockholders and society must bear. These costs are clearly less than those of any alternative means of raising the necessary capital and risk reduction.

The Socialist Firm

In the 1960s the East European states moved away from the system of rigid, centralized planning of the 1950s. Their leaders recognized that the system of planning as practiced in the 1950s had failed to devise an effective incentive and control system to direct production efficiently. In other words, underlying the call for economic reforms in Eastern Europe was a change in the socialist belief that administrative planning is superior to the market-oriented allocations of resources. Economic reforms in Eastern Europe can then be defined as the search for a set of institutions that promise either to improve incentives for business firms to use resources more efficiently (Yugoslavia, Hungary) or to reduce the planners' cost of monitoring the firm's performance (USSR, East Germany) or both (Czechoslovakia, Bulgaria).[12]

Of course, it is easier to announce changes in the system than to implement them. All sorts of problems, including bureaucratic resistance to changes, did indeed arise in Eastern Europe. Predictably, the reforms fell behind schedule in

12 See F. Pryor, *Property and Industrial Organization in Communist and Capitalist Nations* (Bloomington: Indiana University Press, 1973), chap. 7.

most East European countries. Some reforms were revoked and some others never implemented. Yet, the reform drives of the sixties triggered a general process now under way in the socialist world of rethinking the role of market mechanism and price systems, of centralized and decentralized decision making, and of the institution of profit.

Given the failure of the system of administrative planning to direct production efficiently, the future of socialism as a viable alternative to capitalism hinges on the ability of socialist leaders to develop and *actually implement* an economic organization that would improve the allocation and use of resources while, most importantly, retaining the minimum socialist requirement of public ownership in capital goods. From a practical standpoint, the question to ask is, *Have socialist leaders succeeded in developing such a system?* Speculative questions such as, *Can* socialists develop an efficient system? are self-serving, pregnant with normative judgments, and have little to do with positive economic reasoning. Yugoslavia is the only socialist state that has virtually abolished the system of administrative planning while retaining the fundamental socialist requirement of public ownership in capital goods. Thus, the Yugoslav economic system is a *real* socialist alternative to the system of administrative planning. Careful study of the precise advantages and limitations of the Yugoslav economy should then be helpful in evaluating the viability of a decentralized socialist system. The purpose of this section is to suggest an operational theory of the Yugoslav firm. Once again the relevant questions are: What is the content of property rights that defines ownership of the firm in Yugoslavia? Who makes the decisions within the firm? What are the objectives of the decision makers? What is the specific penalty-reward structure that the decision makers face? What are testable implications of their behavior?

Major institutional features of the Yugoslav economic system are (*a*) the state ownership of capital goods, (*b*) the employees' ownership of the returns from capital goods held by their firm, (*c*) the employees' right to approve, police, and enforce the decisions made by the firm's director, and (*d*) the substitution of bank credit for the system of administrative distribution of investable funds. When this institutional framework is translated into the bundle of rights that defines ownership of the firm in Yugoslavia, the following picture emerges: (1) the employees *own* the residual; (2) the employees have the right to *fire* and *hire* cooperating inputs including, most importantly, the firm's director; and (3) the employees can *neither sell the rights specified above nor continue to enjoy them when they leave the employ of the firm.* That is, the right to capture the residual is contingent on the association of one's live labor with the firm's physical assets. When this association ceases to exist, one's right to capture the residual ceases as well. The relationship between the employees and the stock of capital held by the firm is regulated by a legal category, *the right of use.* This right allows the collective to appropriate returns from capital goods. Moreover, the collective can produce, buy, or sell capital goods. However, the firm must maintain the book value of its assets via depreciation or other means (e.g., the firm must reinvest the proceeds from sale of capital goods). In other words, the collective can add to the firm's capital stock, change its composition, but never let its book value fall. To deal with the problems of inflation, the Yugoslav government has periodically revalued the stock of capital held by business firms. If the firm sells an asset to another firm for less than its book value, the difference must be deducted from the residual and earmarked for investment.

In practical terms, employees of the Yugoslav firm have the right to determine the allocation of net profits among the wage fund and retained earnings, decide on the distribution of the wage fund, control the use of retained earnings, replace the firm's director, and approve new investments. With workers given such decision-making powers, questions must arise concerning how the firm is likely to behave.

The expected objective of the Yugoslav firm would appear to be the maximization of the average product of labor. This seems to be a self-evident objective of the employees. The director, who also participates in sharing the residual and can be replaced by the employees, must concur. Given competition, each nonlabor input would be employed up to the point at which the value of the input's marginal product is equal to the given price of the input and the value of the marginal product of labor is equal to the residual-maximizing wage. The wage rate in the firm can be expressed as

$$W = \frac{P \cdot f(L, K^0) - Z}{L},$$

where L = flow of labor services,
K^0= fixed capital stock,
P = commodity price
Z = fixed production expenses of the firm.

The magnitude of Z can be taken as a function of the capital stock. Then, the optimization condition is

$$W^* = P \cdot AP - \frac{Z}{L} = P \cdot MP_L;$$

that is, the value of labor's average physical product minus average fixed cost per unit of labor must be equal to the value of labor's marginal physical product.

It could then be asserted that the Yugoslav system provides incentives for scarce resources to move to their highest-valued uses and ensures a harmony of private and social interests. This rather simplistic view completely ignores, however, the effects of property relations in Yugoslavia on the behavior of the decision makers within the firm. More specifically, the wage maximization hypothesis fails to distinguish between the workers who are employed by the firm and *labor in general.*

This distinction is quite important because the individuals who are current members of the working collective will tend to vote for policies that promote their own welfare, not the welfare of labor in general. Also, the static nature of the wage maximization hypothesis fails to consider the effects of the content of the *right of use* in capital goods on the employees' behavior.

If the initial capital-labor ratio is large and the firm can sell all it wants to sell at the going price, the residual per worker could be increased via an increase in the labor input or a decrease in the stock of capital. We recall that the firm must maintain the value of its stock of capital. Thus, the residual-maximizing behavior would call for hiring additional workers. Every proposed change in the labor force must be evaluated, however, in terms of its expected effects on the "original" group of workers in each of two areas—*productivity* and *policy*.

New workers joining the firm are more than factors of production. They are potential policymakers as well. Any increase in the labor force enlarges the voting base and may cause a shift in the firm's policies (voting patterns). This presents a clear danger to the original group. They cannot, like the residual owners in capitalism, cash in the market value of their rights and leave the firm.

While it is true that the original group might consist of individuals with different utility functions, some minimum agreement by the majority of workers is bound to emerge. The original majority is likely to have (*a*) the length of the planning horizon and (*b*) the economic and social environment to be maintained within the firm during the period. Since an individual has no ownership rights in the firm's capital stock, it would be irrational for him to take the long view in considering the firm's policies. He must secure whatever gains he is to have *during his tenure* with the firm. Thus, the rewards that are meaningful to the worker are the pecuniary and nonpecuniary return that he can obtain during his employ. It follows that the expected tenure with the firm will limit his planning horizon and that he will be willing to trade some pecuniary income from adding to the firm's labor force for the security of common interests provided by the original group. The decision on the hiring of new employees represents a compromise for the original majority. While an enlargement of the firm's labor force may increase the residual per worker, a larger labor force can endanger the attainment of other goals desired by the controlling group. Thus, the value of the marginal product of labor at equilibrium will tend to deviate from the residual-maximizing wage. Similarly, the value of the marginal product of each nonlabor input will not be equal to its price.

In addition to varying the labor force, the collective also has the right to add to the firm's stock of capital. The Yugoslav firm has two major sources of funds: retained earnings and bank credit. At the same time, the employees of the firm face two different wealth-increasing alternatives. They can take the residual out as wages and invest individually in savings accounts, jewelry, or some other assets (taxis, small restaurants, etc.) where the right of private ownership does not necessarily and obviously violate the principle of public ownership in capital goods. Or the workers can leave some fraction of the residual with the firm for joint investment in capital goods and receive returns in the form of incremental wages for as long as they remain with the firm. Given the structure of property rights in Yugoslavia, when the worker leaves the firm he loses all his claims to the future returns from capital stock even though his earlier sacrifice of current income helped the enterprise to purchase additional assets. For convenience we shall refer to these wealth-increasing alternatives as investments in *owned* and *nonowned* assets.[13]

Since the return from joint investment in capital goods via retained earnings is received in the form of incremental wages and for only as long as the worker remains with the firm, the internal rate of return on such investment must be *higher* than the rate of return on owned assets to make the alternative forms of investment equally attractive to the workers. In fact, the precise "equalizing" differential can be determined. To simplify our exposition we assume that the rate of interest (s) on savings accounts represents the highest return available to workers from taking the residual out and investing individually and that owned and nonowned assets are alike in all characteristics (risk level, nonpecuniary returns, etc.) *but* yield. Then, private savings of S dinars in period one permits consumption of $S + {}_sS$ dinars in period two. The same amount of money left with the firm for joint investment in capital assets makes possible a consumption level of ${}_rS$ dinars in the second period. In other words, over a one-period hairpin, a 5 percent return on owned assets is just as appealing as a 105 percent return on self-financed investment in the firm. In general, the conversion formula for an alternative involving the investment outlay S_0 over T-period planning horizon is:

13 For detailed analysis, see E. Furubotn and S. Pejovich, "Property Rights and the Behavior of the Firm in a Socialist State," *Zeitschrift für Nationalökonomie* 30 (1970): 431–54.

$$S_0 = \sum_{t=1}^{T} \frac{r^* S_0}{(1+s)^t},$$

where r^* is the critical rate of return that nonowned assets must yield in order for workers to be indifferent between collective investment in the firm and individual investments at interest rates s. For example, the rates of return that make investment in nonowned assets equally attractive to workers as savings deposits at 5 percent are 23 percent, 19 percent, 13 percent, and 9 percent for time horizons of 5, 6, 10, and 15 years, respectively.[14]

Our equation indicates that unless the interest rate *(s)* is quite small or the planning horizon *(T)* very long, the magnitude of r^* will be substantial. Given the prevailing property relations in Yugoslavia, T is unlikely to be long. Then, with r^* large, the marginal efficiency of investment in the firm r must also be large, or no incentive will exist for workers to save via joint investment in nonowned assets. It follows that if the firm's production function is characterized by constant returns to scale, and the given capital-labor ratio is smaller than the ratio that would maximize the wage per worker the employees can find it advantageous to add to the original capital stock and raise the residual. Yet, the required rate of return, r^*, will make inadequate the adjustment in the K/L ratio via self-financed investment.

The analysis here presents a pessimistic picture concerning the growth of employment and the possibility for self-financed investment by firms in Yugoslavia. An equilibrium may easily be reached where the capital-labor ratio is either smaller or larger than the residual-maximizing ratio determined by the given price structure. The implication is that the community gets less total output from its firms than it could under a different property arrangement.

Given the property rights structure in Yugoslavia, the firms' employment and capital accumulation policies tend to be nonoptimal; for the legal system gives each collective significant decision-making powers and allows workers to reject alternatives that are not favorable to their own welfare, but it also enforces property relations that limit individuals to *the*

14 See S. Pejovich, "The Firm, Monetary Policy and Property Rights in a Planned Economy," *Western Economic Journal* 7 (1969): 193–200.

right of use of capital goods and thus severely reduces the incentives for investment of their nonconsumed income in the firm.

It is certainly surprising that Yugoslav economists as well as government officials expected retained earnings to be the major source of investable funds. The banks were expected merely to provide supplementary funds. Since the average marginal productivity of capital was estimated at close to 30 percent, the economists saw no obstacle to self-finance. However, the share of residual allocated to the investment fund of firms fell from about 40 percent in 1965 to 24 percent in the early 1970s.[15] Moreover, some of this allocation was mandated by the fact that repayment of bank loans is made from the firm's retained earnings. The firms' liquidity position also deteriorated. In the early 1970s about 33 percent of the total value of nonhuman assets held by firms was financed by nonbank debt (primarily via accounts receivable and accounts payable). The average defense interval of business firms, defined as the ratio of the firms' money holdings to their daily cash needs, stood at slightly over three, indicating an extremely low level of liquidity.

It is reasonable to say that the behavior of the Yugoslav firm can be given plausible explanation if the implications of the prevailing property rights structure are examined systematically. It is clear that the bundle of property rights that defines ownership in the Yugoslav firm affects the workers' time preference, hiring policies, and investment decisions in specific and predictable ways; the behavioral model of the Yugoslav firm suggests testable implications. An important implication is that the banking system should be expected to take on a crucial role in freeing the rate of investment from the limitations imposed by inadequate self-finance, as well as in providing firms with needed liquid assets.[16] Indeed, it did.

---

15 All data in this paper concerning the performance of the Yugoslav economy are taken from the *Statistical Yearbook of Yugoslavia*, published annually by the Federal Institute for Statistics in Belgrade; and the *Statistical Bulletin*, published monthly by the Agency for Social Accounting. Since 1973 there has been an increase in the allocation of profits to the investment fund. This change reflects the reimposition of some administrative measures.

16 S. Pejovich, "The Banking System and the Investment Behavior of the Yugoslav Firm," in *Plan and Market*, ed. M. Bornstein (New Haven, Conn.: Yale University Press, 1973).

From 1965 to 1974 the annual volume of long-term and short-term credits to firms increased by 200 percent and over 300 percent, respectively. Also, self-financed investment *inclusive of depreciation* fell from 26 percent to about 20 percent of gross investment in the early 1970s, while the percentage of gross investment financed by bank credit rose from 36 percent to about 50 percent.

The basic reason for the appeal of bank credit to the workers is quite obvious. While self-financed investment requires a reduction of current consumption, bank-financed investment does not. Thus, as long as the cost to the collective of borrowing is less than the increment in the residual generated by additional investment, the workers will seek to expand the firm's capital stock through bank financing. In fact, the collective will want to borrow investable funds up to the point at which the value of the marginal product of credit is equal to the marginal cost of borrowing. Clearly, the availability of bank credit is likely to make the collective's disposition of its residual even more biased against self-financed investment than it would be in the absence of bank credit. This condition is significant because it helps to explain both growing demand by firms for short-term credit and its consequences. As the firm acquires additional capital goods, its scale of operations must increase. That means greater requirements for goods in process, inventories, and liquid holdings. But a reduction in the allocation of the residual to retained earnings must affect the firm's *own* sources of working capital and raise its demand for short-term credit. As long as banks are willing to accommodate firms, a predictable consequence of this expansion of short-term credit is inflation. The rate of inflation in Yugoslavia was close to 20 percent in the 1970s. Importantly, inflationary pressures are inherent in the prevailing property rights structure in Yugoslavia.

This is a logical deduction from the relationship between the bundle of property rights that defines ownership in the Yugoslav firm and the penalty-reward system of the decision makers within the firm. The Yugoslav experience bears it out. The relevant question is now, What are the effects of the firm's dependence on the banking system?

When it is recognized that a positive relationship exists

between the firm's investment in additional fixed assets and its need for liquid assets, it becomes clear that the aggregate demand for investable funds and the marginal efficiency schedule of the firm do not coincide. This raises the problem of assigning a separate rate of return to liquid assets. Lutz and Lutz argue that in a private property, free market community, we can treat those assets as just earning what they cost; that is, the short-term market rate of interest.[17] In that case, the conventional proposition that the firm's rate of investment depends on its schedule of investment opportunities and the market rate of interest remains valid. An important question is, Does economic logic support the extension of this proposition to the investment decision of the Yugoslav firm?

The common feature of those items that are included in our definition of liquid assets (cash balances, near money, inventories) is that they are productive because they help business firms to economize on the high cost of information and to maximize the extent of exchange. In a private property, capitalist economy the firm can use some of its liquid assets to purchase interest-bearing securities (i.e., to hold financial inventories). The distribution of liquid holdings of the capitalist firm between interest-bearing assets (near money) and non-interest-bearing assets such as money balances and physical inventories depends on a multitude of factors, including transaction costs and the market rate of interest; but the essential point is that the enterprise can *choose* to hold some of its liquid assets in interest-bearing securities.[18] The fact that capitalist firms have been consistent in using some of their liquid holdings to purchase interest-bearing securities suggests that they view the alternative of holding all liquid assets in non-interest-bearing forms (i.e., physical inventories and cash) as an inferior (costlier) one.

Financial markets do not exist in socialist states. Assuming that the demand for liquid assets does not differ between the capitalist and the socialist firm, it is then possible to assert that the cost of each given investment in fixed assets is higher

17 F. Lutz and V. Lutz, *The Theory of Investment of the Firm* (Princeton, N.J.: Princeton University Press, 1951), p. 161.

18 W. Baumol, "The Transactions Demand for Cash: An Inventory Theoretical Approach," *Quarterly Journal of Economics* 66 (1952): 545–56.

in socialism, other things being the same. This difference in costs is then a price the socialist state has to pay for its refusal to allow the future consequences of current allocative decisions to be capitalized via the right of private ownership in earning assets.

While better experts might, it is hoped, test the expected consequences of the analysis for finer and more extended applications, the broad facts of Yugoslav experience do not contradict the qualitative results suggested by the model.

The standard theory of production and exchange, modified to take account of the behavioral effects of alternative property rights arrangements, yields interesting, suggestive, and testable propositions concerning the behavior of the modern corporation and the socialist firm in Yugoslavia. Since the modern corporation is the dominant form of business organization in capitalism, and the Yugoslav firm is the only fully tested alternative to the system of administrative controls from the center, the comparison between these two types of firms is useful and important.

The analysis shows that, at equilibrium, the allocation and use of resources by both the modern corporation and the Yugoslav firm does not conform to the equimarginal principle. It also suggests, however, that the deviation from the social optimum is much more serious in the case of the Yugoslav firm. True, the dispersion of stockholding in the modern corporation increases the costs to the owners of policing the behavior of the managers, but the fact that the expected future consequences of the current managerial decisions can be capitalized and that a positive relationship exists between the manager's current performance and his future earnings indicates a reduction in transaction costs. Most significantly, the analysis suggests that an increase in the dispersion of stockholding does not necessarily imply a greater divergence between private and social costs and benefits.

With respect to the Yugoslav variant of a decentralized socialist economy, the analysis shows that, inherent in the structure of property rights that define ownership in the Yugoslav firm, are forces conducive to conflict between the interest of society as a whole and the interests of the collective. The major economic problems in Yugoslavia—inflation, unemployment, the liquidity crisis, low level of self-financed investment, and the virtually complete dependence of business firms on the banks—can be traced to the incentive patterns generated by the prevailing property relations and the absence of capital markets. That is, economic decentralization permitted Yugoslavia to escape the inefficiencies of central planning *at a cost.* The analysis suggests that, if this cost is to be lessened, the government must either grant individuals fuller rights in capital goods or reduce the workers' decision-making powers.[19] The question, Which set of institutions is capable of promoting efficient allocation of resources in a socialist state? is still very much open.

19 E. Furubotn and S. Pejovich, "Property Rights, Economic Decentralization, and the Evolution of the Yugoslav Firm, 1965–1972," *Journal of Law and Economics* 16 (1973): 275–302.

Michael C. Jensen
and William H. Meckling**

Theory of the Firm:

Managerial Behavior, Agency Costs, and Ownership Structure*

> The directors of such [joint-stock] companies, however, being the managers rather of other people's money than of their own, it cannot well be expected, that they should watch over it with the same anxious vigilance with which the partners in a private copartnery frequently watch over their own. Like the stewards of a rich man, they are apt to consider attention to small matters as not for their master's honour, and very easily give themselves a dispensation from having it. Negligence and profusion, therefore, must always prevail, more or less, in the management of the affairs of such a company.
>
> —Adam Smith, *The Wealth of Nations*

1. Introduction and Summary

Motivation of the Paper

In this paper we draw on recent progress in the theory of (1) property rights, (2) agency, and (3) finance to develop a theory of ownership structure for the firm.[1] In addition to tying

* Reprinted, with some changes, by permission of the authors and North-Holland Publishing Co., from the *Journal of Financial Economics* 3 (1976): 305–60. An earlier version of the paper was presented at the First Annual Interlaken Seminar on Analysis and Ideology, Switzerland, June 1974.

** We are indebted to F. Black, E. Fama, R. Ibbotson, W. Klein, M. Rozeff, R. Weil, O. Williamson, an anonymous referee, and our colleagues and members of the Finance Workshop at the University of Rochester—in particular, G. Benston, M. Canes, D. Henderson, K. Leffler, J. Long, C. Smith, R. Thompson, R. Watts, and J. Zimmerman—for their comments and criticisms.

1 We do not use the term *capital structure* because that term usually denotes the relative quantities of bonds, equity, warrants, trade credit, etc., that represent the liabilities of a firm. Our theory implies that there is another important dimension to this problem—namely, the relative amounts of ownership claims held by insiders (management) and outsiders (investors with no direct role in the management of the firm).

together elements of the theory of each of these three areas, our analysis casts new light on and has implications for a variety of issues in the professional and popular literature, such as the definition of the firm, the "separation of ownership and control," the "social responsibility" of business, the definition of a "corporate objective function," the determination of an optimal capital structure, the specification of the content of credit agreements, the theory of organizations, and the supply side of the completeness-of-markets problem.

Our theory helps explain:

1. why an entrepreneur or manager in a firm that has a mixed financial structure (containing both debt and outside equity claims) will choose a set of activities for the firm such that the total value of the firm is *less* than it would be if he were the sole owner and why this result is independent of whether the firm operates in monopolistic or competitive product or factor markets;
2. why his failure to maximize the value of the firm is perfectly consistent with efficiency;
3. why the sale of common stock is a viable source of capital even though managers do not literally maximize the value of the firm;
4. why debt was relied upon as a source of capital before debt financing offered any tax advantage relative to equity;
5. why preferred stock would be issued;
6. why accounting reports would be provided voluntarily to creditors and stockholders and why independent auditors would be engaged by management to testify to the accuracy and correctness of such reports;
7. why lenders often place restrictions on the activities of firms to whom they lend and why firms would themselves be led to suggest the imposition of such restrictions;
8. why some industries are characterized by owner-operated firms whose sole outside source of capital is borrowing;
9. why highly regulated industries such as public utilities or banks will have higher debt-equity ratios for equivalent levels of risk than the average nonregulated firm;
10. why security analysis can be socially productive even if it does not increase portfolio returns to investors.

Theory of the Firm: An Empty Box?

While the literature of economics is replete with references to the "theory of the firm," the material generally subsumed under that heading is not a theory of the firm but actually a theory of markets in which firms are important actors. The firm is a "black box" operated so as to meet the relevant marginal conditions with respect to inputs and outputs, thereby maximizing profits or, more accurately, present value. Except for a few recent and tentative steps, however, we have no theory that explains how the conflicting objectives of the individual participants are brought into equilibrium so as to yield this result. The limitations of this black-box view of the firm have been cited by Adam Smith and Alfred Marshall, among others. More recently, popular and professional debates over the "social responsibility" of corporations and the separation of ownership and control and the rash of reviews of the literature on the "theory of the firm" have evidenced continuing concern with these issues.[2]

A number of major attempts have been made during recent years to construct a theory of the firm by substituting other models for profit or value maximization, each attempt motivated by a conviction that the latter is inadequate to explain managerial behavior in large corporations.[3] Some of

2 Reviews of this literature are given by S. Petersen, "Corporate Control and Capitalism," *Quarterly Journal of Economics* 79 (1965): 1–24; A. A. Alchian, "The Basis of Some Recent Advances in the Theory of Management of the Firm," *Journal of Industrial Economics* 14 (1965): 30–44; idem, "Corporate Management and Property Rights," in *Economic Policy and the Regulation of Corporate Securities,* ed. H. Manne (Washington, D.C.: American Enterprise Institute, 1969); F. Machlup, "Theories of the Firm: Marginalist, Behavioral, Managerial," *American Economic Review* 57 (1967): 1–33; M. Shubik, "A Curmudgeon's Guide to Microeconomics," *Journal of Economic Literature* 8 (1970): 405–34; R. M. Cyert and C. L. Hedrick, "Theory of the Firm: Past, Present and Future," ibid., 10 (1972): 398–412; B. Branch, "Corporate Objectives and Market Performance," *Financial Management* (1973): 24–29; L. E. Preston, "Corporation and Society: The Search for a Paradigm," *Journal of Economic Literature* 13 (1975): 434–53.

3 See O. E. Williamson, *The Economics of Discretionary Behavior: Managerial Objectives in a Theory of the Firm* (Englewood Cliffs, N.J.: Prentice-Hall, 1964); idem, *Corporate Control and Business Behavior* (Englewood Cliffs, N.J.: Prentice-Hall, 1970); idem, *Markets and Hierarchies: Analysis and Antitrust Implications* (New York: Free Press, 1975); R. Marris, *The Economic Theory of Managerial Capitalism* (Glencoe, Ill.: Free Press, 1964); W. J. Baumol, *Business Behavior, Value and Growth* (New York: Macmillan, 1959); E. Penrose, *The Theory of the Growth of the Firm* (New York: Wiley, 1958); R. M. Cyert and J. G. March, *A Behavioral Theory of the Firm* (Englewood Cliffs, N.J.: Prentice-Hall, 1963). Thorough reviews of these and other contribu-

these reformulation attempts have rejected the fundamental principle of maximizing behavior as well as the more specific profit-maximizing model. In the analysis to follow, we retain the notion of maximizing behavior on the part of all individuals.[4]

Property Rights

An independent stream of research with important implications for the theory of the firm has been stimulated by the pioneering work of Coase and has been extended by Alchian, Demsetz, and others.[5] While the focus of this research has been "property rights," the subject matter encompassed

tions are given by F. Machlup, "Theories of the Firm," and Alchian, "Recent Advances."

H. A. Simon, "A Behavioral Model of Rational Choice," *Quarterly Journal of Economics* 69 (1955): 99–118, developed a model of human choice incorporating information (search) and computational costs and also having important implications for the behavior of managers. Unfortunately, Simon's work has often been misinterpreted as a denial of maximizing behavior and has been misused, especially in the marketing and behavioral science literature. His later use of the term *satisficing* has undoubtedly contributed to this confusion because it suggests rejection of maximizing behavior rather than maximization subject to costs of information and of decision making. H. A. Simon, "Theories of Decision Making in Economics and Behavioral Science," *American Economic Review* 49 (1959): 253–83.

4 For the theoretical importance of the assumption of resourceful, evaluative, maximizing behavior on the part of individuals, see W. H. Meckling, "Values and the Choice of the Model of the Individual in the Social Sciences," *Schweizerische Zeitschrift für Volkswirtschaft und Statistik,* 1976, no. 4, pp. 545–59, reprinted in this volume, pp. 00–00. An approach similar to the one embarked on in this paper is taken by W. A. Klein, "Legal and Economic Perspectives on the Firm," unpublished (Los Angeles: University of California, 1976).

5 See R. H. Coase, "The Nature of the Firm," *Economica,* n.s. 4 (1937): 386–405, reprinted in *Readings in Price Theory,* ed. G. J. Stigler and K. Boulding (Homewood, Ill.: Irwin, 1952); idem, "The Federal Communications Commission," *Journal of Law and Economics* 2 (1959): 1–40; idem, "The Problem of Social Costs," ibid., 3 (1960): 1–44; Alchian, "Recent Advances"; idem, "Corporate Management"; A. A. Alchian and R. A. Kessel, "Competition, Monopoly and the Pursuit of Pecuniary Gain," in *Aspects of Labor Economics,* (Princeton, N.J.: Princeton University Press, for the National Bureau of Economic Research, 1962); H. Demsetz, "Toward a Theory of Property Rights," *American Economic Review* 57 (1967): 347–59; A. A. Alchian and H. Demsetz, "Production, Information Costs, and Economic Organization," ibid. 62 (1972): 777–95; R. J. Monsen and A. Downs, "A Theory of Large Managerial Firms," *Journal of Political Economy* 73 (1965): 221–36; M. Silver and R. Auster, "Entrepreneurship, Profit and Limits on Firm Size," *Journal of Business* 42 (1969): 277–81; J. C. McManus, "The Costs of Alternative Economic Organizations," *Canadian Journal of Economics* 8 (1975): 334–50.

A comprehensive survey of this literature is given by E. G. Furubotn and S. Pejovich, "Property Rights and Economic Theory: A Survey of Recent Literature," *Journal of Economic Literature* 10 (1972): 1137–62.

is far broader than that term suggests.[6] What is important for the problems addressed here is that specification of individual rights determines how costs and rewards will be allocated among the participants in any organization. Since the specification of rights is generally effected through contracting (implicit as well as explicit), individual behavior in organizations, including the behavior of managers, will depend upon the nature of these contracts. We focus in this paper on the behavioral implications of the property rights specified in the contracts between the owners and managers of the firm.

Agency Costs

Many problems associated with the inadequacy of the current theory of the firm can also be viewed as special cases of the theory of agency relationships, of which there is a growing literature.[7] This literature has developed independently of the property rights literature even though the problems with which it is concerned are similar; the approaches are in fact highly complementary to each other.

We define an agency relationship as a contract under which one or more persons, the principal(s), engage another person, the agent, to perform some service on their behalf that involves delegating some decision-making authority to the agent. If both parties to the relationship are utility maximizers, there is good reason to believe that the agent will not always act in the best interests of the principal. The *principal* can limit divergences from his interest by establishing appropriate incentives for the agent and by incurring monitoring costs designed to limit the aberrant activities of the agent. In

6 Property rights are, of course, human rights, i.e., rights that are possessed by human beings. The introduction of the wholly false distinction between property rights and human rights in many policy discussions is surely one of the all-time great semantic flimflams.

7 See M. Berhold, "A Theory of Linear Profit-Sharing Incentives," *Quarterly Journal of Economics* 85 (1971): 460–82; S. A. Ross, "The Economic Theory of Agency: The Principals Problems," *American Economic Review* 63 (1973): 134–39; idem, "The Economic Theory of Agency and the Principle of Similarity," in *Essays on Economic Behavior under Uncertainty*, ed. M. D. Balch et al. (Amsterdam: North-Holland, 1974); R. Wilson, "On the Theory of Syndicates," *Econometrica* 36 (1968): 119–32; idem, La decision: Agregation et dynamique des orders de preference (Paris: Editions du Centre National de la Recherche Scientifique, 1969); D. G. Heckerman, "Motivating Managers to Make Investment Decisions," *Journal of Financial Economics* 2 (1975): 273–92.

addition, in some situations it will pay the *agent* to expend resources (bonding costs) to guarantee that he will not take certain actions that would harm the principal or to ensure that the principal will be compensated if he does take such actions. However, it is generally impossible for the principal or the agent at zero cost to ensure that the agent will make optimal decisions from the principal's viewpoint. In most agency relationships the principal and the agent will incur positive monitoring and bonding costs (nonpecuniary as well as pecuniary), and in addition there will be some divergence between the agent's decisions[8] and those decisions that would maximize the welfare of the principal. The dollar equivalent of the reduction in welfare experienced by the principal due to this divergence is also a cost of the agency relationship, and we refer to this latter cost as the residual loss. We define *agency costs* as the sum of:

1. the monitoring expenditures by the principal,[9]
2. the bonding expenditures by the agent, and
3. the residual loss.

Note also that agency costs arise in any situation involving cooperative effort (such as the coauthoring of this paper) by two or more people even though there is no clear-cut principal–agent relationship. Viewed in this light it is clear that our definition of agency costs and their importance to the theory of the firm bears a close relationship to the problem of shirking and monitoring of team production, which Alchian and Demsetz raise in their paper on the theory of the firm.[10]

Since the relationship between the stockholders and manager of a corporation fits the definition of a pure agency relationship, it should be no surprise to discover that the issues associated with the "separation of ownership and control" in the modern diffuse ownership corporation are intimately associated with the general problem of agency. We

8 Given the optimal monitoring and bonding activities by the principal and agent.

9 As it is used in this paper the term *monitoring* includes more than just measuring or observing the behavior of the agent. It includes efforts on the part of the principal to "control" the behavior of the agent through budget restrictions, compensation policies, operating rules, etc.

10 Alchian and Demsetz, "Production."

show below that an explanation of why and how the agency costs generated by the corporate form are borne leads to a theory of the ownership (or capital) structure of the firm.

Before moving on, however, it is worthwhile to point out the generality of the agency problem. The problem of inducing an "agent" to behave as if he were maximizing the "principal's" welfare is quite general. It exists in all organizations and in all cooperative efforts—at every level of management in firms,[11] in universities, in mutual companies, in cooperatives, in governmental authorities and bureaus, in unions, and in relationships normally classified as agency relationships such as are common in the performing arts and the market for real estate. The development of theories to explain the form that agency costs take in each of these situations (where the contractual relations differ significantly), and how and why they are borne, will lead to a rich theory of organizations that is now lacking in economics and the social sciences generally. We confine our attention in this paper to only a small part of this general problem—the analysis of agency costs generated by the contractual arrangements between the owners and top management of the corporation.

Our approach to the agency problem here differs fundamentally from most of the existing literature. That literature focuses almost exclusively on the normative aspects of the agency relationship—that is, how to structure the contractual relation (including compensation incentives) between the principal and agent to provide appropriate incentives for the agent to make choices that will maximize the principal's welfare given uncertainty and imperfect monitoring. We focus almost entirely on the positive aspects of the theory.

11 As we show below, the existence of positive monitoring and bonding costs will result in the manager of a corporation possessing control over some resources that he can allocate (within certain constraints) to satisfy his own preferences. However, to the extent that he must obtain the cooperation of others in order to carry out his tasks (such as divisional vice-presidents) and to the extent that he cannot control their behavior perfectly and costlessly, they will be able to appropriate some of these resources for their own ends. In short, there are agency costs generated at every level of the organization. Unfortunately, the analysis of these more general organizational issues is even more difficult than that of the "ownership and control" issue, because the contractual obligations and rights of the parties are much more varied in nature and generally not as well specified in explicit contractual arrangements. Nevertheless, they exist, and we believe that extensions of our analysis in these directions show promise of producing insights into a viable theory of organization.

That is, we assume individuals solve these normative problems, and given that only stocks and bonds can be issued as claims, we investigate the incentives faced by each of the parties and the elements entering into the determination of the equilibrium contractual form characterizing the relationship between the manager (i.e., agent) of the firm and the outside equity and debt holders (i.e., principals).

Some General Comments on the Definition of the Firm

Ronald Coase, in his seminal paper on the firm, pointed out that economics had no positive theory to determine the bounds of the firm. He characterized the bounds of the firm as that range of exchanges over which the market system was suppressed and resource allocation was accomplished instead by authority and direction. He focused on the cost of using markets to effect contracts and exchanges and argued that activities would be included within the firm whenever the costs of using markets were greater than the costs of using direct authority.[12] Alchian and Demsetz object to the notion that activities within the firm are governed by authority, and they correctly emphasize the role of contracts as a vehicle for voluntary exchange. They emphasize the role of monitoring in situations in which there is joint input or team production.[13] We sympathize with the importance they attach to monitoring, but we believe their emphasis on joint-input production is too narrow and therefore misleading. Contractual relations are the essence of the firm, not only with employees but with suppliers, customers, creditors, etc. The problem of agency costs and monitoring exists for all of these contracts, independent of whether there is joint production in their sense; that is, joint production can explain only a small fraction of the behavior of individuals associated with a firm. A detailed examination of these issues is left to another paper.

It is important to recognize that most organizations are

12 Coase, "Nature of the Firm."

13 Alchian and Demsetz, "Production." They define the classical capitalist firm as a contractual organization of inputs in which there is "(a) joint input production, (b) several input owners, (c) one party who is common to all the contracts of the joint inputs, (d) who has rights to renegotiate any input's contract independently of contracts with other input owners, (e) who holds the residual claim, and (f) who has the right to sell his contractual residual status" (p. 783).

simply *legal fictions that serve as a nexus for a set of contracting relationships among individuals.*[14] This includes firms; non-profit institutions such as universities, hospitals, and foundations; mutual organizations such as mutual savings banks and insurance companies and cooperatives; some private clubs; and even governmental bodies such as cities, states, and the federal government and government enterprises such as the TVA, the Post Office, and transit systems.

The private corporation or firm is simply one form of *legal fiction that serves as a nexus for contracting relationships and is also characterized by the existence of divisible residual claims on the organization's assets and cash flows, which can generally be sold without permission of the other contracting individuals.* While this definition of the firm has little substantive content, emphasizing the essential contractual nature of firms and other organizations focuses attention on a crucial set of questions—why particular sets of contractual relations arise for various types of organizations, what the consequences of these contractual relations are, and how they are affected by changes exogenous to the organization. Viewed this way, it makes little or no sense to try to distinguish those things that are "inside" the firm (or any other organization) from those things that are "outside" of it. There is in a very real sense only a multitude of complex relationships (i.e., contracts) between the legal fiction (the firm) and the owners of labor, material, and capital inputs and the consumers of output.[15]

Viewing the firm as the nexus of a set of contracting relationships among individuals also serves to make it clear that the personalization of the firm implied by asking questions such as, What should be the objective function of the firm? or, Does the firm have a social responsibility? is seriously misleading. *The firm is not an individual.* It is a legal fiction that serves as a focus for a complex process in which the conflicting objectives of individuals (some of whom may

---

14 By *legal fiction* we mean the artificial construct under the law that allows certain organizations to be treated as individuals.

15 For example, we ordinarily think of a product as leaving the firm at the time it is sold, but implicitly or explicitly such sales generally carry with them continuing contracts between the firm and the buyer. If the product does not perform as expected, the buyer often has a right to and can obtain satisfaction. Explicit evidence that such implicit contracts do exist is the practice we occasionally observe of specific provision that "all sales are final."

"represent" other organizations) are brought into equilibrium within a framework of contractual relations. In this sense the "behavior" of the firm is like the behavior of a market, that is, the outcome of a complex equilibrium process. We seldom fall into the trap of characterizing the wheat or stock market as an individual, but we often make this error by thinking about organizations as if they were persons with motivations and intentions.[16]

An Overview of the Paper

We develop the theory in stages. Sections 2 and 4 provide analyses of the agency costs of equity and debt, respectively. These form the major foundation of the theory. Section 3 poses some unanswered questions regarding the existence of the corporate form of organization and examines the role of limited liability. In section 5, the basic concepts derived in sections 2–4 are synthesized into a theory of the corporate ownership structure that takes account of the trade-offs available to the entrepreneur–manager between inside and outside equity and debt. Some qualifications and extensions of the analysis are discussed in section 6, and section 7 contains a brief summary and conclusions.

2. The Agency Costs of Outside Equity

Overview

In this section we analyze the effect of outside equity on agency costs by comparing the behavior of a manager when he owns 100 percent of the residual claims on a firm to his

16 This view of the firm points up the important role of the legal system and the law in social organizations, especially the organization of economic activity. Statutory law sets bounds on the kinds of contracts into which individuals and organizations may enter without risking criminal prosecution. The police powers of the state are available and used to enforce performance of contracts or to enforce the collection of damages for nonperformance. The courts adjudicate conflicts between contracting parties and establish precedents that form the body of common law. All of these government activities affect both the kinds of contracts executed and the extent to which contracting is relied upon. This in turn determines the usefulness, productivity, profitability, and viability of various forms of organization. Moreover, new laws as well as court decisions often can and do change the rights of contracting parties ex post, and they can and do serve as a vehicle for redistribution of wealth. An analysis of some of the implications of these facts is contained in M. C. Jensen and W. H. Meckling, "Can the Corporation Survive?" Center for Research in Government Policy and Business Working Paper no. PPS 76-4 (Rochester, N.Y.: University of Rochester, 1976), and we shall not pursue them here.

behavior when he sells off a portion of those claims to outsiders. If a wholly owned firm is managed by the owner, he will make operating decisions that maximize his utility. These decisions will involve not only the benefits he derives from pecuniary returns but also the utility generated by various nonpecuniary aspects of his entrepreneurial activities, such as the physical appointments of the office, the attractiveness of the secretarial staff, the level of employee discipline, the kind and amount of charitable contributions, personal relations ("love," "respect," etc.) with employees, a larger than optimal computer to play with, and purchase of production inputs from friends. The optimum mix (in the absence of taxes) of the various pecuniary and nonpecuniary benefits is achieved when the marginal utility derived from an additional dollar of expenditure (measured net of any productive effects) is equal for each nonpecuniary item and equal to the marginal utility derived from an additional dollar of after-tax purchasing power (wealth).

If the owner–manager sells equity claims on the corporation that are identical to his (i.e., share proportionately in the profits of the firm and have limited liability), agency costs will be generated by the divergence between his interests and those of the outside shareholders, since he will then bear only a fraction of the costs of any nonpecuniary benefits he takes out in maximizing his own utility. If the manager owns only 95 percent of the stock, he will expend resources to the point where the marginal utility derived from a dollar's expenditure of the firm's resources on such items equals the marginal utility of an additional 95 cents in general purchasing power (i.e., *his* share of the wealth reduction) and not one dollar. Such activities on his part can be limited (but probably not eliminated) by the expenditure of resources on monitoring activities by the outside stockholders. But as we show below, the owner will bear the entire wealth effects of these expected costs as long as the equity market anticipates these effects. Prospective minority shareholders will realize that the owner–manager's interests will diverge somewhat from theirs; hence the price they will pay for shares will reflect the monitoring costs and the effect of the divergence between the manager's interest and theirs. Nevertheless, ignoring for the moment the possibility of borrowing against his wealth, the owner will find it desirable to bear these costs as long as the welfare increment he experiences from converting his claims on the firm into general purchasing power[17] is large enough to offset them.

As the owner–manager's fraction of the equity falls, his fractional claim on the outcomes falls, and this will tend to encourage him to appropriate larger amounts of the corporate resources in the form of perquisites. This also makes it desirable for the minority shareholders to expend more resources in monitoring his behavior. Thus, the wealth costs to the owner of obtaining additional cash in the equity markets rise as his fractional ownership falls.

We shall continue to characterize the agency conflict between the owner–manager and outside shareholders as deriving from the manager's tendency to appropriate perquisites out of the firm's resources for his own consumption. We do not mean to leave the impression, however, that this is the only or even the most important source of conflict. Indeed, it is likely that the most important conflict arises from the fact that as the manager's ownership claim falls, his incentive to devote significant effort to creative activities, such as searching out new profitable ventures, falls. He may in fact avoid such ventures simply because it requires too much trouble or effort on his part to manage or to learn about new technologies. Avoidance of these personal costs and of the anxieties that go with them also represents a source of on-the-job utility to him, and it can result in the value of the firm being substantially lower than it otherwise could be.

A Simple Formal Analysis of the Agency Costs of Equity

In order to develop some structure for the analysis to follow, we make two sets of assumptions. The first set (permanent assumptions) are those carried through almost all of the analysis in sections 2–5. The effects of relaxing some of these are discussed in section 6. The second set (temporary assumptions) are made only for expositional purposes and are relaxed as soon as the basic points have been clarified.

17 For use in consumption, for the diversification of his wealth, or more importantly, for the financing of "profitable" projects that he could not otherwise finance out of his personal wealth. We deal with these issues below after having developed some of the elementary analytical tools necessary to their solution.

Permanent Assumptions:

(P.1) All taxes are zero.

(P.2) No trade credit is available.

(P.3) All outside equity shares are nonvoting.

(P.4) No complex financial claims such as convertible bonds or preferred stock or warrants can be issued.

(P.5) No outside owner gains utility from ownership in a firm in any way other than through its effect on his wealth or cash flows.

(P.6) All dynamic aspects of the multiperiod nature of the problem are ignored by assuming that there is only one production–financing decision to be made by the entrepreneur.

(P.7) The entrepreneur–manager's money wages are held constant throughout the analysis.

(P.8) There exists a single manager (the peak coordinator) with ownership interest in the firm.

Temporary Assumptions:

(T.1) The size of the firm is fixed.

(T.2) No monitoring or bonding activities are possible.

(T.3) No debt financing through bonds, preferred stock, or personal borrowing (secured or unsecured) is possible.

(T.4) All elements of the owner–manager's decision problem involving portfolio considerations induced by the presence of uncertainty and the existence of diversifiable risk are ignored.

Define:

X $= \{x_1, x_2, \ldots, x_n\}$ = vector of quantities of all factors and activities within the firm from which the manager derives nonpecuniary benefits; the x_i are defined such that his marginal utility is positive for each of them;

$C(X)$ = total dollar cost of providing any given amount of these items;

$P(X)$ = total dollar value to the firm of the productive benefits of X;

$B(X) = P(X) - C(X)$ = net dollar benefit to the firm of X, ignoring any effects of X on the equilibrium wage of the manager.

When we ignore the effects of X on the manager's utility and therefore on his equilibrium wage rate, the optimum levels of the factors and activities X are defined by X^* such that

$$\frac{\partial B(X^*)}{\partial X^*} = \frac{\partial P(X^*)}{\partial X^*} - \frac{\partial C(X^*)}{\partial X^*} = 0.$$

Thus, for any vector $X \geqq X^*$ (i.e., where at least one element of X is greater than its corresponding element of X^*), $F \equiv B(X^*) - B(X) > 0$ measures the dollar cost to the firm (net of any productive effects) of providing the increment $X - X^*$ of the factors and activities that generate utility for the manager. We assume henceforth that, for any given level of cost, F, to the firm, the vector of factors and activities on which F is spent are those, $\hat{X}$, which yield the manager maximum utility. Thus $F \equiv B(X^*) - B(\hat{X})$.

We have thus far ignored in our discussion the fact that these expenditures on X occur through time and therefore there are trade-offs to be made across time as well as among alternative elements of X. Furthermore, we have ignored the fact that the future expenditures are likely to involve uncertainty (i.e., they are subject to probability distributions), and therefore some allowance must be made for their riskiness. We resolve both of these issues by defining C, P, B, and F to be the *current market values* of the sequence of probability distributions on the period-by-period cash flows involved.[18]

Given the definition of F as the current market value of the stream of the manager's expenditures on nonpecuniary benefits, we represent the constraint that a single owner–manager faces in deciding how much nonpecuniary income he will extract from the firm by the line $\bar{V}F$ in figure 1. This is analogous to a budget constraint. The market value of the firm is measured along the vertical axis, and the market value of the manager's stream of expenditures on nonpecuniary benefits, F, is measured along the horizontal axis. The value of the firm is $0\bar{V}$ when the amount of nonpecuniary income consumed is zero. By definition V is the maximum

18 And again we assume that, for any given market value of these costs, F, to the firm, the allocation across time and across alternative probability distributions is such that the manager's current expected utility is at a maximum. –

market value of the cash flows generated by the firm for a given money wage for the manager when the manager's consumption of nonpecuniary benefits is zero. At this point all the factors and activities within the firm that generate utility for the manager are at the level X^* defined above. There is a different budget constraint $\overline{V}F$ for each possible scale of the firm (i.e., level of investment, I) and for alternative levels of money wage, W, for the manager. For the moment we pick an arbitrary level of investment (which we assume has already been made) and hold the scale of the firm constant at this level. We also assume that the manager's money wage is fixed at the level W^*, which represents the current market value of his wage contract in the optimal compensation package consisting of both wages, W^*, and nonpecuniary benefits, F^*.[19] Since $1 of current value of nonpecuniary benefits withdrawn from the firm by the manager reduces the market value of the firm by $1, by definition, the slope of $\overline{V}F$ is −1.

The owner–manager's tastes for wealth and nonpecuniary benefits is represented in figure 1 by a system of indifference curves, U_1, U_2, etc.[20] The indifference curves will be convex, as drawn, as long as the owner–manager's marginal rate of substitution between nonpecuniary benefits and wealth diminishes with increasing levels of the benefits. For the 100 percent owner–manager, this presumes that perfect substitutes for these benefits are not available on the outside; that

19 At this stage, when we are considering a 100 percent owner-managed firm, the notion of a "wage contract" with himself has no content. However, the 100 percent owner-managed case is only an expositional device used in passing to illustrate a number of points in the analysis, and we ask the reader to bear with us briefly while we lay out the structure for the more interesting partial ownership case, where such a contract does have substance.

20 The manager's utility function is actually defined over wealth and the future time sequence of vectors of quantities of nonpecuniary benefits, X_t. Although the setting of his problem is somewhat different, Fama analyzes the conditions under which these preferences can be represented as a derived utility function defined as a function of the money value of the expenditures (in our notation, F) on these goods, conditional on the prices of goods. E. F. Fama, "Multiperiod Consumption–Investment Decisions," *American Economic Review* 60 (1970): 163–74; idem, "Ordinal and Measurable Utility," in *Studies in the Theory of Capital Markets*, ed. M. C. Jensen (New York: Praeger, 1972). Such a utility function incorporates the optimization going on in the background that defines $\hat{X}$ discussed above for a given F. In the more general case in which we allow a time series of consumption, $\hat{X}_t$, the optimization is being carried out across both time and the components of X_t for fixed F.

is, to some extent they are job specific. For the fractional owner–manager this presumes that the benefits cannot be turned into general purchasing power at a constant price.[21]

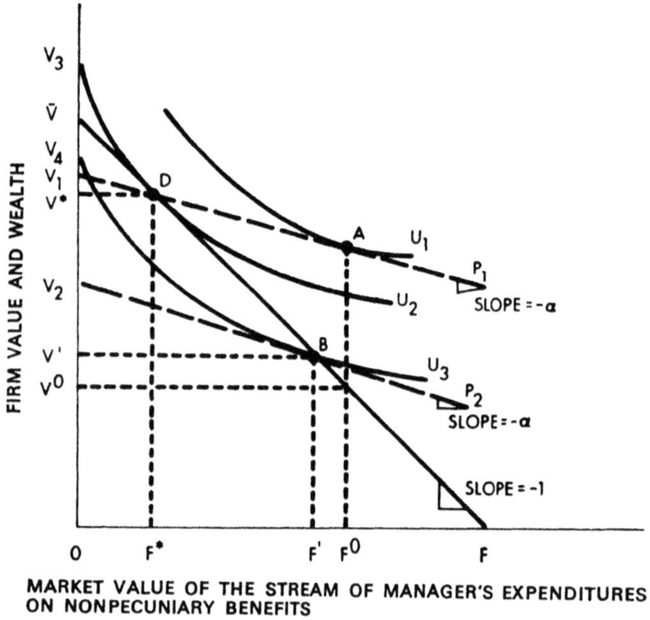

Figure 1. The value of the firm, V, and the level of nonpecuniary benefits consumed, F, when the fraction of outside equity is $(1-\alpha)V$, and $U_j(j = 1, 2, 3)$ represents owner's indifference curves between wealth and nonpecuniary benefits

When the owner has 100 percent of the equity, the value of the firm will be V^*, where indifference curve U_2 is tangent to VF and the level of nonpecuniary benefits consumed is F^*. If the owner sells the entire equity but remains as manager and if the equity buyer can, at zero cost, force the old owner (as manager) to take the same level of nonpecuniary benefits

21 This excludes, for instance, (*a*) the case where the manager is allowed to expend corporate resources on anything he pleases, in which case F would be a perfect substitute for wealth, or (*b*) the case where he can "steal" cash (or other marketable assets) with constant returns to scale—if he could, the indifference curves would be straight lines with slope determined by the fence commission.

as he did as owner, then V^* is the price the new owner will be willing to pay for the entire equity.[22]

In general, however, we would not expect the new owner to be able to enforce identical behavior on the old owner at zero costs. If the old owner sells a fraction of the firm to an outsider, he, as manager, will no longer bear the full cost of any nonpecuniary benefits he consumes. Suppose the owner sells a share of the firm, $1-\alpha$ $(0 < \alpha < 1)$, and retains for himself a share, α. If the prospective buyer believes that the owner–manager will consume the same level of nonpecuniary benefits as he did as full owner, the buyer will be willing to pay $(1-\alpha)V^*$ for a fraction, $1-\alpha$, of the equity. Given that an outsider now holds a claim to $1-\alpha$ of the equity, however, the *cost* to the owner–manager of consuming \$1 of nonpecuniary benefits in the firm will no longer be \$1. Instead, it will be $\alpha \times \$1$. If the prospective buyer actually paid $(1-\alpha)V^*$ for his share of the equity, and if thereafter the manager could choose whatever level of nonpecuniary benefits he liked, his budget constraint would be V_1P_1 in figure 1, with a slope equal to $-\alpha$. Including the payment the owner receives from the buyer as part of the owner's post-sale wealth, his budget constraint, V_1P_1, must pass through D, since he can if he wishes have the same wealth and level of nonpecuniary consumption he consumed as full owner.

But if the owner–manager is free to choose the level of perquisites, F, subject only to the loss in wealth he incurs as

---

22 Point D defines the fringe benefits in the optimal pay package, since the value to the manager of the fringe benefits F^* is greater than the cost of providing them, as is evidenced by the fact that U_2 is steeper to the left of D than the budget constraint with slope equal to -1.

That D is indeed the optimal pay package can easily be seen in this situation, since if the conditions of the sale to a new owner specified that the manager would receive no fringe benefits after the sale, he would require a payment equal to V_3 to compensate him for the sacrifice of his claims to V^* and fringe benefits amounting to F^* (the latter with total value to him of V_3-V^*). But if $F = 0$, the value of the firm is only $\bar{V}$. Therefore, if monitoring costs were zero, the sale would take place at V^* with provision for a pay package that included fringe benefits of F^* for the manager.

This discussion seems to indicate there are two values for the "firm," V_3 and V^*. This is not the case if we realize that V^* is the value of the right to be the residual claimant to the cash flows of the firm, and V_3-V^* is the value of the managerial rights, i.e., the right to make the operating decisions, which include access to F^*. There is at least one other right that has value but plays no formal role in the analysis as yet—the value of the control right. By *control right* we mean the right to hire and fire the manager, and we leave this issue to a future paper.

a part owner, his welfare will be maximized by increasing his consumption of nonpecuniary benefits. He will move to point A, where V_1P_1 is tangent to U_1, representing a higher level of utility. The value of the firm falls from V^* to V^0, that is, by the amount of the cost to the firm of the increased nonpecuniary expenditures, and the owner–manager's consumption of nonpecuniary benefits rises from F^* to F^0.

If the equity market is characterized by rational expectations, the buyers will be aware that the owner will increase his nonpecuniary consumption when his ownership share is reduced. If the owner's response function is known or if the equity market makes unbiased estimates of the owner's response to the changed incentives, the buyer will not pay $(1-\alpha)V^*$ for $1-\alpha$ of the equity.

Theorem. For a claim on the firm of $1-\alpha$, *the outsider will pay only* $(1-\alpha)$ *times the value he expects the firm to have, given the induced change in the behavior of the owner–manager.*

Proof

For simplicity we ignore any element of uncertainty introduced by the lack of perfect knowledge of the owner–manager's response function. Such uncertainty will not affect the final solution if the equity market is large as long as the estimates are rational (i.e., unbiased) and the errors are independent across firms. The latter condition assures that this risk is diversifiable, and therefore equilibrium prices will equal the expected values.

Let W represent the owner's total wealth after he has sold a claim equal to $1-\alpha$ of the equity to an outsider. W has two components. One is the payment, S_0, made by the outsider for $1-\alpha$ of the equity; the rest, S_1, is the value of the owner's (i.e., insider's) share of the firm, so that W, the owner's wealth, is given by

$$W = S_0+S_1 = S_0+\alpha V(F, \alpha),$$

where $V(F, \alpha)$ represents the value of the firm given that the manager's fractional ownership share is α and that he consumes perquisites with current market value of F. Let V_2P_2, with a slope of $-\alpha$, represent the trade-off the owner–manager faces between nonpecuniary benefits and his wealth after the sale. Given that the owner has decided to sell a claim to $1-\alpha$ of the firm, his welfare will be maximized when V_2P_2 is tangent to some indifference curve such as U_3 in figure 1. A price for a claim to $1-\alpha$ of the firm that is satisfactory to both the buyer and the seller will require that this tangency occur along $\bar{V}F$—that is, that the value of the firm be V'. To show this, assume that such is not the case—that the tangency occurs to the left of the point B on the line $\bar{V}F$. Then, since the slope of V_2P_2 is negative, the value of the firm will be larger than V'. The owner–manager's choice of this lower level of consumption of nonpecuniary benefits will imply a higher value both to the firm as a whole and to the fraction of the firm $1-\alpha$ that the outsider has acquired; that is, $(1-\alpha)V' > S_0$. From the owner's viewpoint, he has sold $1-\alpha$ of the firm for less than he could have, given the (assumed) lower level of nonpecuniary benefits he enjoys. On the other hand, if the tangency point B is to the right of the line VF, the owner–manager's higher consumption of nonpecuniary benefits means the value of the firm is less than V', and hence $(1-\alpha)V(F, \alpha) < S_0 = (1-\alpha)V'$. The outside owner then has paid more for his share of the equity than it is worth. S_0 will be a mutually satisfactory price if and only if $(1-\alpha)V' = S_0$. But this means that the owner's postsale wealth is equal to the (reduced) value of the firm V', since

$$W = S_0 + \alpha V' = (1-\alpha)V' + \alpha V' = V'.$$

Q.E.D.

The requirement that V' and F' fall on $\bar{V}F$ is thus equivalent to requiring that the value of the claim acquired by the outside buyer be equal to the amount he pays for it, and conversely for the owner. *This means that the decline in the total value of the firm* (V^*-V') *is entirely imposed on the owner–manager.* His total wealth after the sale of $1-\alpha$ of the equity is V', and the decline in his wealth is V^*-V'.

The distance V^*-V' is the reduction in the market value of the firm engendered by the agency relationship and is a measure of the "residual loss" defined earlier. In this simple example the residual loss represents the total agency costs engendered by the sale of outside equity because monitoring and bonding activities have not been allowed. The welfare loss the owner incurs is less than the residual loss by the value to him of the increase in nonpecuniary benefits ($F'-F^*$). In figure 1 the difference between the intercepts on the Y axis of the two indifference curves U_2 and U_3 is a measure of the owner–manager's welfare loss due to the incurrence of agency costs,[23] and he would sell such a claim only if the increment in welfare he achieves by using the cash amounting to $(1-\alpha)V'$ for other things was worth more to him than this amount of wealth.

Optimal Scale of the Firm with All-Equity Financing

Consider the problem faced by an entrepreneur with initial pecuniary wealth, W, and monopoly access to a project requiring investment outlay, I, subject to diminishing returns to scale in I. Figure 2 portrays the solution to the optimal scale of the firm, taking into account the agency costs associated with the existence of outside equity. The axes are as defined in figure 1 except we now plot on the vertical axis the total wealth of the owner, that is, his initial wealth, W, plus $V(I)-I$, the net increment in wealth he obtains from exploitation of his investment opportunities. The market value of the firm, $V = V(I, F)$, is now a function of the level of investment, I, and the current market value of the manager's expenditures of the firm's resources on nonpecuniary benefits, F. Let $\bar{V}(I)$ represent the value of the firm as a function of the level of investment when the manager's expenditures on nonpecuniary benefits, F, are zero. The schedule in figure 2 with intercept labeled $W+[\bar{V}(I^*)-I^*]$ and slope equal to -1 represents the locus of combinations of postinvestment wealth and dollar cost to the firm of nonpecuniary benefits that are available to the manager when investment is carried to the value-maximizing point, I^*. At this point $\Delta\bar{V}(I)-\Delta I = 0$. If the manager's wealth were large enough to cover the investment required to reach this scale of operation, I^*, he would consume F^* in nonpecuniary benefits and have pecuniary wealth with the value $W+V^*-I^*$. However, if outside financing is required

23 The distance V^*-V' is a measure of what we will call gross agency costs. The distance V_3-V_4 is a measure of what we call net agency costs, and it is this measure of agency costs that will be minimized by the manager in the general case in which we allow investment to change.

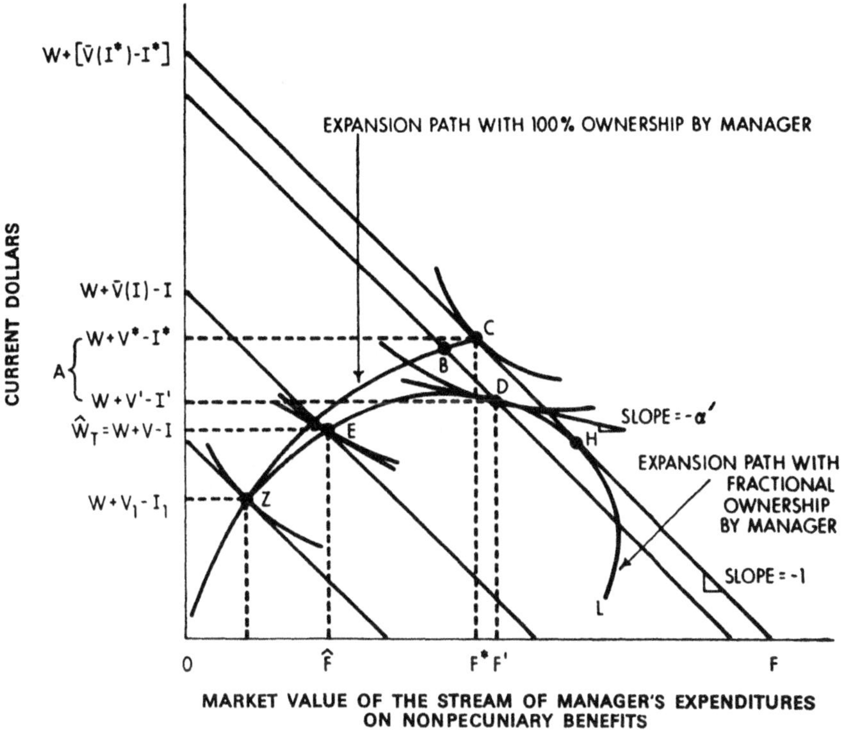

Figure 2. Determination of the optimal scale of the firm in the case where no monitoring takes place. Point *C* denotes optimum investment, I^*, and nonpecuniary benefits, F^*, when investment is 100 percent financed by the entrepreneur. Point *D* denotes optimum investment, I', and nonpecuniary benefits, *F*, when outside equity financing is used to help finance the investment and the entrepreneur owns a fraction, α', of the firm. The distance *A* measures the gross agency costs.

to cover the investment, he will not reach this point if monitoring costs are nonzero.[24]

24 I^* is the value-maximizing and Pareto-optimum investment level that results from the traditional analysis of the corporate investment decision if the firm operates in perfectly competitive capital and product markets and the agency cost problems discussed here are ignored. See G. Debreu, *Theory of Value* (New York: Wiley, 1959), chap. 7; M. C. Jensen and J. B. Long, "Corporate Investment under Uncertainty and Pareto Optimality in the Capital Markets," *Bell Journal of Economics and Management Science* 3 (1972): 151–74; J. B. Long, "Wealth, Welfare, and the Price

The expansion path *OZBC* represents the equilibrium combinations of wealth and nonpecuniary benefits, *F*, that the manager could obtain if he had enough personal wealth to finance all levels of investment up to I^*. It is the locus of points such as *Z* and *C* that represent the equilibrium position for the 100 percent owner–manager at each possible level of investment, *I*. As *I* increases, we move up the expansion path to the point *C*, where $V(I)-I$ is at a maximum. Additional investment beyond this point reduces the net value of the firm, and as it does, the equilibrium path of the manager's wealth and nonpecuniary benefits retraces (in the reverse direction) the curve *OZBC*. We draw the path as a smooth concave function only as a matter of convenience.

If the manager obtained outside financing and if there were zero costs to the agency relationship (perhaps because monitoring costs were zero), the expansion path would also be represented by *OZBC*. Therefore, this path represents what we might call the "idealized" solutions, that is, those which would occur in the absence of agency costs.

Assume the manager has sufficient personal wealth to completely finance the firm only up to investment level I_1, which puts him at point *Z*. At this point $W = I_1$. To increase the size of the firm beyond this point he must obtain outside financing to cover the additional investment required, and this means reducing his fractional ownership. When he does this he incurs agency costs, and the lower is his ownership fraction, the larger are the agency costs he incurs. However, if the investments requiring outside financing are sufficiently profitable, his welfare will continue to increase.

The expansion path *ZEDHL* in figure 2 portrays one possible path of the equilibrium levels of the owner's nonpecuniary benefits and wealth at each possible level of investment higher than I_1. This path is the locus of points such as *E* or *D* where (1) the manager's indifference curve is tangent to a line with slope equal to $-\alpha$ (his fractional claim on the firm

---

of Risk," *Journal of Finance* 27 (1972): 485–88; R. C. Merton and M. G. Subrahmanyam, "The Optimality of a Competitive Stock Market," *Bell Journal of Economics and Management Science* 5 (1974): 145–70; J. Hirschleifer, "On the Theory of Optimal Investment Decisions," *Journal of Political Economy* 66 (1958): 329–52; idem, *Investment, Interest, and Capital* (Englewood Cliffs, N.J.: Prentice-Hall, 1970); E. F. Fama and M. Miller, *The Theory of Finance* (New York: Holt, Rinehart & Winston, 1972).

at that level of investment), and (2) the tangency occurs on the "budget constraint" with slope $= -1$ for the firm value and nonpecuniary benefit trade-off at the same level of investment.[25] As we move along *ZEDHL,* his fractional claim on the firm continues to fall as he raises larger amounts of outside capital. This expansion path represents his complete opportunity set for combinations of wealth and nonpecuniary benefits given the existence of the costs of the agency relationship with the outside equity holders. Point *D,* where this opportunity set is tangent to an indifference curve, represents the solution that maximizes his welfare. At this point, the level of investment is I', his fractional ownership share in the firm is α', his wealth is $W+V'-I'$, and he consumes a stream of nonpecuniary benefits with current market value of F'. The gross agency costs (denoted by A) are equal to $(V^*-I^*)-(V'-I')$. Given that no monitoring is possible, I' is the socially optimal level of investment as well as the privately optimal level.

We can characterize the optimal level of investment as that point, I', which satisfies the following condition for small changes:

$$\Delta V - \Delta I + \alpha' \Delta F = 0. \tag{1}$$

$\Delta V - \Delta I$ is the change in the net market value of the firm, and $\alpha' \Delta F$ is the dollar value to the manager of the incremental

25 Each equilibrium point such as that at E is characterized by $(\hat{a}, \hat{F}, \hat{W}_T)$, where $\hat{W}_T$ is the entrepreneur's postinvestment financing wealth. Such an equilibrium must satisfy each of the following four conditions:

(1) $$\hat{W}_T + F = \overline{V}(I) + W - I = \overline{V}(I) - K,$$

where $K \equiv I - W$ is the amount of outside financing required to make the investment I. If this condition is not satisfied, there is an uncompensated wealth transfer (in one direction or the other) between the entrepreneur and outside equity buyers.

(2) $$U_F(\hat{W}_T, \hat{F})/U_{W_T}(\hat{W}_T, \hat{F}) = \hat{a},$$

where U is the entrepreneur's utility function on wealth and perquisites, U_F and U_{W_T} are marginal utilities, and $\hat{a}$ is the manager's share of the firm.

(3) $$(1-\hat{a})V(I) = (1-\hat{a})[V(I)-\hat{F}] \geqq K,$$

which says the funds received from outsiders are at least equal to K, the minimum required outside financing.

(4) Among all points $(\hat{a}, \hat{F}, \hat{W}_T)$ satisfying conditions (1)–(3), $(\alpha, F, \hat{W}_T)$ gives the manager highest utility. This implies that $(\hat{a}, \hat{F}, \hat{W}_T)$ satisfy condition (3) as an equality.

fringe benefits he consumes (which cost the firm ΔF dollars).[26] Furthermore, recognizing that $V = \overline{V} - F$, where $\overline{V}$ is the value of the firm at any level of investment when $F = 0$, we can substitute into the optimum condition to get

$$(\Delta\overline{V} - \Delta I) - (1 - \alpha')\Delta F = 0 \tag{3}$$

as an alternative expression for determining the optimum level of investment.

The idealized or zero agency cost solution, I^*, is given by the condition $\Delta\overline{V} - \Delta I = 0$; and since ΔF is positive, the actual welfare-maximizing level of investment I' will be less than I^*, because $\Delta\overline{V} - \Delta I$ must be positive at I' if (3) is to be satisfied. Since $-\alpha'$ is the slope of the indifference curve at the optimum and therefore represents the manager's demand price for incremental nonpecuniary benefits, ΔF, we know that $\alpha'\Delta F$ is the dollar value to him of an increment of fringe benefits costing the firm ΔF dollars. The term $(1 - \alpha')\Delta F$ thus measures the dollar "loss" to the firm (and himself) of an additional ΔF dollars spent on nonpecuniary benefits. The term $\Delta\overline{V} - \Delta I$ is the gross increment in the value of the firm, ignoring any changes in the consumption of nonpecuniary benefits. Thus, the manager stops increasing the size of the firm when the gross increment in value is just offset by the incremental "loss" involved in the consumption of additional fringe benefits due to his declining fractional interest in the firm.[27]

---

26 *Proof.* Note that the slope of the expansion path (or locus of equilibrium points) at any point is $(\Delta V - \Delta I)/\Delta F$, and at the optimum level of investment this must be equal to the slope of the manager's indifference curve between wealth and the market value of fringe benefits, F. Furthermore, in the absence of monitoring, the slope of the indifference curve, $\Delta W/\Delta F$, at the equilibrium point, D, must be equal to $-\alpha'$. Thus,

$$(\Delta V - \Delta I)/\Delta F = -\alpha' \tag{2}$$

is the condition for the optimal scale of investment, and this implies that condition (1) holds for small changes at the optimum level of investment, I'.

27 Since the manager's indifference curves are negatively sloped, we know that the optimum scale of the firm, point D, will occur in the region where the expansion path has negative slope; i.e., the market value of the firm will be declining and the *gross* agency costs, A, will be increasing, and thus the manager will not minimize them in making the investment decision (even though he will minimize them for any *given* level of investment). However, we define the *net* agency cost as the dollar equivalent of the welfare loss the manager experiences because of the agency rela-

The Role of Monitoring and Bonding Activities in Reducing Agency Costs

In the above analysis we have ignored the potential for controlling the behavior of the owner–manager through monitoring and other control activities. In practice, it is usually possible by expending resources to alter the opportunity the owner–manager has for capturing nonpecuniary benefits. These methods include auditing, formal control systems, budget restrictions, and the establishment of incentive compensation systems that serve to identify the manager's interests more closely with those of the outside equity holders, etc. Figure 3 portrays the effects of monitoring and other control activities in the simple situation portrayed in figure 1. The two figures are identical except for the curve *BCE* in figure 3, which depicts a "budget constraint" derived when monitoring possibilities are taken into account. Without monitoring, and with outside equity of $1-\alpha$, the value of the firm will be V' and nonpecuniary expenditures F'. By incurring monitoring costs, M, the equity holders can restrict the manager's consumption of perquisites to amounts less than F'. Let $F(M, \alpha)$ denote the maximum perquisites the manager can consume for alternative levels of monitoring expenditures, M, given his ownership share α. We assume that increases in monitoring reduce F, and reduce it at a decreasing rate; that is, $\partial F/\partial M < 0$ and $\partial^2 F/\partial M^2 > 0$.

Since the current value of expected future monitoring expenditures by the outside equity holders reduces the value to them, dollar for dollar, of any given claim on the firm, the outside equity holders will take this into account in determin-

tionship evaluated at $F = 0$ (the vertical distance between the intercepts on the Y axis of the two indifference curves on which points C and D lie). The optimum solution, I', does satisfy the condition that net agency costs are minimized. But this simply amounts to a restatement of the assumption that the manager maximizes his welfare.

Finally, it is possible for the solution point D to be a corner solution, and in this case the value of the firm will not be declining. Such a corner solution can occur, for instance, if the manager's marginal rate of substitution between F and wealth falls to zero fast enough as we move up the expansion path or if the investment projects are "sufficiently" profitable. In these cases the expansion path will have a corner that lies on the maximum-value budget constraint with intercept $V(I^*)-I^*$, and the level of investment will be equal to the idealized optimum, I^*. However, the market value of the residual claims will be less than V^* because the manager's consumption of perquisites will be larger than F^*, the zero agency cost level.

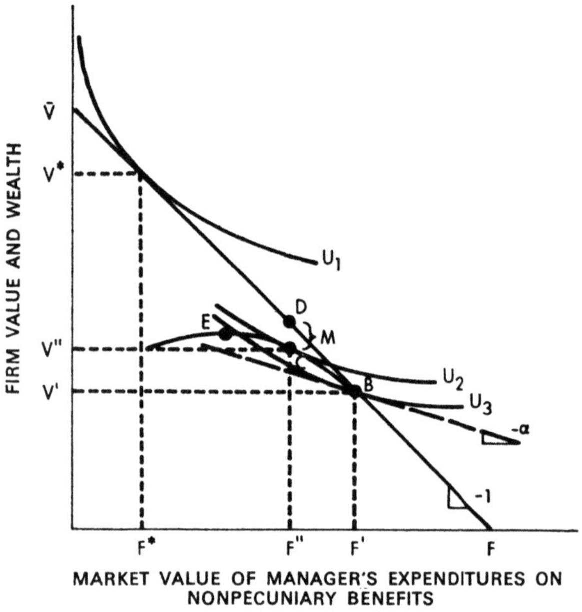

Figure 3. The value of the firm, V, and level of nonpecuniary benefits, F, when outside equity is $1-\alpha$; U_1, U_2, U_3 represent owner's indifference curves between wealth and nonpecuniary benefits; and monitoring (or bonding) activities impose opportunity set BCE as the trade-off constraint facing the owner.

ing the maximum price they will pay for any given fraction of the firm's equity. Therefore, given positive monitoring activity, the value of the firm is given by $V = \bar{V} - F(M, \alpha) - M$, and the locus of these points for various levels of M and for a given level of α lie on the line BCE in figure 3. The vertical difference between the $\bar{V}F$ and BCE curves is M, the current market value of the future monitoring expenditures.

If it is possible for the outside equity holders to make these monitoring expenditures and thereby to impose the reductions in the owner–manager's consumption of F, he will voluntarily enter into a contract with the outside equity holders that gives them the rights to restrict his consumption of nonpecuniary items to F''. He finds this desirable because it will cause the value of the firm to rise to V''. Given the contract, the optimal monitoring expenditure on the part of the outsiders, M, is the amount $D-C$. The entire increase in the value of the firm that accrues will be reflected in the owner's wealth, but his welfare will be increased by less than this because he forgoes some nonpecuniary benefits he previously enjoyed.

If the equity market is competitive and makes unbiased estimates of the effects of the monitoring expenditures on F and V, potential buyers will be indifferent between the following two contracts:

(i) Purchase of a share $1-\alpha$ of the firm at a total price of $(1-\alpha)V'$ and no rights to monitor or control the manager's consumption of perquisites
(ii) Purchase of a share $1-\alpha$ of the firm at a total price of $(1-\alpha)V''$ and the right to expend resources up to an amount equal to $D-C$ that will limit the owner–manager's consumption of perquisites to F''

Given contract (ii) the outside shareholders would find it desirable to monitor to the full rights of their contract because it will pay them to do so. However, if the equity market is competitive, the total benefits (net of the monitoring costs) will be capitalized into the price of the claims. Thus, not surprisingly, the owner–manager reaps all the benefits of the opportunity to write and sell the monitoring contract.[28]

An Analysis of Bonding Expenditures

We can also see from the analysis of figure 3 that it makes no difference who actually makes the monitoring expendi-

28 The careful reader will note that point C will be the equilibrium point only if the contract between the manager and outside equityholders specifies with no ambiguity that they have the right to monitor in order to limit his consumption of perquisites to an amount no less than F''. If there is any ambiguity in this contract regarding these rights, then there arises another source of agency costs that is symmetrical to our original problem. If they could do so, the outside equityholders would monitor to the point where the net value of *their* holdings, $(1-\alpha)V-M$, was maximized, and this would occur when $(\partial V/\partial M)(1-\alpha)-1 = 0$, which would be at some point between points C and E in fig. 3. Point E denotes the point where the value of the firm net of the monitoring costs is at a maximum, i.e., where $\partial V/\partial M-1 = 0$. But the manager would be worse-off than in the zero-monitoring solution if the maximum point for $(1-\alpha)V-M$ were to the left of the intersection between BCE and the indifference curve U_3 passing through point B (which denotes the zero-monitoring level of welfare). Thus, if the manager could not eliminate enough of the ambiguity in the contract to push the equilibrium to the right of the intersection of the curve BCE with indifference curve U_3, he would not engage in any contract that allowed monitoring.

tures—in all cases, the owner bears the full amount of these costs as a wealth reduction. Suppose that the owner–manager could expend resources to guarantee to the outside equity holders that he would limit his activities that cost the firm F. We call these expenditures bonding costs, and they would take such forms as contractual guarantees to have the financial accounts audited by a public accountant, explicit bonding against malfeasance on the part of the manager, and contractual limitations on the manager's decision-making power (which limitations impose costs on the firm because they reduce his ability to take full advantage of some profitable opportunities, as well as limiting his ability to harm the stockholders while making himself better-off).

If the incurrence of the bonding costs were entirely under the control of the manager and if they yielded for him the same opportunity set BCE in figure 3, he would incur them in amount $D-C$. This would limit his consumption of perquisites to F'' from F', and the solution is exactly the same as if the outside equity holders had performed the monitoring. The manager finds it in his interest to incur these costs as long as the net increments in his wealth that they generate (by reducing the agency costs and therefore increasing the value of the firm) are more valuable than the perquisites given up. This optimum occurs at point C in both cases under our assumption that the bonding expenditures yield the same opportunity set as the monitoring expenditures. In general, of course, it will pay the owner–manager to engage in bonding activities and to write contracts that allow monitoring as long as the marginal benefits of each are greater than their marginal cost.

Optimal Scale of the Firm with Monitoring and Bonding Activities

If we allow the outside owners to engage in (costly) monitoring activities to limit the manager's expenditures on nonpecuniary benefits and we allow the manager to engage in bonding activities to guarantee to the outside owners that he will limit his consumption of F, we get an expansion path such as that on which Z and G lie in figure 4. We have assumed in drawing figure 4 that the cost functions involved in monitoring and bonding are such that some positive levels of the activities are desirable—that is, yield benefits greater than their cost. If this is not true, the expansion path generated by the expenditure of resources on these activities would lie below ZD, and no such activity would take place at any level of investment. Points Z, C, and D and the two expansion paths on which they lie are identical to those portrayed in figure 2. Points Z and C lie on the 100 percent ownership expansion path, and points Z and D lie on the fractional ownership, zero-monitoring and bonding activity expansion path.

The path on which points Z and G lie is the one given by the locus of equilibrium points for alternative levels of investment characterized in figure 3 by the point labeled C, which denotes the optimal level of monitoring and bonding activity and the resulting values of the firm and nonpecuniary benefits to the manager given a fixed level of investment. If any monitoring or bonding is cost effective, the expansion path on which Z and G lie must over some range be above the nonmonitoring expansion path. Furthermore, if it lies anywhere to the right of the indifference curve passing through point D (the zero monitoring–bonding solution), the final solution to the problem will involve positive amounts of monitoring or bonding activities. Based on the discussion above, we know that as long as the contracts between the manager and outsiders are unambiguous regarding the rights of the respective parties, the final solution will be at that point where the new expansion path is just tangent to the highest indifference curve. At this point the optimal levels of monitoring and bonding expenditures are M'' and b''; the manager's postinvestment-financing wealth is given by $W+V''-I''-M''-b''$, and his nonpecuniary benefits are F''. The total gross agency costs, A, are given by $A(M'', b'', \alpha'', I'') = (V^*-I^*)-(V''-I''-M''-b'')$.

Pareto Optimality and Agency Costs in Manager-Operated Firms

In general we expect to observe both bonding and external monitoring activities, and the incentives are such that the levels of these activities will satisfy the conditions of efficiency. They will not, however, result in the firm being run in a manner so as to maximize its value. The difference between V^*, the efficient solution under zero monitoring and bonding costs (and therefore zero agency costs), and V'', the value of the firm given positive monitoring costs, is the total gross agency costs defined earlier in the introduction. These are the costs of the "separation of ownership and control," which Adam Smith focused on in the passage quoted at the beginning of this paper and which Berle and Means popularized 157 years later.[29] The solutions outlined above to our highly simplified problem imply that agency costs will be positive as long as monitoring costs are positive—which they certainly are.

The reduced value of the firm caused by the manager's consumption of perquisites outlined above is "nonoptimal" or inefficient only in comparison to a world in which we could obtain compliance of the agent to the principal's wishes at zero cost or in comparison to a *hypothetical* world in which the agency costs were lower. But these costs (monitoring and bonding costs and "residual loss") are an unavoidable result of the agency relationship. Furthermore, since they are borne entirely by the decision maker (in this case, the original owner) responsible for creating the relationship, he has the incentives to see that they are minimized (because he captures the benefits from their reduction). In addition, these agency costs will be incurred only if the benefits to the owner–manager from their creation are great enough to outweigh them. In our current example these benefits arise from the availability of profitable investments requiring capital investment in excess of the original owner's personal wealth.

In conclusion, finding that agency costs are nonzero (i.e., that there are costs associated with the separation of ownership and control in the corporation) and concluding therefrom that the agency relationship is nonoptimal, wasteful, or inefficient is equivalent in every sense to comparing a world in which iron ore is a scarce commodity (and therefore costly) to a world in which it is freely available at zero resource cost and concluding that the first world is "nonoptimal"—a perfect example of the fallacy criticized by Coase and what Demsetz characterizes as the "Nirvana" form of analysis.[30]

29 A. A. Berle, Jr., and G. C. Means, *The Modern Corporation and Private Property* (New York: Macmillan, 1932).

30 R. H. Coase, "Discussion," *American Economic Review* 54 (1964): 194–97; H. Dem-

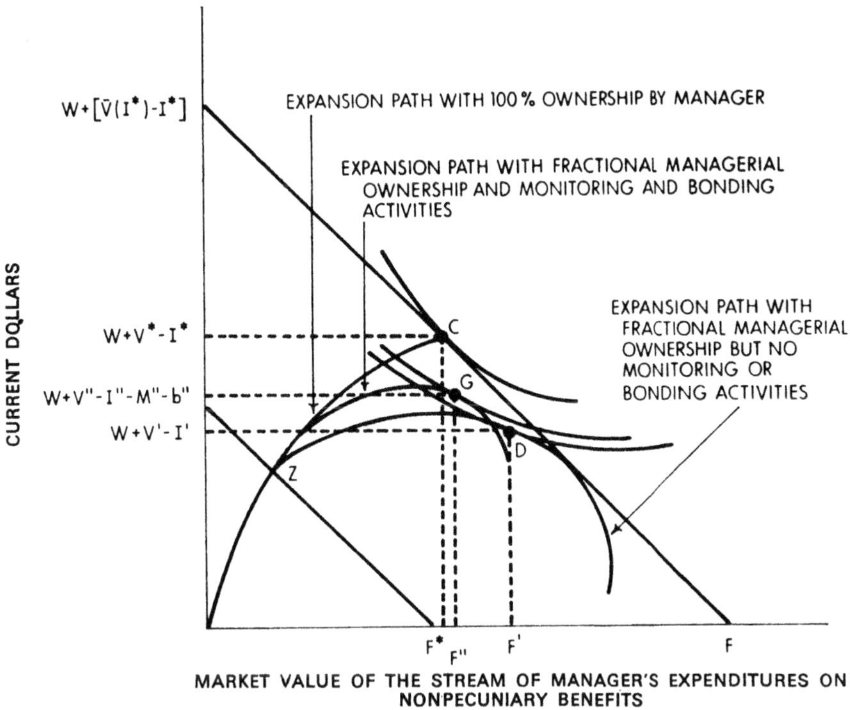

Figure 4. Determination of optimal scale of the firm allowing for monitoring and bonding activities. Optimal monitoring costs are *M''*; bonding costs are *b''*; and the equilibrium scale of firm, manager's wealth, and consumption of nonpecuniary benefits are at point *G*.

Factors Affecting the Size of the Divergence from Ideal Maximization

The magnitude of the agency costs discussed above will vary from firm to firm. It will depend on the tastes of managers, the ease with which they can exercise their own preferences

setz, "Information and Efficiency: Another Viewpoint," *Journal of Law and Economics* 12 (1969): 1–22.

If we could establish the existence of a feasible set of alternative institutional arrangements that would yield net benefits from the reduction of these costs, we could legitimately conclude that the agency relationship engendered by the corporation was not Pareto-optimal. However, we would then be left with the problem of explaining why these alternative institutional arrangements have not replaced the corporate form of organization.

as opposed to value maximization in decision making, and the costs of monitoring and bonding activities.[31] The agency costs will also depend upon the cost of measuring the manager's (agent's) performance and evaluating it, the cost of devising and applying an index for compensating the manager that correlates with the owner's (principal's) welfare, and the cost of devising and enforcing specific behavioral rules or policies. Where the manager has less than a controlling interest in the firm, these costs will also depend upon the market for managers. Competition from other potential managers limits the costs of obtaining managerial services (including the extent to which a given manager can diverge from the idealized solution that would obtain if all monitoring and bonding costs were zero). The size of the divergence (the agency costs) will be directly related to the cost of replacing the manager. If his responsibilities require very little knowledge specialized to the firm, if it is easy to evaluate his performance, and if replacement search costs are modest, the divergence from the ideal will be relatively small, and vice versa.

The divergence will also be constrained by the market for the firm itself, that is, by capital markets. Owners always have the option of selling their firm, either as a unit or piecemeal. Owners of manager-operated firms can and do sample the capital market from time to time. If they discover that the value of the future earnings stream to others is higher than the value of the firm to them given that it is to be manager-operated, they can exercise their right to sell. It is conceivable that other owners could be more efficient at monitoring or even that a single individual with appropriate managerial talents and with sufficiently large personal wealth would elect to buy the firm. In this latter case the purchase by such a single individual would completely eliminate the agency costs. If there were a number of such potential owner–manager purchasers (all with talents and tastes identical to the current manager), the owners would receive in the sale price of the firm the full value of the residual claimant rights,

31 The monitoring and bonding costs will differ from firm to firm depending on such things as the inherent complexity and geographical dispersion of operations, the attractiveness of perquisites available in the firm (consider the mint), etc.

including the capital value of the eliminated agency costs plus the value of the managerial rights.

It is frequently argued that the existence of competition in product (and factor) markets will constrain the behavior of managers to idealized value maximization, that is, that monopoly in product (or monopsony in factor) markets will permit larger divergences from value maximization.[32] Our analysis does not support this hypothesis. The owners of a firm with monopoly power have the same incentives to limit divergences of the manager from value maximization (i.e., the ability to increase their wealth) as do the owners of competitive firms. Furthermore, competition in the market for managers will generally make it unnecessary for the owners to share rents with the manager. The owners of a monopoly firm need only pay the supply price for a manager.

Since the owner of a monopoly has the same wealth incentives to minimize managerial costs as would the owner of a competitive firm, both will undertake that level of monitoring which equates the marginal cost of monitoring to the marginal wealth increment from reduced consumption of perquisites by the manager. Thus, the existence of monopoly will not increase agency costs.

Furthermore, the existence of competition in product and factor markets will not eliminate the agency costs due to managerial control problems, as has often been asserted.[33] If my competitors all incur agency costs equal to or greater than mine, I will not be eliminated from the market by their competition.

---

32 See, for example, Williamson, *Discretionary Behavior:*

"Where competitors are numerous and entry is easy, persistent departures from profit maximizing behavior inexorably leads to extinction. Economic natural selection holds the stage. In these circumstances, the behavior of the individual units that constitute the supply side of the product market is essentially routine and uninteresting and economists can confidently predict industry behavior without being explicitly concerned with the behavior of these individual units.

"When the conditions of competition are relaxed, however, the opportunity set of the firm is expanded. In this case, the behavior of the firm as a distinct operating unit is of separate interest. Both for purposes of interpreting particular behavior within the firm as well as for predicting responses of the industry aggregate, it may be necessary to identify the factors that influence the firm's choices within this expanded opportunity set and embed these in a formal model." [P. 2]

33 For example, M. Friedman, "The Social Responsibility of Business Is to Increase Its Profits," *New York Times Magazine*, Sept. 13, 1970, pp. 32 ff.

The existence and size of the agency costs depend on the nature of the monitoring costs, the tastes of managers for nonpecuniary benefits, and the supply of potential managers who are capable of financing the entire venture out of their personal wealth. If monitoring costs are zero, agency costs will be zero; or if there are enough 100 percent owner–managers available to own and run all the firms in an industry (competitive or not), then agency costs in that industry will also be zero.[34]

3. Some Unanswered Questions Regarding the Existence of the Corporate Form

The Question

The analysis up to this point has left us with a basic puzzle: Why, given the existence of positive costs of the agency relationship, do we find so widely prevalent the usual corporate form of organization with widely diffuse ownership? If one takes seriously much of the literature regarding the "discretionary" power held by managers of large corporations, it is difficult to understand the historical fact of enormous growth in equity in such organizations, not only in the United States, but throughout the world. Paraphrasing Alchian: How does it happen that millions of individuals are willing to turn over a significant fraction of their wealth to organizations run by managers who have so little interest in their welfare? What is even more remarkable, Why are they willing to make these commitments purely as residual claimants, that is, on the anticipation that managers will operate the firm so that earnings will accrue to the stockholders?[35]

There is certainly no lack of alternative ways that individuals might invest, including entirely different forms of organizations. Even if consideration is limited to corporate organizations, there are clearly alternative ways capital might be raised—through fixed claims of various sorts, bonds, notes, mortgages, etc. Moreover, the corporate income tax

34 Assuming there are no special tax benefits to ownership nor utility of ownership other than that derived from the direct wealth effects of ownership, such as might be true for professional sports teams, race horse stables, firms that carry the family name, etc.

35 Alchian, "Corporate Management."

seems to favor the use of fixed claims since interest is treated as a tax-deductible expense. Those who assert that managers do not behave in the interest of stockholders have generally not addressed a very important question: Why, if non-manager-owned shares have such a serious deficiency, have they not long since been driven out by fixed claims?[36]

Some Alternative Explanations of the Ownership Structure of the Firm

The Role of Limited Liability

Manne and Alchian and Demsetz argue that one of the attractive features of the corporate form vis-à-vis individual proprietorships or partnerships is the limited liability of equity claims in corporations. Without this provision, each and every investor purchasing one or more shares of a corporation would be potentially liable for the debts of the corporation to the full extent of his personal wealth. Few individuals would find this a desirable risk to accept, and the major benefits to be obtained from risk reduction through diversification would be to a large extent unobtainable.[37] This argument, however, is incomplete, since limited liability does not eliminate the basic risk—it merely shifts it. The argument must rest ultimately on transactions costs. If all stockholders of GM were liable for GM's debts, the maximum liability for an individual shareholder would be greater than if his shares had limited liability. However, given that many other stockholders also existed and that each was liable for the unpaid claims in proportion to his ownership, it is highly unlikely that the maximum payment each would have to make would be large in the event of GM's bankruptcy, since the total wealth of those stockholders would also be large. Nevertheless, the existence of unlimited liability would impose incentives for each shareholder to keep track of both the liabilities of GM and the wealth of the other GM owners. It is easily conceivable that the costs of so doing would, in the aggregate, be much higher than simply paying a premium in

36 Marris, *Managerial Capitalism,* pp. 7–9, is the exception, although he argues that there exists some "maximum leverage point" beyond which the chances of "insolvency" are in some undefined sense too high.

37 H. G. Manne, "Our Two Corporate Systems: Law and Economics," *Virginia Law Review* 53 (1967): 259–84; Alchian and Demsetz, "Production."

the form of higher interest rates to the creditors of GM in return for their acceptance of a contract granting limited liability to the shareholders. The creditors would then bear the risk of any nonpayment of debts in the event of GM's bankruptcy.

It is also not generally recognized that limited liability is merely a necessary condition, not a sufficient condition, for explaining the magnitude of the reliance on equities. Ordinary debt also carries limited liability.[38] If limited liability is all that is required, why don't we observe large corporations, individually owned, with a tiny fraction of the capital supplied by the entrepreneur and the rest simply borrowed?[39] At first this question seems silly to many people (as does the question regarding why firms would ever issue debt or preferred stock under conditions where there are no tax benefits obtained from the treatment of interest or preferred-dividend payments[40]). We have found that oftentimes this question is misinterpreted to be one regarding why firms obtain capital. The issue is not why they obtain capital but why they obtain it through the particular forms we have

38 By *limited liability* we mean the same conditions that apply to common stock. Subordinated debt or preferred stock could be constructed so as to carry with it liability provisions; i.e., if the corporation's assets were insufficient at some point to pay off all prior claims (trade credit, accrued wages, senior debt, etc.) and if the personal resources of the "equityholders" were also insufficient to cover these claims, the holders of this "debt" would be subject to assessments beyond the face value of their claim (assessments that might be limited or unlimited in amount).

39 Alchian and Demsetz, "Production," p. 709, argue that one can explain the existence of both bonds and stock in the ownership structure of firms as the result of differing expectations regarding the outcomes for the firm. They argue that bonds are created and sold to "pessimists" and stocks with a residual claim with no upper bound are sold to "optimists."

As long as capital markets are perfect with no taxes or transactions costs and individual investors can issue claims on distributions of outcomes on the same terms as firms, such actions on the part of firms cannot affect their values. The reason is simple. Suppose such "pessimists" did exist and yet the firm issues only equity claims. The demand for those equity claims would reflect the fact that the individual purchaser could on his own account issue "bonds" with a limited and prior claim to the distribution of outcomes on the equity that is exactly the same as that which the firm could issue. Similarly, investors could easily unlever any position by simply buying a proportional claim to both the bonds and stocks of a levered firm. Therefore, a levered firm could not sell at a different price than an unlevered firm solely because of the existence of such differential expectations. See Fama and Miller, *Theory of Finance*, chap. 4, for an excellent exposition of these issues.

40 Corporations did use both prior to the institution of the corporate income tax in the United States, and preferred dividends have never, with minor exceptions, been tax-deductible.

observed for such long periods of time. The fact is that no well-articulated answer to this question currently exists in the literature of either finance or economics.

The "Irrelevance" of Capital Structure

In their pathbreaking 1958 article on the cost of capital, Modigliani and Miller demonstrated that in the absence of bankruptcy costs and tax subsidies on the payment of interest, the value of the firm is independent of the financial structure. They later demonstrated that the existence of tax subsidies on interest payments would cause the value of the firm to rise with the amount of debt financing by the amount of the capitalized value of the tax subsidy.[41] But this line of argument implies that the firm should be financed almost entirely with debt. Realizing the inconsistency with observed behavior, Modigliani and Miller commented:

> It may be useful to remind readers once again that the existence of a tax advantage for debt financing . . . does not necessarily mean that corporations should at all times seek to use the maximum amount of debt in their capital structures. . . . there are as we pointed out, limitations imposed by lenders . . . as well as many other dimensions (and kinds of costs) in real-world problems of financial strategy which are not fully comprehended within the framework of static equilibrium models, either our own or those of the traditional variety. These additional considerations, which are typically grouped under the rubric of "the need for preserving flexibility," will normally imply the maintenance by the corporation of a substantial reserve of untapped borrowing power.[42]

Modigliani and Miller are essentially left without a theory of the determination of the optimal capital structure, and Fama and Miller, commenting on the same issue, reiterate this conclusion:

> And we must admit that at this point there is little in the way of convincing research, either theoretical or empirical, that explains the amounts of debt that firms do decide to have in their capital structure.[43]

41 F. Modigliani and M. H. Miller, "The Costs of Capital, Corporation Finance, and the Theory of Investment," *American Economic Review* 48 (1958): 261–97; idem, "Corporate Income Taxes and the Cost of Capital," ibid., 53 (1963): 433–43.

42 Modigliani and Miller, "Corporate Income Taxes," p. 442.

43 Fama and Miller, *Theory of Finance*, p. 173.

The Modigliani–Miller theorem is based on the assumption that the probability distribution of the cash flows to the firm is independent of the capital structure. It is now recognized that the existence of positive costs associated with bankruptcy and the presence of tax subsidies on corporate interest payments will invalidate this irrelevance theorem precisely because the probability distribution of future cash flows changes as the probability of the incurrence of the bankruptcy costs changes, that is, as the ratio of debt to equity rises. We believe the existence of agency costs provides stronger reasons for arguing that the probability distribution of future cash flows is *not* independent of the capital, or ownership, structure.

While the introduction of bankruptcy costs in the presence of tax subsidies leads to a theory that defines an optimal capital structure,[44] we argue that this theory is seriously incomplete since it implies that no debt should ever be used in the absence of tax subsidies if bankruptcy costs are positive. Since we know debt was commonly used prior to the existence of the current tax subsidies on interest payments, this theory does not capture what must be some important determinants of the corporate capital structure.

In addition, neither bankruptcy costs nor the existence of tax subsidies can explain the use of preferred stock or warrants that have no tax advantages, and there is no theory that tells us anything about what determines the fraction of equity claims held by insiders as opposed to outsiders, which our analysis in section 2 indicates is so important. We return to these issues later after analyzing in detail the factors affecting the agency costs associated with debt.

4. The Agency Costs of Debt

In general, if the agency costs engendered by the existence of outside owners are positive, it will pay the absentee owner (i.e., shareholders) to sell out to an owner–manager who can avoid these costs.[45] This could be accomplished in principle

44 See A. Kraus and R. Litzenberger, "A State Preference Model of Optimal Financial Leverage," *Journal of Finance* 28 (1973): 911–22; P. Lloyd-Davies, "Risk and Optimal Leverage," unpublished (Rochester, N.Y.: University of Rochester, 1975).

45 And if there is competitive bidding for the firm from potential owner–managers, the absentee owner will capture the capitalized value of these agency costs.

by having the manager become the sole equity holder by repurchasing all of the outside equity claims with funds obtained through the issuance of limited liability debt claims and through the use of his own personal wealth. This single-owner corporation would not suffer the agency costs associated with outside equity. Therefore, there must be some compelling reasons why we find so prevalent as an organizational form the diffuse-owner corporate firm financed by equity claims.

An ingenious entrepreneur, eager to expand, has the opportunity to design a whole hierarchy of fixed claims on assets and earnings, with premiums paid for different levels of risk.[46] Why don't we observe large corporations individually owned, with a tiny fraction of the capital supplied by the entrepreneur in return for 100 percent of the equity and the rest simply borrowed? We believe there are a number of reasons: (1) the incentive effects associated with highly leveraged firms, (2) the monitoring costs these incentive effects engender, and (3) bankruptcy costs. Furthermore, all of these costs are simply particular aspects of the agency costs associated with the existence of debt claims on the firm.

The Incentive Effects Associated with Debt

We don't find many large firms financed almost entirely with debt-like claims (i.e., nonresidual claims) because of the effect such a financial structure would have on the owner–manager's behavior. Potential creditors will not loan $100 million to a firm in which the entrepreneur has an investment of $10,000. With that financial structure the owner–manager will have a strong incentive to engage in activities (investments) that promise very high payoffs if successful even if they have a very low probability of success. If they

46 The spectrum of claims that firms can issue is far more diverse than is suggested by our two-way classification—fixed vs. residual. There are convertible bonds, equipment trust certificates, debentures, revenue bonds, warrants, etc. Different bond issues can contain different subordination provisions with respect to assets and interest. They can be callable or noncallable. Preferred stocks can be "preferred" in a variety of dimensions and contain a variety of subordination stipulations. In the abstract, we can imagine firms issuing claims contingent on a literally infinite variety of states of the world such as those considered in the literature on the time–state preference models. See K. J. Arrow, "The Role of Securities in the Optimal Allocation of Risk Bearing," *Review of Economic Studies* 31 (1964): 91–96; Debreu, *Theory of Value;* Hirschleifer, *Investment, Interest, and Capital.*

turn out well, he captures most of the gains; if they turn out badly, the creditors bear most of the costs.[47]

To illustrate the incentive effects associated with the existence of debt and to provide a framework within which we can discuss the effects of monitoring and bonding costs, wealth transfers, and the incidence of agency costs, we again consider a simple situation. Assume we have a manager-owned firm with no debt outstanding, in a world in which there are no taxes. The firm has the opportunity to take one of two mutually exclusive equal-cost investment opportunities, each of which yields a random payoff, $\tilde{X}_j$, T periods in the future ($j = 1, 2$). Production and monitoring activities take place continuously between time 0 and time T, and markets in which the claims on the firm can be traded are open continuously over this period. After time T the firm has no productive activities, so the payoff $\tilde{X}_j$ includes the distribution of all remaining assets. For simplicity, we assume that the two distributions are log-normally distributed and have the same expected total payoff, $E(\tilde{X})$, where $\tilde{X}$ is defined as the logarithm of the final payoff. The distributions differ only by their variances with $\sigma_1^2 < \sigma_2^2$. The systematic, or covariance, risk of each of the distributions, β_j, in the Sharpe-Lintner capital asset–pricing model is assumed to be identical.[48] Assuming that asset prices are determined according to the capital asset–pricing model, the preceding assumptions imply that the total market value of each of these distributions is identical, and we represent this value by V.

If the owner–manager has the right to decide which investment program to take, and if after he decides this he has the opportunity to sell part or all of his claims on the outcomes in the form of either debt or equity, he will be indifferent between the two investments.[49] However, if the owner

47 An apt analogy is the way one would play poker on money borrowed at a fixed interest rate, with one's own liability limited to some very small stake. Fama and Miller, *Theory of Finance*, pp. 179–80, also discuss and provide a numerical example of an investment decision that illustrates very nicely the potential inconsistency between the interests of bondholders and stockholders.

48 W. F. Sharpe, "Capital Asset Prices: A Theory of Market Equilibrium under Conditions of Risk," *Journal of Finance* 19 (1964): 425–42; J. Lintner, "Security Prices, Risk, and Maximal Gains from Diversification," ibid., 20 (1965): 587–616.

49 The portfolio diversification issues facing the owner–manager are brought into the analysis in sec. 5 below.

has the opportunity to *first* issue debt, then to decide which of the investments to take, and then to sell all or part of his remaining equity claim on the market, he will not be indifferent between the two investments. The reason is that by promising to take the low-variance project, selling bonds, and then taking the high-variance project he can transfer wealth from the (naïve) bondholders to himself as equity holder.

Let X^* be the amount of the "fixed" claim in the form of a non-coupon-bearing bond sold to the bondholders such that the total payoff to them, R_j ($j = 1, 2$, denotes the distribution the manager chooses), is

$$\begin{aligned} R_j &= X^*, \quad \text{if} \quad \tilde{X}_j \geqq X^*, \\ &= X_j, \quad \text{if} \quad \tilde{X}_j \leqq X^*. \end{aligned}$$

Let B_1 be the current market value of bondholder claims if investment 1 is taken, and let B_2 be the current market value of bondholder claims if investment 2 is taken. Since in this example the total value of the firm, V, is independent of the investment choice and also of the financing decision, we can use the Black-Scholes option-pricing model to determine the values of the debt, B_j, and equity, S_j, under each of the choices.[50]

Black and Scholes derive the solution for the value of a European call option (one that can be exercised only at the maturity date) and argue that the resulting option-pricing equation can be used to determine the value of the equity claim on a levered firm. That is, the stockholders in such a firm can be viewed as holding a European call option on the total value of the firm with exercise price equal to X^* (the face value of the debt), exercisable at the maturity date of the debt issue. More simply, the stockholders have the right to buy the firm back from the bondholders for a price of X^* at time T. Merton shows that, as the variance of the outcome

50 F. Black and M. Scholes, "The Pricing of Options and Corporate Liabilities," *Journal of Political Economy* 81 (1973): 637–54. See C. Smith, "Option Pricing: A Review," *Journal of Financial Economics* 3 (1976): 3–52, for a review of the option-pricing literature and its applications; and see D. Galai and R. W. Masulis, "The Option Pricing Model and the Risk Factor of Stock," ibid., pp. 53–82, for an application of the model to mergers and corporate investment decisions.

distribution rises, the value of the stock (i.e., call option) rises;[51] since our two distributions differ only in their variances, $\sigma_2^2 < \sigma_1^2$, the equity value S_1 is less than S_2. This implies $B_1 > B_2$, since $B_1 = V - S_1$ and $B_2 = V - S_2$.

Now if the owner–manager could sell bonds with face value X^* under the conditions that the potential bondholders believed this to be a claim on distribution 1, he would receive a price of B_1. After selling the bonds, his equity interest in distribution 1 would have value S_1. But we know S_2 is greater than S_1, and thus the manager can make himself better-off by changing the investment to take the higher-variance distribution 2, thereby redistributing wealth from the bondholders to himself. All this assumes, of course, that the bondholders could not prevent him from changing the investment program. *If the bondholders cannot do so, and if they perceive that the manager has the opportunity to take distribution* 2, *they will pay the manager only* B_2 *for the claim* X^*, *realizing that his maximizing behavior will lead him to choose distribution* 2. In this event there is no redistribution of wealth between bondholders and stockholders (and in general with rational expectations there never will be) and no welfare loss. It is easy to construct a case, however, in which these incentive effects do generate real costs.

Let cash flow distribution 2 in the previous example have an expected value, $E(X_2)$, which is lower than that of distribution 1. Then we know that $V_1 > V_2$, and if ΔV, which is given by

$$\Delta V = V_1 - V_2 = (S_1 - S_2) + (B_1 - B_2),$$

is sufficiently small relative to the reduction in the value of the bonds, the value of the stock will increase.[52] If we re-

51 R. C. Merton, "The Theory of Rational Option Pricing," *Bell Journal of Economics and Management Science* 4 (1973): 141–83; idem, "On the Pricing of Corporate Debt: The Risk Structure of Interest Rates," *Journal of Finance* 29 (1974): 449–70.

52 While we used the option-pricing model above to motivate the discussion and to provide some intuitive understanding of the incentives facing the equityholders, the solutions of Black and Scholes, "Pricing of Options," do not apply when incentive effects cause V to be a function of the debt-equity ratio, as it is in general and in this example. J. B. Long, "Discussion," *Journal of Finance* 27 (1974): 485–88, points out this difficulty with respect to the usefulness of the model in the context of tax subsidies on interest and of bankruptcy cost. The results of Merton, "Pricing of Corporate Debt," and Galai and Masulis, "Option Pricing Model," must be interpreted with care, since the solutions are strictly incorrect in the context of tax subsidies or agency costs.

arrange the expression for ΔV, the difference between the equity values for the two investments is given by

$$S_2 - S_1 = (B_1 - B_2) - (V_1 - V_2),$$

and the term $B_1 - B_2$ is the amount of wealth "transferred" from the bondholders, and $V_1 - V_2$ is the reduction in overall firm value. Since we know $B_1 > B_2$, $S_2 - S_1$ can be positive even though the reduction in the value of the firm, $V_1 - V_2$, is positive.[53] Again, the bondholders will not actually lose as long as they accurately perceive the motivation of the equity-owning manager and his opportunity to take project 2. They will presume he will take investment 2 and hence will pay no more than B_2 for the bonds when they are issued.

In this simple example the reduced value of the firm, $V_1 - V_2$, is the agency cost engendered by the issuance of debt, and it is borne by the owner–manager.[54] If he could finance the project out of his personal wealth, he would clearly choose project 1, since its investment outlay was assumed equal to that of project 2 and its market value, V_1, was

53 The numerical example of Fama and Miller, *Theory of Finance*, pp. 179–80, is a close representation of this case in a two-period state model. However, they go on to make the following statement on p. 180:

"From a practical viewpoint, however, situations of potential conflict between bondholders and shareholders in the application of the market value rule are probably unimportant. In general, investment opportunities that increase a firm's market value by more than their cost both increase the value of the firm's shares and strengthen the firm's future ability to meet its current bond commitments."

This first issue regarding the importance of the conflict of interest between bondholders and stockholders is an empirical one, and the last statement is incomplete—in some circumstances the equityholders could benefit from projects whose net effect was to reduce the total value of the firm—as they and we have illustrated. The issue cannot be brushed aside so easily.

54 Myers points out another serious incentive effect on managerial decisions of the existence of debt that does not occur in our simple single-decision world. He shows that if the firm has the option to take future investment opportunities, the existence of debt that matures after the options must be taken will cause the firm (using an equity-value-maximizing investment rule) to refuse to take some otherwise profitable projects because they would benefit only the bondholders and not the equityholders. This will (in the absence of tax subsidies to debt) cause the value of the firm to fall. Thus (although he doesn't use the term) these incentive effects also contribute to the agency costs of debt in a manner perfectly consistent with the examples discussed in the text. S. C. Myers, "A Note on the Determinants of Corporate Debt Capacity," unpublished (London: London Graduate School of Business Studies, 1975).

greater. This wealth loss, $V_1 - V_2$, is the "residual loss" portion of what we have defined as agency costs, and it is generated by the cooperation required to raise the funds to make the investment. Another important part of the agency costs is monitoring and bonding costs, and we now consider their role.

The Role of Monitoring and Bonding Costs

In principle it would be possible for the bondholders, by the inclusion of various covenants in the indenture provisions, to limit the managerial behavior that results in reductions in the value of the bonds. Provisions imposing constraints on management's decisions regarding such things as dividends, future debt issues, and maintenance of working capital are not uncommon in bond issues.[55] To completely protect the bondholders from the incentive effects, these provisions would have to be incredibly detailed and cover most operating aspects of the enterprise, including limitations on the riskiness of the projects undertaken. The costs involved in writing such provisions, the costs of enforcing them, and the reduced profitability of the firm (induced because the covenants occasionally limit management's ability to take optimal actions on certain issues) would likely be nontrivial. In fact, since management is a continuous decision-making process, it will be almost impossible to completely specify such conditions without having the bondholders actually perform the management function. All costs associated with such covenants are what we mean by monitoring costs.

The bondholders will have incentives to engage in the writing of such covenants and in monitoring the actions of the manager to the point where the "nominal" marginal cost to them of such activities is just equal to the marginal benefits they perceive from engaging in them. We use the word *nominal* here because debtholders will not in fact bear these costs. As long as they recognize their existence, they will take them into account in deciding the price they will pay for any given

55 Black and Scholes, "Pricing of Options," discuss the ways in which dividend and future financing policy can redistribute wealth between classes of claimants on the firm. F. Black, M. H. Miller, and R. A. Posner, "An Approach to the Regulation of Bank Holding Companies," unpublished (Chicago: University of Chicago, 1974), discuss many of these issues with particular reference to their topic.

debt claim,[56] and therefore the seller of the claim (the owner) will bear the costs just as in the equity case discussed in section 2.

In addition, the manager has incentives to take into account the costs imposed on the firm by covenants in the debt agreement that directly affect the future cash flows of the firm, since they reduce the market value of his claims. Because both the external and internal monitoring costs are imposed on the owner–manager, it is in his interest to see that the monitoring is performed in the lowest-cost way. Suppose, for example, that the bondholders (or outside equity holders) would find it worthwhile to produce detailed financial statements such as those contained in the usual published accounting reports as a means of monitoring the manager. If the manager himself can produce such information at lower costs than they (perhaps because for his own internal decision-making purposes he is already collecting much of the data they desire), it would pay him to agree in advance to incur the cost of providing such reports and to have their accuracy testified to by an independent outside auditor. This is an example of what we refer to as bonding costs.[57]

56 In other words, these costs will be taken into account in determining the yield to maturity on the issue. For an examination of the effects of such enforcement costs on the nominal interest rates in the consumer small-loan market, see G. Benston, "The Impact of Maturity Regulation on High Interest Rate Lenders and Borrowers," *Journal of Financial Economics* 4 (1977): 23–49.

57 To illustrate the fact that it will sometimes pay the manager to incur "bonding" costs to guarantee the bondholders that he will not deviate from his promised behavior, let us suppose that for an expenditure of $\$b$ of the firm's resources he can guarantee that project 1 will be chosen. If he spends these resources and takes project 1, the value of the firm will be V_1-b; and clearly, as long as $(V_1-b) > V_2$ or, alternatively, $(V_1-V_2) > b$, he will be better-off, since his wealth will be equal to the value of the firm minus the required investment, I (which we assumed for simplicity to be identical for the two projects).

On the other hand, to prove that the owner–manager prefers the lowest-cost solution to the conflict, let us assume he can write a covenant into the bond issue that will allow the bondholders to prevent him from taking project 2 if they incur monitoring costs of $\$m$, where $m < b$. If he does this, his wealth will be higher by the amount $b-m$. To see this, note that if the bond market is competitive and makes unbiased estimates, potential bondholders will be indifferent between:

(i) a claim X^* with no covenant (and no guarantees from management) at a price of B_2,

(ii) a claim X^* with no covenant (and guarantees from management, through bonding expenditures by the firm of $\$b$, that project 1 will be taken) at a price of B_1, and

Bankruptcy and Reorganization Costs

We argue in section 5 that, as the debt in the capital structure increases beyond some point, the marginal agency costs of debt begin to dominate the marginal agency costs of outside equity; the result of this is the generally observed phenomenon of the simultaneous use of both debt and outside equity. Before considering these issues, however, we consider here the third major component of the agency costs of debt, which helps to explain why debt doesn't completely dominate capital structures—the existence of bankruptcy and reorganization costs.

It is important to emphasize that bankruptcy and liquida-

(iii) a claim X^*, with a covenant and the opportunity to spend m on monitoring (to guarantee that project 1 will be taken) at a price of $B_1 - m$.

The bondholders will realize that (i) in fact represents a claim on project 2 and that (ii) and (iii) represent a claim on project 1 and will thus be indifferent between the three options at the specified prices. The owner–manager, however, will not be indifferent between incurring the bonding costs, b, directly, or including the covenant in the bond indenture and letting the bondholders spend m to guarantee that he take project 1. His wealth in the two cases will be given by the value of his equity plus the proceeds of the bond issue less the required investment, and if $m < b < V_1 - V_2$, then his post-investment-financing wealth, W, for the three options will be such that $W_i < W_{ii} < W_{iii}$. Therefore, since it would increase his wealth, he would voluntarily include the covenant in the bond issue and let the bondholders monitor.

Without going into the problem in detail, we mention another issue. Similar to the case in which the outside equityholders are allowed to monitor the manager–owner, the agency relationship between the bondholders and stockholders has a symmetry if the rights of the bondholders to limit actions of the manager are not perfectly spelled out. Suppose the bondholders, by spending sufficiently large amounts of resources, could force management to take actions that would transfer wealth from the equityholders to the bondholders (by taking sufficiently less risky projects). One can easily construct situations in which such actions could make the bondholders better-off, hurt the equityholders, and actually lower the total value of the firm. Given the nature of the debt contract, the original owner–manager might maximize his wealth in such a situation by selling off the equity and keeping the bonds as his "owner's" interest. If the nature of the bond contract is given, this may well be an inefficient solution, since the total agency costs (i.e., the sum of monitoring and value loss) could easily be higher than the alternative solution. However, if the owner–manager could strictly limit the rights of the bondholders (perhaps by inclusion of a provision that expressly reserves for the equityholder all rights not specifically granted to the bondholder), he would find it in his interest to establish the efficient contractual arrangement, since by minimizing the agency costs he would be maximizing his wealth. These issues involve the fundamental nature of contracts, and for now we simply assume that the "bondholders' " rights are strictly limited and unambiguous and all rights not specifically granted them are reserved for the "stockholders"—a situation descriptive of actual institutional arrangements. This allows us to avoid the incentive effects associated with "bondholders" potentially exploiting "stockholders."

tion are very different events. The legal definition of bankruptcy is difficult to specify precisely. In general, it occurs when the firm cannot meet a current payment on a debt obligation,[58] or one or more of the other indenture provisions providing for bankruptcy is violated by the firm. In this event the stockholders have lost all claims on the firm,[59] and the remaining loss, the difference between the face value of the fixed claims and the market value of the firm, is borne by the debtholders. Liquidation of the firm's assets will occur only if the market value of the future cash flows generated by the firm is less than the opportunity cost of the assets, that is, the sum of the values that could be realized if the assets were sold piecemeal.

If there were no costs associated with the event called bankruptcy, the total market value of the firm would not be affected by increasing the probability of its incurrence. However, it is costly, if not impossible, to write contracts representing claims on a firm and clearly delineating the rights of holders for all possible contingencies. Thus, even if there were no adverse incentive effects in expanding fixed claims relative to equity in a firm, the use of such fixed claims would be constrained by the costs inherent in defining and enforcing those claims. Firms incur obligations daily to suppliers, to employees, to different classes of investors, etc. So long as the firm is prospering, the adjudication of claims is seldom a problem. When the firm has difficulty meeting some of its obligations, however, the issue of the priority of those claims can pose serious problems. This is most obvious in the extreme case in which the firm is forced into bankruptcy. If bankruptcy were costless, the reorganization would be accompanied by an adjustment of the claims of various parties, and the business could, if that proved to be in the interest of

58 If the firm were allowed to sell assets to meet a current debt obligation, bankruptcy would occur when the total market value of the future cash flows expected to be generated by the firm is less than the value of a current payment on a debt obligation. Many bond indentures do not, however, allow for the sale of assets to meet debt obligations.

59 We have been told that while this is true in principle, the actual behavior of the courts frequently appears to involve the provision of some settlement to the common stockholders even when the assets of the company are not sufficient to cover the claims of the creditors.

the claimants, simply go on (although perhaps under new management).[60]

In practice, bankruptcy is not costless but generally involves an adjudication process that itself consumes a fraction of the remaining value of the assets of the firm. Thus the cost of bankruptcy will be of concern to potential buyers of fixed claims in the firm, since their existence will reduce the payoffs to them in the event of bankruptcy. These are examples of the agency costs of cooperative efforts among individuals (although in this case, perhaps *noncooperative* would be a better term). The price buyers will be willing to pay for fixed claims will thus be inversely related to the probability of the incurrence of these costs—that is, to the probability of bankruptcy. Using a variant of the argument employed above for monitoring costs, it can be shown that the total value of the firm will fall and the owner–manager equityholder will bear the entire wealth effect of the bankruptcy costs as long as potential bondholders make unbiased estimates of their magnitude at the time they initially purchase bonds.[61]

Empirical studies of the magnitude of bankruptcy costs are almost nonexistent. Warner, in a study of 11 railroad bankruptcies between 1930 and 1955, estimates the average costs of bankruptcy as a fraction of the value of the firm three years prior to bankruptcy to be 2.5 percent (with a range of 0.4–5.9 percent). The average dollar costs were $1.88 million.[62] Both of these measures seem remarkably

60 If under bankruptcy the bondholders have the right to fire the management, the management will have some incentives to avoid taking actions that increase the probability of this event (even if it is in the best interest of the equityholders) if they (the management) are earning rents or if they have human capital specialized to this firm or if they face large adjustment costs in finding new employment. A detailed examination of this issue involves the value of the control rights (the rights to hire and fire the manager), and we leave it to a subsequent paper.

61 Kraus and Litzenberger, "Optimal Financial Leverage," and Lloyd-Davies, "Risk and Optimal Leverage," demonstrate that the total value of the firm will be reduced by these costs.

62 J. B. Warner, "Bankruptcy Costs, Absolute Priority, and the Pricing of Risky Debt Claims," unpublished (Chicago: University of Chicago, 1975). Average costs of bankruptcy included only payments to all parties for legal fees, professional services, trustees' fees, and filing fees. They did not include the costs of management time or changes in cash flows due to shifts in the firm's demand or cost functions, discussed below.

small and are consistent with our belief that bankruptcy costs themselves are unlikely to be the major determinant of corporate capital structures. It is also interesting to note that the annual amount of defaulted funds has fallen significantly since 1940.[63] One possible explanation for this phenomenon is that firms are using mergers to avoid the costs of bankruptcy. This hypothesis seems even more reasonable if, as is frequently the case, reorganization costs represent only a fraction of the costs associated with bankruptcy.

In general, the revenues or the operating costs of the firm are not independent of the probability of bankruptcy and thus the capital structure of the firm. As the probability of bankruptcy increases, both the operating costs and the revenues of the firm are adversely affected, and some of these costs can be avoided by merger. For example, a firm with a high probability of bankruptcy will also find that it must pay higher salaries to induce executives to accept the higher risk of unemployment. Furthermore, in certain kinds of durable-goods industries the demand function for the firm's product will not be independent of the probability of bankruptcy. The computer industry is a good example. There, the buyer's welfare is dependent to a significant extent on the ability to maintain the equipment and on continuous hardware and software development. Furthermore, the owner of a large computer often receives benefits from the software developments of other users. Thus, if the manufacturer leaves the business or loses his software support and development experts because of financial difficulties, the value of the equipment to his users will decline. The buyers of such services have a continuing interest in the manufacturer's viability not unlike that of a bondholder, except that their benefits come in the form of continuing services at lower cost rather than principal and interest payments. Service facilities and spare parts for automobiles and machinery are other examples.

In summary, then, the agency costs associated with debt[64] consist of:

63 T. R. Atkinson, *Trends in Corporate Bond Quality,* Studies in Corporate Bond Finance 4 (New York: National Bureau of Economic Research, 1967).

64 Which, incidentally, exist only when the debt has some probability of default.

1. the opportunity wealth loss caused by the impact of debt on the investment decisions of the firm,
2. the monitoring and bonding expenditures by the bondholders and the owner–manager (i.e., the firm),
3. the bankruptcy and reorganization costs.

Why Are the Agency Costs of Debt Incurred?

We have argued that the owner–manager bears the entire wealth effects of the agency costs of debt and captures the gains from reducing them. Thus, the agency costs associated with debt, discussed above, will tend, in the absence of other mitigating factors, to discourage the use of corporate debt. What are the factors that encourage its use?

One factor is the tax subsidy on interest payments. (This will not explain preferred stock where dividends are not tax-deductible.[65]) Modigliani and Miller originally demonstrated that the use of riskless perpetual debt will increase the total value of the firm (ignoring the agency costs) by an amount equal to τB, where τ is the marginal and average corporate tax rate and B is the market value of the debt. Fama and Miller demonstrate that for the case of risky debt the value of the firm will increase by the market value of the (uncertain) tax subsidy on the interest payments.[66] Again, these gains will accrue entirely to the equity and will provide an incentive to utilize debt to the point where the marginal

65 Our theory is capable of explaining why, in the absence of the tax subsidy on interest payments, we would expect to find firms using both debt and preferred stocks—a problem that has long puzzled at least one of the authors. If preferred stock has all the characteristics of debt except for the fact that its holders cannot put the firm into bankruptcy in the event of nonpayment of the preferred dividends, then the agency costs associated with the issuance of preferred stock will be lower than those associated with debt by the present value of the bankruptcy costs.

However, these lower agency costs of preferred stock exist only over some range if, as the amount of such stock rises, the incentive effects caused by their existence impose value reductions that are larger than those caused by debt (including the bankruptcy costs of debt). There are two reasons for this. First, the equityholders' claims can be eliminated by the debtholders in the event of bankruptcy, and second, the debtholders have the right to fire the management in the event of bankruptcy. Both of these will tend to become more important as an advantage to the issuance of debt as we compare situations with large amounts of preferred stock to equivalent situations with large amounts of debt, because they will tend to reduce the incentive effects of large amounts of preferred stock.

66 Modigliani and Miller, "Corporate Income Taxes"; Fama and Miller, *Theory of Finance,* chap. 4.

wealth benefits of the tax subsidy are just equal to the marginal wealth effects of the agency costs discussed above.

Even in the absence of these tax benefits, however, debt would be utilized if the ability to exploit potentially profitable investment opportunities were limited by the resources of the owner. If the owner of a project cannot raise capital, he will suffer an opportunity loss represented by the increment in value offered to him by the additional investment opportunities. Thus, even though he will bear the agency costs from selling debt, he will find it desirable to incur them to obtain additional capital as long as the marginal wealth increments from the new investment projects are greater than the marginal agency costs of debt and these agency costs are, in turn, less than those caused by the sale of additional equity, discussed in section 2. Furthermore, this solution is optimal from the social viewpoint. However, in the absence of tax subsidies on debt, these projects must be unique to this firm,[67] or they would be taken by other competitive entrepreneurs (perhaps new ones) who possessed the requisite personal wealth to fully finance the projects[68] and were therefore able to avoid the existence of debt or outside equity.

5. A Theory of the Corporate Ownership Structure

In the previous sections we discussed the nature of agency costs associated with outside claims on the firm—both debt

67 One other condition also has to hold to justify the incurrence of the costs associated with the use of debt or outside equity in our firm. If there are other individuals in the economy who have sufficiently large amounts of personal capital to finance the entire firm, our capital-constrained owner can realize the full capital value of his current and prospective projects and avoid the agency costs by simply selling the firm (i.e., the right to take these projects) to one of these individuals. He will then avoid the wealth losses associated with the agency costs caused by the sale of debt or outside equity. If no such individuals exist, it will pay him (and society) to obtain the additional capital in the debt market. This implies, incidentally, that it is somewhat misleading to speak of the owner–manager as the individual who bears the agency costs. One could argue that it is the project that bears the costs, since if it is not sufficiently profitable to cover all the costs (including the agency costs), it will not be taken. We continue to speak of the owner–manager bearing these costs to emphasize the more correct and important point that he has the incentive to reduce them because, if he does, his wealth will be increased.

68 We continue to ignore for the moment the additional complicating factor involved with the portfolio decisions of the owner and the implied acceptance of potentially diversifiable risk by such 100 percent owners in this example.

and equity. Our purpose here is to integrate these concepts into the beginnings of a theory of the corporate ownership structure. We use the term *ownership structure* rather than *capital structure* to highlight the fact that the crucial variables to be determined are not just the relative amounts of debt and equity but also the fraction of the equity held by the manager. Thus, for a given size firm we want a theory to determine three variables:[69]

S_i : inside equity (held by the manager),
S_0 : outside equity (held by anyone outside of the firm),
B : debt (held by anyone outside of the firm).

The total market value of the equity is $S = S_i + S_0$, and the total market value of the firm is $V = S + B$. In addition, we also wish to have a theory that determines the optimal size of the firm, that is, its level of investment.

The Optimal Ratio of Outside Equity to Debt

Consider first the determination of the optimal ratio of outside equity to debt, S_0/B. To do this, let us hold the size of the firm constant. V, the actual value of the firm for a given size, will depend on the agency costs incurred; hence, for our index of size we use V^*, the value of the firm at a given scale when agency costs are zero. For the moment we also hold the amount of outside financing, $B + S_0$, constant. Given that a specified amount of financing, $B + S_0$, is to be obtained externally, our problem is to determine the optimal fraction $E^* \equiv S_0^*/(B + S_0)$ to be financed with equity.

We argued above that, (1) as long as capital markets are efficient (i.e., characterized by rational expectations), the prices of assets such as debt and outside equity will reflect unbiased estimates of the monitoring costs and redistributions that the agency relationship will engender, and (2) the selling owner–manager will bear these agency costs. Thus, from the owner–manager's standpoint the optimal proportion of outside funds to be obtained from equity (versus debt) *for a given level of internal equity* is that E which results in minimum total agency costs.

69 We continue to ignore such instruments as convertible bonds and warrants.

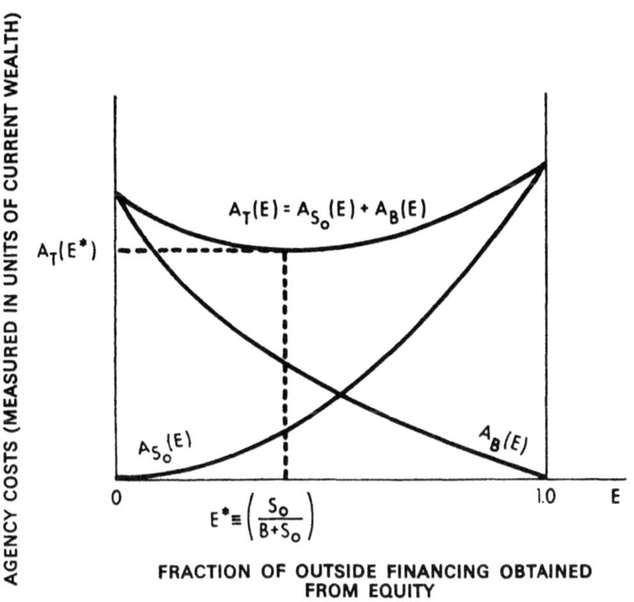

Figure 5. Total agency costs, $A_T(E)$, as a function of the ratio of outside equity to total outside financing, $E \equiv S_o/(B+S_o)$, for a given firm size V^* and given total amounts of outside financing, $B+S_o$. $A_{So}(E) \equiv$ agency costs associated with outside equity, $A_B(E) \equiv$ agency costs associated with debt, B. $A_T(E^*) =$ minimum total agency costs at optimal fraction of outside financing E^*.

Figure 5 presents a breakdown of the agency costs into two separate components: Define $A_{So}(E)$ as the total agency costs (a function of E) associated with the "exploitation" of the outside equityholders by the owner–manager, and define $A_B(E)$ as the total agency costs associated with the presence of debt in the ownership structure. $A_T(E) = A_{So}(E)+A_B(E)$ is the total agency cost.

Consider the function $A_{So}(E)$. When $E \equiv S_o/(B+S_o)$ is zero—that is, when there is no outside equity—the manager's incentives to exploit the outside equity is at a minimum (zero), since the changes in the value of the *total* equity are equal to the changes in *his* equity.[70] As E increases to 100

70 Note, however, that even when outsiders own none of the equity, if there is any risky debt outstanding, the stockholder–manager still has some incentives to engage

percent, his incentives to exploit the outside equityholders increase, and hence the agency costs $A_{So}(E)$ increase.

The agency costs associated with the existence of debt, $A_B(E)$, are composed mainly of the value reductions in the firm and the monitoring costs caused by the manager's incentive to reallocate wealth from the bondholders to himself by increasing the value of his equity claim. They are at a maximum where all outside funds are obtained from debt, that is, where $S_o = E = 0$. As the amount of debt declines to zero, these costs also go to zero, because as E goes to 1, his incentive to reallocate wealth from the bondholders to himself falls. These incentives fall for two reasons: (1) the total amount of debt falls, and therefore it is more difficult to reallocate any given amount away from the debtholders; (2) his share of any accomplished reallocation is falling, since S_o is rising and therefore $S_i/(S_o+S_i)$, his share of the total equity, is falling.

The curve $A_T(E)$ represents the sum of the agency costs from various combinations of outside equity and debt financing, and as long as $A_{So}(E)$ and $A_B(E)$ are as we have drawn them, the minimum total agency cost for a given size firm and outside financing will occur at some point such as $A_T(E^*)$ with a mixture of both debt and equity.[71]

Before proceeding further, we issue a caveat. The exact shape of the functions drawn in figure 5 and several others discussed below is essentially an open question at this time. In the end, their shape is a question of fact and can only be

---

in activities yielding him nonpecuniary benefits but reducing the value of the firm by more than he personally values the benefits. Any such actions that reduce the value of the firm, V, tend to reduce the value of the bonds as well as the value of the equity. Although the option-pricing model does not in general apply exactly to the problem of valuing the debt and equity of the firm, it can be useful in obtaining some qualitative insights into matters such as this. In that model, $\partial S/\partial V$ indicates the rate at which the stock value changes per dollar change in the value of the firm (and similarly for $\partial B/\partial V$). Both of these terms are less than unity (see Black and Scholes, "Pricing of Options"). Therefore, any action of the manager that reduces the value of the firm, V, tends to reduce the value of both the stock and the bonds, and the larger is the total debt-equity ratio, the smaller is the impact of any given change in V on the value of the equity and, therefore, the lower is the cost to him of consuming nonpecuniary benefits.

71 This occurs, of course, not at the intersection of $A_{So}(E)$ and $A_B(E)$, but at the point where the absolute value of the slopes of the functions are equal, i.e., where $A'_{So}(E) + A'_B(E) = 0$.

settled by empirical evidence. We outline some a priori arguments that we believe lead to some plausible hypotheses about the behavior of the system, but confess that we are far from understanding the many conceptual subtleties of the problem. We are fairly confident of our arguments regarding the signs of the first derivatives of the functions, but the second derivatives are also important to the final solution, and much more work (both theoretical and empirical) is required before we can have much confidence regarding these parameters. We anticipate the work of others as well as our own to cast more light on these issues. Moreover, we suspect the results of such efforts will generate revisions of the details of what follows. We believe it is worthwhile to delineate the overall framework in order to demonstrate, if only in a simplified fashion, how the major pieces of the puzzle fit together into a cohesive structure.

Effects of the Scale of Outside Financing

In order to investigate the effects of increasing the amount of outside financing, $B+S_0$, and therefore reducing the amount of equity held by the manager, S_i, we continue to hold the scale of the firm, V^*, constant. Figure 6 presents a plot of the agency cost functions, $A_{S0}(E)$, $A_B(E)$, and $A_T(E) = A_{S0}(E)+A_B(E)$, for two different levels of outside financing. Define an index of the amount of outside financing to be

$$K = (B+S_0)/V^*,$$

and consider two different possible levels of outside financing K_0 and K_1 for a given scale of the firm such that $K_0 < K_1$.

As the amount of outside equity increases, the owner's fractional claim on the firm, α, falls. He will be induced thereby to take additional nonpecuniary benefits out of the firm because his share of the cost falls. This also increases the marginal benefits from monitoring activities and therefore will tend to increase the optimal level of monitoring. Both of these factors will cause the locus of agency costs $A_{S0}(E; K)$ to shift upward as the fraction of outside financing, K, increases. This is depicted in figure 6 by the two curves representing the agency costs of equity, one for the low level

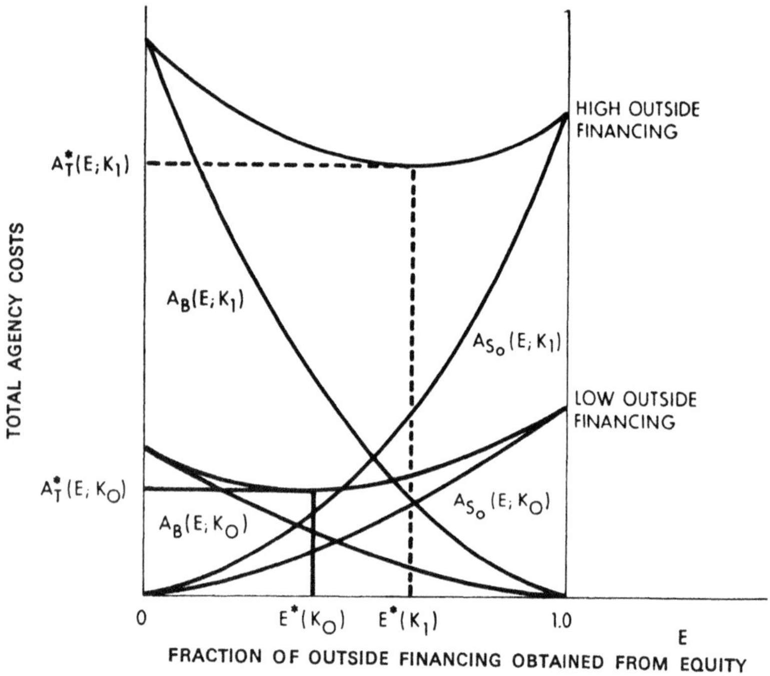

Figure 6. Agency cost functions and optimal outside equity as a fraction of total outside financing, $E^*(K)$, for two different levels of outside financing, K, for a given size firm, V^*: $K_1 > K_0$.

of outside financing, $A_{S0}(E;\ K_0)$, the other for the high level of outside financing, $A_{S0}(E;\ K_1)$. The locus of the latter lies above the former everywhere except at the origin, where both are 0.

The agency cost of debt will similarly rise as the amount of outside financing increases. This means that the locus of $A_B(E;\ K_1)$ for high outside financing, K_1, will lie above the locus of $A_B(E;\ K_0)$ for low outside financing, K_0, because the total amount of resources that can be reallocated from bondholders increases as the total amount of debt increases. However, since these costs are zero when the debt is zero for both K_0 and K_1, the intercepts of the $A_B(E;\ K)$ curves coincide at the right axis.

The net effect of the increased use of outside financing given the cost functions assumed in figure 6 is to: (1) increase

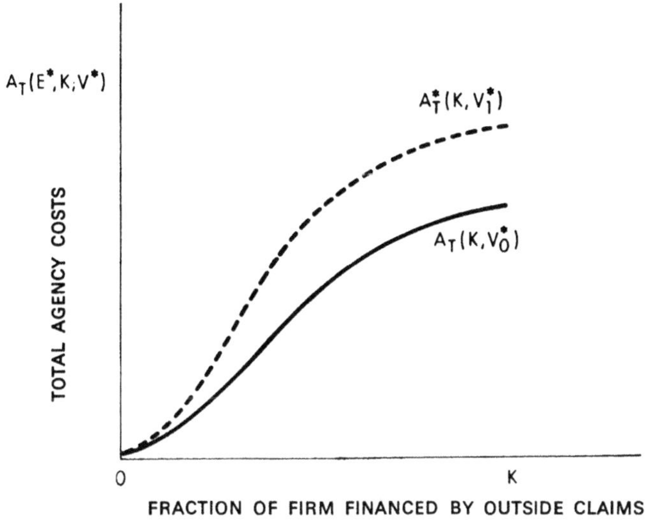

Figure 7. Total agency costs as a function of the fraction of the firm financed by outside claims for two firm sizes, $V_1^* > V_0^*$

the total agency costs from $A_T(E^*; K_0)$ to $A_T(E^*; K_1)$, and (2) to increase the optimal fraction of outside funds obtained from the sale of outside equity. We draw these functions for illustration only and are unwilling to speculate at this time on the exact form of $E^*(K)$ that gives the general effect of increasing outside financing on the relative quantities of debt and equity.

The locus of points, $A_T(E^*; K)$, where agency costs are minimized (not drawn in fig. 6) determines $E^*(K)$, the optimal proportions of equity and debt to be used in obtaining outside funds as the fraction of outside funds, K, ranges from 0 to 100 percent. The solid line in figure 7 is a plot of the minimum total agency costs as a function of the amount of outside financing for a firm with scale V_0^*. The dotted line shows the total agency costs for a larger firm with scale $V_1^* > V_0^*$. That is, we hypothesize that the larger the firm becomes, the larger are the total agency costs because it is likely that the monitoring function is inherently more difficult and expensive in a larger organization.

Risk and the Demand for Outside Financing

The model we have used to explain the existence of minority shareholders and debt in the capital structure of corporations implies that the owner–manager, if he resorts to any outside funding, will have his entire wealth invested in the firm. The reason is that he can thereby avoid the agency costs imposed by additional outside funding. This suggests that he would not resort to outside funding until he had invested in the firm 100 percent of his personal wealth—an implication that is not consistent with what we generally observe. Most owner–managers hold personal wealth in a variety of forms, and some have only a relatively small fraction of their wealth invested in the corporation they manage.[72] Diversification on the part of owner–managers can be explained by risk aversion and optimal portfolio selection.

If the returns from assets are not perfectly correlated, an individual can reduce the riskiness of the returns on his portfolio by dividing his wealth among many different assets, that is, by diversifying.[73] Thus a manager who invests all of his wealth in a single firm (his own) will generally bear a welfare loss (if he is risk averse) because he is bearing more risk than necessary. He will, of course, be willing to pay something to avoid this risk, and the costs he must bear to accomplish this diversification will be the agency costs outlined above. He will suffer a wealth loss as he reduces his fractional ownership because prospective shareholders and bondholders will take into account the agency costs. Nevertheless, the manager's desire to avoid risk will contribute to his becoming a minority stockholder.

The Optimal Amount of Outside Financing, K^*

Assume for the moment that the owner of a project (i.e., the owner of a prospective firm) has enough wealth to finance the entire project himself. The optimal scale of the corpora-

72 On the average, however, top managers seem to have substantial holdings in absolute dollars. A survey by Wytmar (*Wall Street Journal,* August 13, 1974, p. 1) found that the median value of 826 chief executive officers' stock holdings in their companies at year end 1973 was $557,000 and $1.3 million at year end 1972.

73 These diversification effects can be substantial. It has been shown that on the average, for New York Stock Exchange securities, approximately 55 percent of the total risk (as measured by standard deviation of portfolio returns) can be eliminated

tion is then determined by the condition that $\Delta V - \Delta I = 0$. In general, if the returns to the firm are uncertain, the owner–manager can increase his welfare by selling off part of the firm either as debt or equity and reinvesting the proceeds in other assets. If he does this with the optimal combination of debt and equity (as in fig. 6) the total wealth reduction he will incur is given by the agency cost function, $A_T(E^*, K; V^*)$ in figure 7. The functions $A_T(E^*, K; V^*)$ will be S-shaped (as drawn) if total agency costs for a given scale of firm increase at an increasing rate at low levels of outside financing and at a decreasing rate for high levels of outside financing as monitoring imposes more and more constraints on the manager's actions.

Figure 8 shows marginal agency costs as a function of K, the fraction of the firm financed with outside funds assuming the total agency cost function is as plotted in figure 7 and assuming the scale of the firm is fixed. The demand by the owner–manager for outside financing is shown by the remaining curve in figure 8. This curve represents the marginal value of the increased diversification that the manager can obtain by reducing his ownership claims and optimally constructing a diversified portfolio. It is measured by the amount he would pay to be allowed to reduce his ownership claims by a dollar in order to increase his diversification. If the liquidation of some of his holdings also influences the owner–manager's consumption set, the demand function plotted in figure 8 also incorporates the marginal value of these effects. The intersection of these two schedules determines the optimal fraction of the firm to be held by outsiders, and this in turn determines the total agency costs borne by the owner. This solution is Pareto-optimal; there is no way to reduce the agency costs without making someone worse-off.

The Optimal Scale of the Firm

While the details of the solution of the optimal scale of the firm are complicated when we allow for the issuance of debt, equity, and monitoring and bonding, the general structure

by following a naïve strategy of dividing one's assets equally among 40 randomly selected securities. J. L. Evans and S. H. Archer, "Diversification and the Reduction of Dispersion: An Empirical Analysis," *Journal of Finance* 23 (1968): 761–768.

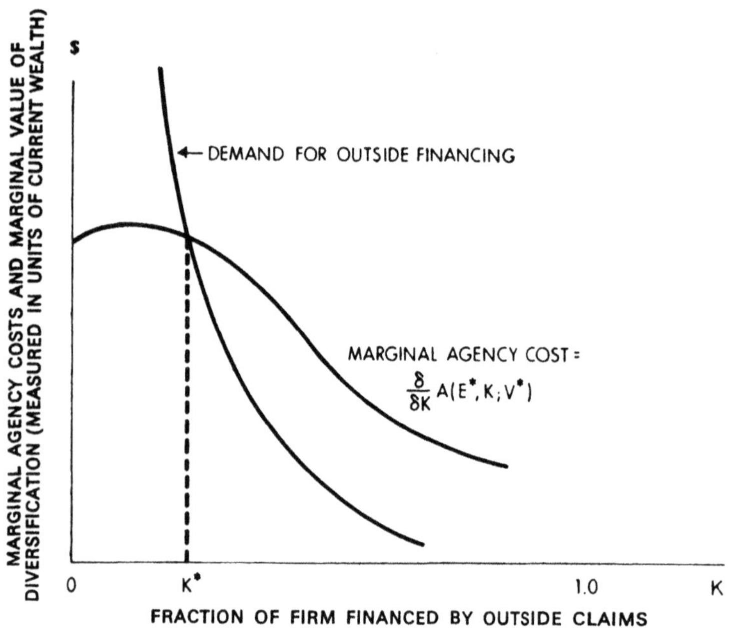

Figure 8. Determination of the optimal amount of outside financing, K^*, for a given scale of firm

of the solution is analogous to the case in which monitoring and bonding are allowed for the outside equity example (see fig. 4).

If it is optimal to issue any debt, the expansion path taking full account of such opportunities must lie above the curve *ZG* in figure 4. If this new expansion path lies anywhere to the right of the indifference curve passing through point *G*, debt will be used in the optimal financing package. Furthermore, the optimal scale of the firm will be determined by the point at which this new expansion path touches the highest indifference curve. In this situation the resulting level of the owner–manager's welfare must, therefore, be higher.

6. Qualifications and Extensions of the Analysis

Multiperiod Aspects of the Agency Problem

We have assumed throughout our analysis that we are dealing only with a single investment-financing decision by the entrepreneur and have ignored the issues associated with the incentives affecting future financing–investment decisions that might arise after the initial set of contracts are consummated between the entrepreneur–manager, outside stockholders, and bondholders. These are important issues left for future analysis.[74] Their solution will undoubtedly introduce some changes in the conclusions of the single-decision analysis. It seems clear, for instance, that the expectation of future sales of outside equity and debt will change the costs and benefits facing the manager in making decisions that benefit himself at the (short-run) expense of the current bondholders and stockholders. If he develops a reputation for such dealings, he can expect this to influence unfavorably the terms at which he can obtain future capital from outside sources. This will tend to increase the benefits associated with "sainthood" and will tend to reduce the size of the agency costs. Given the finite life of any individual, however, such an effect cannot reduce these costs to zero, because at some point these future costs will begin to weigh more heavily on his successors, and therefore the relative benefits to him of acting in his own best interests will rise.[75] Furthermore, it will generally be impossible for him to fully guarantee to the outside interests that his successor will continue to follow his policies.

The Control Problem and Outside Owner's Agency Costs

The careful reader will notice that nowhere in the analysis thus far have we taken into account many of the details of the relationship between the part owner–manager and the outside stockholders and bondholders. In particular, we have assumed that all outside equity is nonvoting. If such equity does have voting rights, then the manager will be

74 The recent work of Myers, "Corporate Debt Capacity," which views future investment opportunities as options and investigates the incentive effects of the existence of debt in such a world where a sequence of investment decisions is made, is another important step in the investigation of the multiperiod aspects of the agency problem and the theory of the firm.

75 A special case of this problem, involving the use of nonvested pension rights to help correct for this end-game play in the law enforcement area, is analyzed by G. S. Becker and G. J. Stigler, "Law Enforcement, Corruption and Compensation of Enforcers" (Paper presented at the Conference on Capitalism and Freedom, Charlottesville, Va., Oct. 1972).

concerned about the effects on his long-run welfare of reducing his fractional ownership below the point at which he loses effective control of the corporation—that is, below the point at which it becomes possible for the outside equityholders to fire him. A complete analysis of this issue will require a careful specification of the contractual rights involved on both sides, the role of the board of directors, and the coordination (agency) costs borne by the stockholders in implementing policy changes. This latter point involves consideration of the distribution of the outside ownership claims. Simply put, forces exist to determine an equilibrium distribution of outside ownership. If the costs of reducing the dispersion of ownership are lower than the benefits to be obtained from reducing the agency costs, it will pay some individual or group of individuals to buy shares in the market to reduce the dispersion of ownership. We occasionally witness these conflicts for control, which involve outright market purchases, tender offers, and proxy fights. Further analysis of these issues is left to the future.

Inside Debt and the Use of Convertible Financial Instruments

We have been asked why debt held by the manager (i.e., "inside debt") plays no role in our analysis.[76] We have as yet been unable to formally incorporate this dimension into our analysis in a satisfactory way. The question is a good one and suggests some potentially important extensions of the analysis. For instance, it suggests an inexpensive way for the owner–manager with both equity and debt outstanding to eliminate a large part (perhaps all) of the agency costs of debt. If he binds himself contractually to hold a fraction of the total debt equal to his fractional ownership of the total equity, he would have no incentive whatsoever to reallocate wealth from the debtholders to the stockholders. Consider the case where

$$B_i/S_i = B_0/S_0, \tag{4}$$

where S_i and S_0 are as defined earlier, B_i is the dollar value of the inside debt held by the owner–manager, and B_0 is the

76 By our colleague David Henderson.

debt held by outsiders. In this case, if the manager changes the investment policy of the firm to reallocate wealth between the debt- and equityholders, the net effect on the total value of his holdings in the firm will be zero. Therefore, his incentives to perform such reallocations are zero.[77]

Why, then, don't we observe practices or formal contracts that accomplish this elimination or reduction of the agency costs of debt? Maybe we do for smaller privately held firms (we haven't attempted to obtain these data), but for large diffuse owner corporations the practice does not seem to be common. One reason for this, we believe, is that in some respects the claim that the manager holds on the firm in the form of his wage contract has some of the characteristics of debt.[78] If true, this implies that, even with zero holdings of formal debt claims, he still has positive holdings of a quasi-debt claim, and this may accomplish the satisfaction of condition (4). The problem here is that any formal analysis of this issue requires a much deeper understanding of the relationship between formal debt holdings and the wage contract; that is, how much debt is it equivalent to?

This line of thought also suggests some other interesting issues. Suppose the implicit debt characteristics of the manager's wage contract result in a situation equivalent to

$$B_i/S_i > B_o/S_o.$$

Then he would have incentives to change the operating characteristics of the firm (i.e., reduce the variance of the outcome distribution) to transfer wealth from the stockholders to the debtholders, which is the reverse of the situation we examined in section 4. Furthermore, this seems to capture some of the concern often expressed regarding the fact that managers of large publicly held corporations seem to behave

77 This also suggests that *some* outside debtholders can protect themselves from "exploitation" by the manager by purchasing a fraction of the total equity equal to their fractional ownership of the debt. All debtholders, of course, cannot do this unless the manager does so also. In addition, such an investment rule restricts the portfolio choices of investors and therefore would impose costs if followed rigidly. Thus, the agency costs will not be eliminated this way either.

78 Consider the stituation in which the bondholders have the right in the event of bankruptcy to terminate his employment and therefore to terminate the future returns to any specific human capital or rents he may be receiving.

in a risk-averse way, to the detriment of the equityholders. One solution to this would be to establish incentive compensation systems for the manager or to give him stock options, which in effect give him a claim on the upper tail of the outcome distribution. This also seems to be a commonly observed phenomenon.

This analysis also suggests some additional issues regarding the costs and benefits associated with the use of more complicated financial claims such as warrants, convertible bonds, and convertible preferred stock, which we have not formally analyzed as yet. These have some of the characteristics of nonvoting shares, although they can be converted into voting shares under some terms. Alchian and Demsetz provide an interesting analysis regarding the use of nonvoting shares.[79] They argue that some shareholders with strong beliefs in the talents and the judgments of the manager will want to be protected against the possibility that some other shareholders will take over and limit the actions of the manager (or fire him). Given that the securities exchanges prohibit the use of nonvoting shares by listed firms, the use of option-like securities might be a substitute for these claims.

In addition, warrants represent a claim on the upper tail of the distribution of outcomes, and convertible securities can be thought of as securities with nondetachable warrants. It seems that the incentive effects of warrants would tend to offset to some extent the incentive effects of the existence of risky debt, because the owner–manager would be sharing with the warrant holders part of the proceeds associated with a shift in the distribution of returns. Thus, we conjecture that potential bondholders will find it attractive to have warrants attached to the risky debt of firms in which it is relatively easy to shift the distribution of outcomes to expand the upper tail of the distribution and transfer wealth from bondholders. It would then be attractive also to the owner–manager because of the reduction in the agency costs that he would bear. This argument also implies that it would make little difference if the warrants were detachable (and therefore saleable separately from the bonds), since their mere existence would reduce the incentives of the manager (or stockholders) to increase the riskiness of the firm (and there-

79 Alchian and Demsetz, "Production."

fore increase the probability of bankruptcy). Furthermore, the addition of a conversion privilege to fixed claims such as debt or preferred stock would also tend to reduce the incentive effects of the existence of such fixed claims and therefore lower the agency costs associated with them. The theory predicts that these phenomena should be more frequently observed when the incentive effects of such fixed claims are high than when they are low.

Monitoring and the Social Product of Security Analysts

One of the areas in which further analysis is likely to lead to high payoffs is that of monitoring. We currently have little that could be glorified by the title of a "theory of monitoring," and yet this is a crucial building block of the analysis. We would expect monitoring activities to become specialized to those institutions and individuals who possess comparative advantages in these activities. A large role in these activities seems to be played by the security analysts employed by institutional investors, brokers, and investment advisory services, as well as by individual investors in the normal course of investment decision making.

A large body of evidence indicates that security prices incorporate in an unbiased manner all publicly available information and much of what might be called "private information."[80] There is also a large body of evidence indicating that the security-analysis activities of mutual funds and other institutional investors are not reflected in portfolio returns; that is, they do not increase risk-adjusted portfolio returns over a naïve random-selection, buy-and-hold strategy.[81] Therefore, some have been tempted to conclude that the resources expended on such research activities to find under- or overvalued securities is a social loss. Jensen argues, however, that this conclusion cannot be unambiguously drawn because there is a large consumption element in the demand for these services.[82]

80 See E. F. Fama, "Efficient Capital Markets: A Review of Theory and Empirical Work," *Journal of Finance* 25 (1970): 383–417.

81 For an example of this evidence and for references, see M. C. Jensen, "Risk, the Pricing of Capital Assets, and the Evaluation of Investment Portfolios," *Journal of Business* 42 (1969): 167–247.

82 M. C. Jensen, "Tests of Capital Market Theory and Implications of the Evidence," Graduate School of Management Working Paper Series no. 7414 (Rochester, N.Y.: University of Rochester, 1974).

Furthermore, the analysis of this paper would seem to indicate that, to the extent that security-analysis activities reduce the agency costs associated with the separation of ownership and control, they are indeed socially productive. Moreover, if this is true, we expect the major benefits of these activities to be reflected in the higher capitalized value of the ownership claims to corporations and *not* in the period-to-period portfolio returns of the analyst. Equilibrium in the security-analysis industry requires that the private returns to analysis (i.e., portfolio returns) must be just equal to the private costs of such activity,[83] and this will not reflect the social product of this activity, which will consist of larger output and higher *levels* of the capital value of ownership claims. Therefore, the argument implies that if there is a nonoptimal amount of security analysis being performed, it is too much,[84] not too little (since the shareholders would be willing to pay directly to have the "optimal" monitoring performed, and we don't seem to observe such payments).

Specialization in the Use of Debt and Equity

Our previous analysis of agency costs suggests at least one other testable hypothesis—that in those industries in which the incentive effects of outside equity or debt are widely different, we would see specialization in the use of the low–agency cost financing arrangement. In industries in which it is relatively easy for managers to lower the mean value of the outcomes of the enterprise by outright theft, special treatment of favored customers, consumption of leisure on the job, etc. (for example, the bar and restaurant industry), we would expect to see the ownership structure of firms characterized by relatively little outside equity (i.e., 100 percent ownership of the equity by the manager), with almost all outside capital obtained through the use of debt.

The theory predicts that the opposite would be true when the incentive effects of debt are large relative to the incentive effects of equity. Firms like conglomerates, in which it would be easy to shift outcome distributions adversely for bondholders (by changing the acquisition or divestiture policy),

83 Ignoring any pure consumption elements in the demand for security analysis.

84 Again ignoring the value of the pure consumption elements in the demand for security analysis.

should be characterized by relatively lower utilization of debt. Conversely, in industries in which the freedom of management to take riskier projects is severely constrained (for example, regulated industries such as public utilities) we should find more intensive use of debt financing.

The analysis suggests that, in addition to the fairly well understood role of uncertainty in the determination of the quality of collateral, there is at least one other element of great importance—the ability of the owner of the collateral to change the distribution of outcomes by shifting either the mean outcome or the variance of the outcomes. A study of bank lending policies should reveal these to be important aspects of the contractual practices observed there.

The Large Diffuse-Ownership Corporation

While we believe the structure outlined in the preceding pages is applicable to a wide range of corporations, it is still in an incomplete state. One of the most serious limitations of the analysis as it stands is that we have not worked out in this paper its application to the very large modern corporation whose managers own little or no equity. We believe our approach can be applied to this case, but space limitations preclude discussion of these issues here. They remain to be worked out in detail and will be included in a future paper.

The Supply Side of the Incomplete Markets Question

The analysis of this paper is also relevant to the incomplete market issue.[85] The problems addressed in this literature derive from the fact that, whenever the available set of financial claims on outcomes in a market fails to span the underlying state space, the resulting allocation is Pareto-inefficient.[86] A disturbing element in this literature is that the

85 See, among others, K. J. Arrow, "Role of Securities"; P. A. Diamond, "The Role of a Stock Market in a General Equilibrium Model with Technological Uncertainty," *American Economic Review* 57 (1967): 759–76; N. H. Hakansson, "The Superfund: Efficient Paths toward a Complete Financial Market," unpublished (University of California, Berkeley, 1974); idem, "Ordering Markets and the Capital Structures of Firms with Illustrations," Institute of Business and Economic Research Working Paper no. 24 (Berkeley: University of California, 1974); M. Rubenstein, "A Discrete-Time Synthesis of Financial Theory," ibid., nos. 20, 21 (1974); S. A. Ross, "Options and Efficiency," Rodney L. White Center for Financial Research Working Paper no. 3-74 (Philadelphia: University of Pennsylvania, 1974).

86 See Arrow, "Role of Securities," and Debreu, *Theory of Value*.

inefficiency conclusion is generally drawn without explicit attention in the analysis to the costs of creating new claims or of maintaining the expanded set of markets called for to bring about the welfare improvement.

The demonstration of a possible welfare improvement from the expansion of the set of claims by the introduction of new basic contingent claims or options can be thought of as an analysis of the demand conditions for new markets. Viewed from this perspective, what is missing in the literature on this problem is the formulation of a positive analysis of the supply of markets (or the supply of contingent claims). That is, what is it in the maximizing behavior of individuals in the economy that causes them to create and sell contingent claims of various sorts?

The analysis in this paper can be viewed as a small first step in the direction of formulating such an analysis based on the self-interested maximizing behavior of individuals. We have shown why it is in the interest of a wealth-maximizing entrepreneur to create and sell claims such as debt and equity. Furthermore, as we have indicated above, it appears that extensions of these arguments will lead to a theory of the supply of warrants, convertible bonds, and convertible preferred stock. We are not suggesting that the specific analysis offered above is likely to be sufficient to lead to a theory of the supply of the wide range of contracts (both existing and merely potential) in the world at large. However, we do believe that framing the question of the completeness of markets in terms of the joining of both the demand and supply conditions, instead of implicitly assuming that new claims spring forth from some (costless) wellhead of creativity unaided or unsupported by human effort, will be very fruitful.

7. Conclusions

The publicly held business corporation is an awesome social invention. Millions of individuals voluntarily entrust billions of dollars, francs, pesos, etc., of personal wealth to the care of managers on the basis of a complex set of contracting relationships that delineate the rights of the parties involved. The growth in the use of the corporate form as well as the growth in market value of established corporations suggest that, at least up to the present, creditors and investors have by and large not been disappointed with the results, despite the agency costs inherent in the corporate form.

Agency costs are as real as any other costs. The level of agency costs depends, among other things, on statutory and common law and human ingenuity in devising contracts. Both the law and the sophistication of contracts relevant to the modern corporation are the products of a historical process in which there were strong incentives for individuals to minimize agency costs. Moreover, there were alternative organizational forms available and opportunities to invent new ones. Whatever its shortcomings, the corporation has thus far survived the market test against potential alternatives.

Armen A. Alchian

Some Implications of Recognition of Property Right Transactions Costs*

The list of fields of economics in the Directory of the American Economic Association contains no references to transactions costs or to property, despite much recent interest and research in that area. Probably the paper in *recent* times that most stimulated progress was Coase's "The Problem of Social Costs."[1] It demonstrated that, with costless exchange transactions and well-defined and transferable property rights, resource uses—aside from wealth effects on relative consumption demands—are independent of initial rights assignments. This statement signifies that transactions costs —the *costs* attendant to transferring entitlements or rights— destroy the classic standard theorems on market exchange efficiency. It indicates that many so-called market failures are failures of *existence* of markets or, more accurately, are results of obstacles (costs) to transactions, agreements, contracts, or understandings about uses of resources. These costs arise because of difficulties of communication, information collation, contract stipulation, ambiguities of entitlements or rights that might be traded. A host of activities are encompassed by the rubric "transactions costs."

* Presented at the First Annual Interlaken Seminar on Analysis and Ideology, Switzerland, June, 1974.

1 Ronald H. Coase, *Journal of Law and Economics* 3 (1960): 1–5.

Transactions

An oral tradition (a euphemism for a rubric of terminology, conjectures, and plausible assertions) exists on the role of entitlement and transactions costs. The conception of transactions remains sufficiently indefinite to permit superficial reference to "transactions costs" as the key to any paradox, externality, public goods provision, etc.

The following activities seem to be worth noting in the transactions conception:

1. *Search* over society for *who* has what rights. The cost of this search is reduced by specialists—as for nearly all activity. For land or houses, there are real estate agents and for stocks, stockbrokers. Employment agencies, yellow pages, and advertising convey information about *who* has what rights available for transfer.

2. The investigation of *what rights* each person has in each case. Title search firms identify rights holders and their entitlements. Automobile registration gives clearer evidence. Retail merchants provide assurance that goods are not stolen or of bad title, and we can't forget lawyers.

3. Technological *attributes* of goods. Investigation of physical attributes is sometimes sufficiently expensive to interdict transactions. Advertising or display of a good or of evidence about its characteristics is often provided by specialist "middlemen" who trade in the good. Indeed, this is a major function of merchants. Should we (a) include only the costs of conveying information about attributes of the goods or (b) take the state of knowledge as exogenous and include only the costs of providing risk-sharing provisions, guarantees, assurances, or remedies—if attributes are not as represented? For the moment, we include both and dub the first "attribute determination" and the second "risk sharing." Means for providing attribute information are diverse as well as specialized; examples are brand names, franchises, warranties, guarantees, commitments of wealth to a long-run venture (a means of self-imposed losses for bad performance, which thus serves to inform potential customers of the greater loss the seller will incur for unreliable performance), free trials, advertising of attributes, and governmentally imposed standards.

4. *Price search* and *price predictability*. The discovery of

bid and offer prices is facilitated by essentially the same procedures as the search for rights holders. Centralized markets and quick public reporting of actual prices benefit those who create markets as well as the public. Stockbrokers specialize in "making" a predictable market for specific stocks. "Scalping" on the futures markets provides more price predictability. Specialists (retailers, wholesalers, brokers) who make a market or maintain inventories and contribute to price predictability thereby reduce costs of search and planning. Futures markets provide more predictability. If prices were revised instantly and unpredictably to constantly clear markets, their reduced predictability would make planning and optimizing more difficult and would induce more pretransaction search. For example, an architect can design a house more efficiently the more accurately he can predict the prices of alternative components at construction time. Predictability over time is of greater value where planning preparation costs are more sensitive to haste, where larger inventories are held, or where adjustment costs in switching to other sellers are greater.

A geographical—or temporal—distribution of potential prices with a higher mean, *but smaller variance,* can be efficient. For example, resale price maintenance over a set of retailers is, in some cases, a price-search economizing device, which is more economical for people whose search time is valuable and for purchases of low value relative to search-time costs—where the gains from marginal search per unit time are therefore low. Constancy of prices, despite queues of random length and timing, provide price predictability at the expense of unpredictability of queue times. Clearly, it seems inappropriate to expect fluctuating, instantaneously market-clearing prices, for that would induce more costly search and adjustment than would a combination of both greater predictability and queuing, depending upon costs of search relative to costs of queuing and the gains from predictability. Long-term constant (though lower) wages with secure employment is a means of providing predictability to employees.

5. *Contract stipulation.* The complexity of contract stipulations depends on the rights being transferred, objective predictability and measurability of performance, and the contingencies for which advance provision is made. Many

contingencies are met by ex post settlement in the way they would have been met if anticipated—using goodwill as a reward for mutually satisfactory settlements. Contract formation or stipulation includes specification of performance conditions and the allocation of risk resulting from the unpredictability of actual performance. These conditions are as significant as the price, since the price itself will depend upon those terms and conditions. (The activity referred to here is not that of *reaching agreement* on what to include in the conditions but that of making those conditions objectively testable, unambiguous, and measurable.)

If all contingencies could be stipulated unambiguously *and enforced costlessly,* then the quality attributes of any good could be left unknown to any or all parties, with payment being determined by actual subsequent performance. But "of course," since that stipulation and enforcement is not costless, the cost of discerning attributes of a good cannot be treated as unessential or unimportant. Some techniques for economizing on stipulative activity are the use of standard forms, or conventions, of explicit contract laws, and of agreements to submit to arbitration. Continued sales relations between the parties make satisfactory performance desirable to preserve the capital value of anticipated future sales. Undoubtedly, the vast majority of contracts contain incomplete specification of performance conditions, relying instead on the loss of goodwill wealth consequent to a termination of sales or purchases if performance deviates from the predicted performance.

Complex performance or a long-term performance will not necessarily be associated with long-term or complex contracts. If the performance, however complex, can be detected sequentially, payment can be provided sequentially in accord with performance. It is not so much the length of the activity to be agreed upon in a transaction as the costs of detecting the quality of continuing performance that seems to suggest the complex variety of detailed, contractual arrangements. For example, labor employment arrangements often contemplate a long-term relationship; yet no long-term contracts are formalized. Instead, the pay and termination conditions are *expressed* in short-term contracts, but the terms of pay and termination are those that would typify a long-term contract if such contracts were formalized. This view of employment contracts will go far to explain types of unemployment, layoffs, seniority, and relatively constant wages and pay patterns over time. One of the major efforts of this study proposal will be centered on employment transactions costs.[2]

6. *Contract performance.* Without monitors, controls, and ex post adjustments, incentives exist to shirk or neglect performance. Techniques for detecting or measuring performance and for providing payment in accord with performance will be varied and will be used only insofar as they are worth the costs. In some situations, failure to watch pay and performance will cause a loss of future contracts and impose a "goodwill" or "present value" loss on negligent parties. In other cases, a contractual system of rewards or payment procedures will be devised to monitor or facilitate mutual performance or appropriate revisions in subsequent exchange rates.

Some Categories of Property Rights

A transaction culminates in a rights or entitlements transfer. What is a "property right"? In the *rights* of a person to a resource we include the probability that his decision about demarcated uses of the resource will determine the use, in the sense that his decision dominates that of any other person. If my decisions about some use or condition of a car dominate those of all other persons—so that their decisions are ineffective in upsetting or attenuating my decisions—then I, rather than they, have a property right to the car. The decision class of demarcated uses or actions or conditions appurtenant to that resource identifies the *domain* of rights held in that resource, not the strength of the right. If the probability is one—certainty—that my decision will dominate, I have an "absolute" right with respect to the demarcated class of conditions or uses to which the rights apply. For example, I may have an "absolute" right to pick apples off a tree, but not to prune the tree. I may have an absolute right to drive an automobile, but not to have it repainted some other color. The domain or scope of demarcated uses or con-

2 See D. Gordon, "The Neo-Classical Theory of Keynesian Unemployment," *Economic Inquiry* 12 (1974): 431–459.

ditions of a good can be partitioned among several people. Call this *use-domain partitioning.*

Distinct from the partitions of the domain of uses of an entity is the *decision sharing* with other people with whom some rights over the same domain of uses are jointly held. A shared *decision process* states the procedure whereby those persons shall identify a decision to which all are bound. Majority vote is but one example whereby several joint holders identify or achieve a decision (which is not necessarily "agreement"). All engage in the *process* of selecting a decision even though not all may have preferred the resultant decision. Sharing a decision right with other people reduces the probability that any one sharer's preference will determine the decision, but it does not reduce the probability of a reached decision being effective. Though sharing of decision authority attenuates individual power to determine decisions with respect to some resource, that power often is thereby spread over a wider set of resources, as when a larger group shares a larger pooled set of assets.

In decision-shared rights we must consider the probability that one sharer's preference among potential decisions will be the selected decision, as determined by the decision-process arrangement, not by the personality or persuasive powers of the individual, however strong those might be. We are here referring, not to what determines each individual's preference ordering of decisions, but instead, to what role his preference (however influenced) has in determining the group's selected decision.

Related, but different, is the consequence sharing of the resulting use or saleable value of the resource. How these *consequences* are shared is not necessarily the same as for the *decision* sharing. One "vote" per head (or share of common stock) does not require that the consequences be shared equally per capita (or per share).

If we were to try to categorize or differentiate property rights, we would, we conjecture, do so on the basis of a vector of characteristics including at least: (1) the domain of activities or uses over which a decision may be assigned, (2) the process of reaching a decision for a group of sharing rights holders, (3) the rules for assigning consequences to sharing members, and (4) the transferability of each of these elements (entitlements) to other people.

A right will be said to be broader, the broader its decision domain. The less a potential domain is partitioned to others, the broader the property right. Authority to decide who will be allowed to rent "my" house and at what price is more partitioned by fair-housing and rent-control and zoning laws, which transfer to political processes some decision authority. The wider the set of possible uses that are collected into one domain or set of uses, the broader the domain of the property right. But what makes it more private?

We seem to use also the degree of decision sharing (number of sharers in the decision process) as a criterion. A private property right can refer to the fact that one person holds the decision rights alone, rather than severally with others. Or *private* can identify the indefinitely large domain of uses that are collected into one parcel of rights, so that we could set as a limiting form, *unlimited* indefinite domain of uses to be decided by *one* person. These *two* components—(*a*) *unlimited domain* and (*b*) *single*-person, unshared decision processes—seem to be characteristics of "private" property rights.

Ability to *transfer* (or alienate) decision authority to another is also an attribute characterizing private property rights. Another characteristic is *responsibility*, which means that the technological or exchange-value consequences of his decisions about his goods are to be borne by the decision maker. If the good changes value in use, or in exchange, the decision maker has that value of use or of exchange. No other person has to transfer some rights to him in order to compensate him for loss because of inappropriate decision, nor can others compel unilateral transfer of value from him. In sum, all persons are bound by the same class of rights in the goods in which they are said to possess rights. Thus, (1) indefiniteness of use domain, (2) nonsharing of decisions, (3) responsibility, and (4) transferability are elements heavily weighted in the *private* property conception.

If decisions are shared, the property could be corporate or partnership, although still characterized as "private" property. If the shares are not alienable, the term "private" property seems at odds with common usage.

Now let us contrast this rubric of private property with public property, in order to identify some differences.

Public and private property

Compare a privately owned with a publicly owned golf course (or auditorium, bus service, water service, garbage-collection service, airport, school, or even spaghetti factory). There are differences in their operation; at least anyone who has ever compared them will think so. Why do these differences occur?

Preliminary investigation suggests, for example, that the difference between a privately owned corporation with 1,000 owners and a state-owned entity in a democracy with 1,000 citizens is quite significant, because the 1,000 individuals are furthering their own individual interests in each entity under different systems of property rights. In economic jargon, "the opportunity sets differ." A desire to avoid, or suppress, the effects of the profit-making incentive is often a reason for resort to public property. The objectives sought via public property, however, cannot merely be announced to the managers or operators with the expectation that exhortation will be either sufficient or necessary to achieve the objective.

Public property entitlements and consequences must be borne by all members of the public; none can divest himself of any portion of that ownership. A person must move from one town to another to change his ownership in public property. But while one lives in any community with public property, he has rights in that community's property and cannot divest himself of that public entitlement; but, by definition, he can sell and shift private property rights without also having to leave the community.[3]

To see what difference is made by the right to transfer ownership shares, suppose public ownership could be sold. With capitalized profits or losses accruing to the owners, will incentives be any different?

---

3 It is tempting to emphasize the possibility, under public ownership, of someone joining the community and thereby acquiring a share of public ownership, without payment to any of the existing owners. This dilution of a person's share of ownership is presumably absent in private ownership. Of course, a community could close off immigration or require purchase of land, but public ownership would continue even if this dilution effect were important. Furthermore, many corporations issue new shares without preemptive rights to incumbents. Still, even if dilution of public ownership were eliminated by restriction of entry, the inability to sell one's share in public property rights remains a factor in the costs-reward system impinging on all members of the public and on the employees and administrators of the governmental institution.

An answer is suggested by two implications of the specialization of "ownership," which is similar to the familiar specialization of other kinds of skills or activities. The two are: rewards and costs are *more* strongly imposed on each person responsible for them (1) via (*a*) concentration of rights and (*b*) capitalization of future effects into present sales value and (2) via comparative-advantage effects of (*a*) specialized knowledge in control and (*b*) specialized risk bearing.

Concentration

Greater concentration of rewards and costs means that a person's wealth is more dependent upon his activities. The more he concentrates his wealth holding in particular resources, the larger is his wealth response to his own activities in those areas. For example, suppose there are 100 people in a community, with ten separate enterprises; and suppose each person, holding a 1 percent interest in each, could, by devoting one-tenth of his attention to some one enterprise, produce a saving or gain of $1,000. Since the individual is a one-hundredth part owner, he will acquire $10. If he does this for each of the ten different enterprises, his total wealth gain will be $100, with the rest of the wealth increment, $9,900, going to the other 99 people. Of course, if the other 99 people act in the same way, he will get from their activities an increase of wealth of $990,000/100 = $9,900, which gives him a total of $10,000. This is exactly equal to his own marginal product, most of which was spread over the other owners.

Let us now suppose a more concentrated holding; each person owns a one-tenth part of *one* enterprise only (which means that ownership has been reshuffled from pro rata equal shares in all ten enterprises to a concentration in one enterprise by each person. He will now be assumed to devote all his attention to one enterprise, so he again produces $10,000. Of this he gets $1,000. The remaining $9,000 goes to the other owners. The difference is that, now, $1,000 is dependent upon his own activities whereas formerly only $10 was. Or, more pertinently, the amount dependent upon the activities of other people is reduced from $9,900 to $9,000.

If we go to the extreme where the 10 enterprises are divided into 100, with each person as the sole owner of 1 enterprise, then all $10,000 of his year's wealth increase will be his to keep. The first of these three examples corresponds to "public property rights," the second to corporate joint private rights, and the third to sole proprietorship.

If public property rights were saleable, they would in effect become capitalizable private ownership rights, and there would be a movement toward concentration of ownership. Why? The wealth that a person can get or lose is more dependent upon his own activities. If, however, people prefer to collect a major portion of their wealth gain from other people's activities, the total wealth gain would decrease, since everyone would have less incentive to work. It suffices that there be at least one person who prefers to make himself less dependent upon other people's activities and who prefers at least some more wealth to some more leisure. He will then be prepared to buy up some property rights and pay a higher price for them than they are worth to some other people in their current forms of property.

Capitalization

Capitalization of values of future service into *present* exchange values of rights, and hence capitalization on the present wealth of rights owners, is more complete (i.e., less expensive to realize) for private than for public property rights. This means that, in making present decisions, foreseen future consequences are more fully heeded for private than for public property resources. The weaker impact on present values of marketable wealth reduces incentives to heed market values of both present and future consequences. One would therefore conjecture that privately owned resources will be used and priced differently from publicly owned insofar as these differences are differential responses to potential marketable values. Briefly, the wealth incentive is less strongly applicable for public property.

Comparative advantage in ownership: control

The preceding example did not involve differences of abilities, knowledge, beliefs, or attitudes toward risk. But if people differ in any of these respects, specialization in various tasks—including owning—will increase wealth. This is simply an extension of the logical theorem of gains from comparative advantage, which we shall not explain here.

The usual discussion of comparative advantage ignores "ownership" productivities. But people differ in their talents as owners—as monitors and decision makers. Owners bear the risk of value changes and make the decisions about how much to produce, how much to invest, how it shall be produced, and who shall be employed as laborers and managers.[4] Ownership ability includes attitude toward risk bearing, knowledge of and monitoring of different people's productive performance, foresight, and, of course, decision "judgment." These talents differ among people according to the particular industry, type of product, or productive resource associated with that industry. Differences in these skills make comparative advantage in property rights pertinent. If property rights are transferable, people will concentrate and use their property rights in those areas in which they believe they have a comparative advantage. Just as specialization in typing, music, or various types of labor is more productive, so is specialization in ownership. Some people specialize in electronics industry knowledge, some in airlines, some in dairies, some in retailing, etc. Private property owners can specialize in knowledge about electronics, devoting much of their effort and study to learning which electronic devices show promise, which are now most efficient in various uses, which should be produced in larger numbers, where investment should take place, what kinds of research and development to finance, etc. But public ownership reduces (by high transactions costs) specialization among owners—though not among employees in the publicly owned venture.

A person who is very knowledgeable about woodworking and cabinet or furniture building would have an advantage as an owner of a furniture company. He would, by being a stockholder, not necessarily make the company any better, but instead he would choose the better company—in terms of his knowledge—as one in which to own shares. The relative rise in the price of such companies enables the existing owners to issue new shares, borrow money more readily, and retain control. In this way the differences in knowledge enable people to specialize in the application of that knowledge

4 Armen A. Alchian and Harold Demsetz, "Production, Information Costs, and Economic Organization," *American Economic Review* 62 (1972): 777–793.

to the management and operation of the company—albeit, sometimes by indirect lines.

Comparative advantage in ownership: risk and beliefs

A second aspect of ownership specialization is risk bearing. If various ventures or resources represent different prospects of values, then exchange of ownership will enable a wealth-increasing reallocation of rights among people, leading to greater utility in the same sense that exchange of goods does. In addition, people differ in beliefs about the prospects of future values of the assets whose ownership can be transferred. Differences in "knowledge" can be used not only in an effort to be more productive but also as a means for distinguishing different prospect situations. For example, I may be the top administrator of the Carnation Milk Company, but I may hold stocks in some electronics company because I prefer the risk pattern provided by that combination rather than by holding Carnation stock also. In this way a person can separate the productivity of knowledge and effort (received as salary) from the risk bearing. I can, if I want, combine them by holding stock in a company in which I am active. This possibility of separating the *control* (effective administration or operation of the company—an activity that rewards comparative superiority in ability and knowledge) from *risk* and *beliefs* is, of course, regarded as an advantage by those who act as employed managers or administrators and by those who choose to act as corporate stockowners without also bothering to exercise their vote or worry about control. Yet it is often criticized as undesirable.

Not all of the stockholders have to exercise voting rights effectively to exert an influence on management. Most stockholders may go along simply because they believe the prospects for profits and losses are sufficiently promising relative to other assets they could own. If losses eventuate, their pertinent alternative is to sell out. To whom? To other buyers who, because of the reduced profit prospects, will offer only a lower price. These "nonactive" owners perform a function in that, at least, they provide the willingness to bear some of the value consequences. So long as scarce resources *exist,* value changes *will* occur. The question left is, then, who is to bear the reduced value; someone has to.

Often it is said that joint ownership in the modern corporation has separated ownership and control. What this means is that risk bearing and management are more independent. This is correct in the sense that each stockholder does not have the same kind of control as does a sole owner. But it is a long normative leap to decrying this. Specialization in risk bearing and in managerial decision making about uses of resources in now possible. Complete separation of the two does not exist for *every* joint stockholder, for to the extent that some share owners are inactive or indifferent to alternative choices or management problems, other stockholders (joint owners) will be more influential. In effect, the "passive" owners are betting on the decisions of "active" owners —"betting" in the sense that they are prepared to pay for any losses produced by these "activists" and in turn collect some of the profits, if any. In the absence of any right to buy and sell shared rights, everyone would have to bet on the activists as a group (the case of public property). The right to sell concentrates this betting on those who are prepared to pay the most (or demand the least) for the right to do so. And it concentrates the control or management with those who believe they are relatively most able at that task—with the less able being eliminated more surely in private, transferable rights than in public because: (1) evidence of poor management and the opportunity to capture profits by eliminating it is revealed to outsiders by the lower selling price of the ownership rights; (2) the specialization of ownership functions is facilitated; and (3) the possibility of concentrating one's wealth in certain areas permits greater correlation of personal interest and effort in line with wealth holdings.

We conjecture: *Under public community rights the consequences of any decision are less fully thrust upon the decision maker than under private property.* They are *less* fully borne than if the same action were taken in a private property institution, with a similar number of owners. One would expect that public agencies would, in order to offset or counterbalance this reduced cost bearing, impose special constraints on public employees or agents. Public agents who are authorized to spend public funds will be more severely constrained with extra restrictions because costs of their actions are less effectively thrust upon them.

Some Suggested Analytical Interpretations

Transactions costs and their relationship to property rights suggest several ramifications that may merit some attention.

1. It is often said that someone who pollutes the air—or disturbs the peace and quiet—should not do so or should buy rights for doing so. Why? Because he is presumed not to own the resource being abused. The tacit assumption is that air is owned by nondrivers of autos, that rights to the use of land are owned by residers on the land and not by those who put noise or smoke on it. This is a sheer presumption about where rights "should" be assigned. Commentators have jumped to the conclusion that, because no one now is explicitly assigned those rights, the rights belong to those who have no reason to change the prior existing state of resources or that the rights should be assigned to political agents. If auto drivers owned the air, so that people who wanted less smog or cleaner air had to buy the air rights (to cleaner air) from drivers, the results would be no different from the results if rights were initially assigned the opposite way—*absent transactions costs!* Since smoke and smog are produced in the act of increasing someone's utility, the reduction of clean air is no different from the reduction of my leisure when I work for the university rather than relaxing on the golf course, contemplating the path of my golf ball. So I contend that the university imposes pollution on me.

Clearly, the growing concern about various forms of "pollution" and environmental law—and even torts—indicates the value of developing an understanding of the factors contributing to "transactions costs" and of the institutions and means for adapting to or reducing them.

2. Because the world is not characterized by costlessly "well-defined" property rights and costless transactions activity, some resources appear to be used wastefully or inappropriately. Apparently some desirable revisions of resource use are apparent (to observers) and, if brought about, would produce gains beyond the sacrificed values of current uses—if only the people could be made aware of and *responsive* to these potentialities, as could be done if the costs of reaching a contract and enforcing it were not so high. Coase illustrated ways in which these potential gains, if not achieved by voluntary contracts among the parties, were

often achieved by judicial settlements or by direction of law. Jurists often enforce the highest-valued uses by assigning disputed entitlements or rights to the persons whose interest it was to use resources in that way (or whose interest it would have been to buy those use rights had the market been sufficiently well organized and rights sufficiently well defined to permit transferability).

An explicit conjecture is that over decades, judicial evolution is toward well-defined rights in the sense of making them more definite, secure, and cheaply transferable. The conjecture is that this would tend toward *private* property rights. But this conjecture remains to be evaluated.

3. The well-known Modigliani-Miller theorem that the value of an enterprise is independent of its form of financing is a special application of the Coase theorem; absent transactions costs, rights will be partitioned in their highest-valued ways and thereby have the highest values.[5] So long as entitlements are well defined, partitionable, and transferable, under the motive of enhanced wealth they will be revised and used in the maximum-valued ways—if transactions costs are absent. Their initial sale value will be capitalized to reflect those values.

In fact, of course, rights are not costlessly transferable or revisable. Therefore, what forms of rights are most appropriately issued initially by, say, a new corporation? Bonds, common stocks, preferreds, convertibles, warrants? Are there any factors that would explain the optimal initial mix, given transactions costs of subsequent revisions or transfers? We conjecture that differences in beliefs by investors about the potential performance of the enterprise can account for differences in appropriate initial mixes—given transactions costs that are not insignificant.

4. A remaining vestige of confusion about the meaning of the propositions about effects of transactions costs arises from "blackmail" or nuisance liability problems. Smith would threaten to impose larger damages on Jones at trivial cost to Smith—say by cheaply creating smoke or by revealing secret, malign information about Jones. Similarly, the low cost of creating smoke to extract preventive payment from

5 Franco Modigliani and Merton Miller, "The Cost of Capital, Corporation Finance and the Theory of Investment," *American Economic Review* 48 (1958): 268–297.

the threatened party was believed, erroneously, to upset the "costless" transactions analysis. What the blackmail or nuisance threats do, however, is simply reveal that rights to the land's condition are not held by the threatened party but are instead *distributed* among many other people no *one* of whom can by agreement with the threatened party and the others exclude other parties from creating smoke. (From every other party, the rights would have to be purchased by one agent who could exercise or transfer exclusive authority.) There exists the problem of assembling all the dispersed entitlements from the various holders into one general exclusion right. Thus, if there were many neighbors of my land, each of whom had a nonexclusive entitlement to dump smoke on my land (i.e., could not prevent others from doing so), and if the sum of values to each person of dumping his smoke was less than the damage to me, it would pay me to buy and consolidate the rights from all the neighbors (the rest of the society).

If it be thought that each would have an incentive to hold out for the total value and thereby obstruct agreement, it should be recognized that this so-called blackmail is really "bargaining." Each party tries to obtain most of the value of the land use—whether by threatening to withhold agreement or, in so-called blackmail cases, by threatening to destroy potential use value by dumping smoke. But this really is only the classic bilateral monopoly bargaining problem, common in many other areas. It does not depend on the rights assignments; it instead reflects an obstacle to achieving an agreed-upon price. The parties are "bargaining" over the exchange rate for transfer of rights. With "pure" competition on both sides, the exchange rate would be uniquely determined by rivalry of alternative bidders and sellers. But otherwise, there is a *range* of mutually beneficial exchange prices. When threatening to quit while bargaining over my salary I am imposing a bargaining cost and trying to obtain more of the transactions surplus. When I threaten not to accept an offer, I am "blackmailing" my employer (given that I would have accepted his initial offer if I knew for sure that there was no possibility of getting more from that employer). *This* so-called blackmail becomes merely the costs of bilateral monopoly-monopsony bargaining.

But there is another kind of problem that should not be

confused with "the" blackmail problem. Suppose rights to privacy were deemed to exist and to be held by the person himself but were inadequately guarded by state legal action, with less than adequate compensation for invasion of privacy (even though the revealers were punished). Since state punishment does not guarantee complete deterrence, some whose privacy is threatened will add private action. Society may deem some of such private action *improper* because of its perverse effects of *inducing* activity designed to penetrate privacy. For example, suppose thieves could resell stolen goods to victims (at a price less than the owner's costs of going to the state for protection and recovery). Such private actions would undermine the punitive state-provided system of deterrence and protection. In a collusive agreement of protected people, although it pays individuals to break the agreement privately, it pays even more for the group not to. Lacking a theory of government and social norms, we can only call attention to the differences between the monopoly-monopsony bargaining case and this blackmail undermining of state-enforced deterrence. Do not confuse the two.

5. Another consequence of the entitlements–transactions costs analysis has been to aid the *formal* economic analysis of liability rules. Is the producer liable or is the consumer? The employer or the employee? The driver of this car or that car or neither? Unfortunately, the term *liability* is ambiguous. If the consumer is liable, does it mean that in the absence of contracts to the contrary he is presumed to bear the losses of contingent events? Does it mean that he cannot legally contract with a seller about the risks of consequences of future performance? If the former, it merely identifies a presumed contractual condition *in the absence of specific contract terms* to the contrary. It presumably is an approximation to terms that a majority of contracts would contain and thereby reduces contract stipulation costs.

If, on the other hand, *liability* means stipulation of conditions that *must* be included in any contract, does the imposed liability rule make a difference? In what effects? Other terms of the contract, as when employer liability for accidents is imposed, can be altered to reduce wages that compensated for self-insurance against accidents. What is changed is only the *system* of insurance for accidents. Employees now must purchase group insurance via lower wages, whereas formerly they could accept higher wages and *either* pay for group insurance *or* self-insure. To *impose* a mandatory contract stipulation in all employee-employer contracts is to impose prohibitively high transactions cost for some contract revisions. Employees must buy employer-administered group insurance. Only if transactions costs (*including* legal restrictions on rights transfers) are absent, are *initial* assignments of liabilities irrelevant, for they can be renegotiated. With costs of renegotiation, initial rights allocation does alter the end result. In sum, since "bearing the liability" is merely another way to say something about who starts with what rights, the *rule* of liability is a negotiable, initial provision in a contract.

If (*a*) it is a negotiable, initial suggestion that will hold only in the absence of explicit provisions to the contrary, nothing is changed if there are no costs of making contracts. If (*b*) the specified liability is not negotiable and *must* be included in all *new* contracts, then other negotiable conditions will offset the imposed conditions so as to more closely, though not completely, achieve the results that would have been achieved in the absence of the imposed stipulations. If (*c*) new stipulations are imposed on *existing* contracts without any permissible revisions in the continuing contract, the rule of liability matters (at least) for the duration of the contract. With transactions costs present, as they always are, *imposed* rules of liabilities or rights make a difference in who takes what kind of, more, or less preventive or precautionary action.

6. Another major clarification consequent to the analysis of the costs of transfer of rights was that of "externalities," which are now explained or interpreted as consequences of poorly defined, poorly assured property rights, which implies high transactions costs. It became clear also that the Pigou tradition of "externalities" as something to be handled by taxes, subsidies, or government activity was inappropriate. It is neither obvious nor demonstrable that all government processes would induce a "better" allocation than had been achieved already. Furthermore, an alternative to *that* kind of governmental action is making the property rights better defined, transferable, and secure and easier to enforce at law. This second facet attracted significant empirical study beyond that being given to other political means of meeting

the problem of "externalities." The implications for basic reinterpretation of the tort laws are wide ranging.

The concept of externalities is bankrupt because of its ambiguity. Buchanan and Stubblebine restructured the term *externalities* in such a way as to permit its graceful abandonment—via the route of adding adjectives, adverbs, and other modifiers to distinguish the various subconcepts and thereby exposing the many inconsistent meanings of *externality*.[6] In one sense, almost all human actions have externalities in that one person's acts affect other people. Sometimes only those acts that affect the technological production function of other people are called externalities—though Viner was considerate enough to call these "technological external diseconomies"[7]—a conception that is well worth retaining. Sometimes *externalities* has been used to describe only unheeded effects on other people. Whatever the terminology, it is worth distinguishing the case in which someone else would benefit from my actions, but by less than the cost to me, from those cases in which the marginal effects on others have a value in excess of the value to me, but in which there are costs of communicating or negotiating an enforceable agreement between the interacting parties. In this case, it seems the issue is usefully describable, not as one of "externalities," but as one of communication, contracting, or property rights costs, all mingled in the term *transactions costs*.

7. The above suggests a new question: What institutional arrangements have evolved to reduce the costs of communicating information, of contracting, and of defining and enforcing property rights so as to induce potentially mutually beneficial resource uses and activity? (The question is *not*, What if, miraculously, all those costs were absent? This latter query is equivalent to asking for zero costs of steel, cloth, and food. We would be richer, obviously.)

We have analytically explored one facet of this pertinent question with a proposition that what is known as a firm is essentially a contractual arrangement for reducing the costs

6 James Buchanan and Craig Stubblebine, "Externality," *Economica* 29 (1962): 371–384.

7 Jacob Viner, "Cost Curves and Supply Curves," *Zeitschrift für Nationalokonomie* 3 (1931): 23–46.

of detecting and monitoring (adjusting rewards appropriately) joint production performance. This explanation, though not inconsistent with the elements contained in the interpretations of Knight and Coase,[8] does provide refutable implications. It does so by moving beyond the idea that transactions costs are obstacles to the pure market economy's assigning every resource use via pairwise market contracting. Also, a definition of a firm is provided. And implications are derived about whom the control monitor is responsible to, who will receive the residual, the assets that will be owned by that firm's owner, the types of activities that will be more likely managed by partnerships, and some differences among profit sharing, nonprofit, corporate, socialist, cooperative, and governmentally owned firms.

And of course, we need not emphasize the problems into which socialists have been led. The Czechoslovaks were moving toward a market system—as some Russians would like to do—but the Czechs faced up to the issue more bluntly and with less political opposition and perceived that more private rights are necessary for a market pricing system to work as desired. Younger plant managers were pushing in that direction for efficiency incentives. Power would be transferred from the political authorities to individual businessmen. A continuation of that trend would weaken the socialist party control. That handwriting on the wall clearly predicted, and "justified," the Russian invasion. In Yugoslavia, property rights in resources are persistently being privatized—that is, removed from political agents. In every Communist country, there will develop a conflict between the new aspiring plant managers who see ways to improve operations and increase their wealth if only they could reap more of the harvests of their increased output. The necessity for rights to be transferable if the market is to be used is the dilemma the Russian economists are slowly discerning. The conflict between a potential rising entrepreneurial class and the political authorities is inevitable. And it is pathetic to observe Russian economists in their agonizing, awakening awareness of this dependence of an "efficient" market system on a system of transferable private property rights. They

8 Frank H. Knight, "Fallacies in the Interpretation of Social Costs," *Quarterly Journal of Economics* 38 (1924): 524-606; Ronald H. Coase, "The Nature of the Firm," *Economica* 4 (1937): 368–405.

struggle to avoid the term *property rights,* just as they avoid the term *interest;* but they have accepted the latter under the name of *efficiency index*—which is, admittedly, a pretty good name. What will they call the private property rights in productive assets in Russia?

8. Another clarification stemming from a formal analysis of property rights and their transfer costs pertains to the public-good *analytic* concept. If heavy goods involved greater transactions costs than lighter goods, market forces would have less influence on the use of heavy goods; if animate services had higher transactions costs, they would be allocated less by individual exchange in private markets. For any goods with higher transactions costs, the same would follow. The implication is that a public-private goods *technological* distinction provides in itself *no implications whatsoever* about efficient or "appropriate means of disposition, production, or control of public and private goods." Literally, nothing makes the public-versus-private good *technological* attribute an appropriate criterion for political or market control—despite articles by the "high" and "low" to that effect—unless that technological characteristic is merely a name for high transactions costs.

A technological characteristic is relevant if and only if it correlates with—and then only as a proxy for—transactions costs. Wild animals, airplane airspace, underground oil and gas, all have relatively high cost components in the transactions rubric, and that makes them more fit for group or nonmarket control. Some technologically public goods involve lower property rights and transactions costs than some private goods; the consequence should not be missed for analysis of procedures of control.

Many policies about problems of "free riders" or of reaching agreements about production and uses of public goods presume that government activities provide superior methods of overcoming these questions. As yet, no clear theory of government behavior has been established on the basis of which to derive such presumptions. The private sector does have much that serves to meet many so-called free riders and the problem of reaching agreements. Direct attention to transactions costs under various forms of property rights will avoid at least the technological fallacy.

9. Taking a lesson from the public goods–private goods misclassification, we can ask if there is any significance to the private *property*–public *property* distinction. Is there any reason to believe the incidence of the private-public good characteristic is correlated with transactions costs? We think so. And if it is correlated with transactions costs, we should expect to be able to derive contrasting implications about behavior and uses of resources under public and private property rights.

Harold Demsetz

The Antitrust Dilemma*

The execution of U.S. antitrust laws has been directed against three targets. The first is collusion. The attempt to collude in setting industry price has become illegal *per se* under these laws, much as it had been in the common law prior to the passage of the Sherman Antitrust Act. The second target has been a variety of pricing and marketing practices that have been and are used by U.S. business firms, including the setting of different prices for different customers, the use of tie-in sales, the utilization of "requirements" contracts, and the adoption of full-line forcing. The stated reason for prohibiting or limiting these marketing practices is to prevent them from creating (additional) monopoly power. The third target has been large firms occupying industries whose output is concentrated in the hands of a few firms—oligopolistic industry structures; here, the attempt has been to restructure industries in the expectation that a reduction in concentration will yield an increase in competition.

Indeed, the threat to large firms in concentrated industries has found new sources in potential legislation. For example, Senate Bill 1167, known as the Hart bill, would have established a rebuttable presumption that monopoly power is possessed and that reorganization of the industry is called for when four or fewer firms account for 50 percent—or more —of sales in any line of commerce in any section of the country in any year of the three years immediately preceding the filing of the complaint. While that bill is now defunct, there

* Presented at the First Annual Interlaken Seminar on Analysis and Ideology, Switzerland, June 1974.

have arisen new legislative efforts, primarily authored by Senator Gary Hart, to create a new commission for the study of competition and industry structure.

The dilemma that faces U.S. antitrust policy is the likely sacrifice of efficiency implied by continued attempts to accomplish the second and third targets of antitrust.

The emphasis on deconcentration found in antitrust decisions has derived intellectual support from a doctrine—which I have elsewhere labeled the market concentration doctrine[1] —asserting not only monopoly power and market concentration are correlated but that market concentration creates monopoly power. The doctrine has become popular partly because there have been many statistical studies that have found a positive correlation between profit rates, which are taken as an index of monopoly power, and measures of market concentration. There have been a minority of studies that have failed to find such a correlation, but the larger share of the evidence seems to establish such a correlation. In recent years there have been a few studies, particularly those of Professor Brozen, that have tended to undercut this evidence.[2] In one of his papers, Brozen failed to find any long-run persistence in the correlations uncovered by some of the more important earlier studies, and in a second paper he found that an important study by Bain[3] overestimated the amount by which profit rates in concentrated industries exceeded those in unconcentrated industries. The primary reason for this overestimation was the small (and apparently nonrepresentative) sample of industries relied upon by Bain.

The second reason for the doctrine's popularity has been the belief that increased market concentration makes successful price collusion easier to obtain and to enforce. The major contribution to this theoretical position was provided by Professor Stigler,[4] but Stigler did not discuss two impor-

1 Harold Demsetz, *The Market Concentration Doctrine*, AEI-Hoover Domestic Policy Studies (Washington, D.C.: American Enterprise Institute, 1973).

2 Yale Brozen, "The Antitrust Task Force Deconcentration Recommendation," *Journal of Law and Economics* 13 (1970), and "Bain's Concentration and Rates of Return Revisited," *Journal of Law and Economics* 14 (1971).

3 Joe Bain, "Relation of Profit Rate to Industry Concentration," *Quarterly Journal of Economics* 65 (1951).

4 George J. Stigler, "A Theory of Oligopoly," *Journal of Political Economy* 72 (1964).

tant problems facing any attempt to collude: How to discipline those who choose not to participate? What to do about entry by newcomers seeking to take advantage of high prices? In general, other theoretical work done in this area suffers the same (and graver) defects; the structure of the industry is taken as given, and then alterations in given structures are examined to ascertain the impact of structure on price and output. For each alternative structure, however, the possibility that high prices will attract entrants is ignored. Theoretical support for the validity of the doctrine, because of defects such as these, has not been very strong.

Many of the earlier studies measured industry profit rates on the basis of the accounting rates of return of only the larger firms in the industries examined, or they weighted large-firm profit rates more heavily, so that correlations uncovered were mainly between profit rates of *large* firms and industry concentration. If collusion, *and only collusion,* is the cause of the correlations between concentration and profit rates that were found in many earlier studies, then we should be able to observe these correlations for any size class of firms. Collusion should work to the advantage of small and medium-sized firms as well as large firms. I recently looked at what the data show us about this relationship.[5] Table 1 presents a more recent and more accurate tabulation of profit rates and concentration. In this table,

TABLE 1

Rates of Return by Size and Concentration

C_4	No. of Industries	R_1	R_2	R_3	R_4
0–20%	14	+7.3%	+9.5%	+10.6%	+ 8.1%
20–30	25	+4.6	+8.7	+10.0	+10.5
34–40	22	+5.0	+9.0	+ 9.3	+11.7
40–50	21	+4.9	+9.3	+11.0	+ 9.1
50–60	10	−0.3	+9.8	+11.0	+13.5
Over 60	3	+5.0	+8.6	+10.4	+21.6

5 Harold Demsetz, "Industry Structure, Market Rivalry, and Public Policy," *Journal of Law and Economics* 16 (1973), and "Two Systems of Belief about Monopoly," in *Industrial Concentration: The New Learning,* ed. H. J. Goldschmid, H. M. Mann, and J. F. Weston (Boston: Little, Brown, 1974).

C_4 measures the percentage of output produced by the four largest firms in Internal Revenue Service minor industries. R_1 through R_4 measure profit rates for different-size firms measured by dollar value of assets: R_1 less than \$500,000, R_2 = \$500,000 to \$5,000,000, R_3 = \$5,000,000 to \$50,000,000, and R_4 greater than \$50,000,000. No positive correlation seems to be present for the three smaller-size classes; indeed, there is a slight (but not statistically significant) negative correlation for the smallest. Similar results have been found when the largest size class is increased to \$100,000,000 and above, and other investigators have found confirming evidence elsewhere.

In view of this evidence, it is unlikely that collusion is the only factor at work, if it is at work at all, in producing the statistical relationships uncovered by the older studies. There may be more collusion in more concentrated industries (or there may not), but it seems that large firms in concentrated industries produce at lower cost than small firms in these industries, whereas this does not seem to be the case for unconcentrated industries. Hence, as concentration increases from industry to industry, the cost performance of large firms relative to smaller firms seems to improve; profit rates of smaller firms are not greater in concentrated industries than unconcentrated, while profit rates of large firms do tend to be higher in concentrated industries. Table 2 offers more extensive data in support of these findings. Correlations between profit rate and concentration tend to be consistently positive (but not always significantly) only for the largest firms. It is this large-firm characteristic that accounts for the significant positive correlations found in industry data when firms of all sizes are grouped together (see data row for all asset sizes in table 2). Professor Round has recently completed a study using Australian data that supports the findings just reported.[6]

These data indicate that a deconcentration policy may very well raise the cost of production by reducing the share of industry output produced by relatively efficient firms. If concentrated industries do not collude more successfully than unconcentrated industries, then it is only the relative

6 D. K. Round, "Industry Structure, Market Rivalry, and Public Policy: Some Australian Evidence," *Journal of Law and Economics* 18 (1975).

TABLE 2

Correlation between Rate of Return and Concentration by Asset Size of Firms

Asset Size ($000)	No. of Industries / Year	116 / 1963	116 / 1966	116 / 1967	76[1] / 1970
$0–500		−0.19[2]	−0.09	−0.01	−0.38[3]
500–5'000		− .00	− .06	− .07	− .01
5,000–50,000		+ .11	+ .04	− .05	− .00
50,000–100,000		+ .01	+ .09	+ .10	− .03
100,000 and up		+ .16	+ .16	+ .16	+ .28[2]
All asset sizes		+ .35[3]	+ .20[3]	+ .19[2]	+ .27[2]

[1]The 76 industries tabulated in 1970 is the counterpart of the 116 industries tabulated earlier; the changed number results from new industry definitions.

[2]Significant at 5 percent confidence level.

[3]Significant at 1 percent confidence level.

efficiency of large firms in concentrated industries that accounts for the data, or it is merely an accounting bias in the profit reports of large firms. In the first case, deconcentration imposes a clear short-run loss on the economy, and in the second case it produces no short-run gain. In the long run, the growth of efficient firms will be discouraged. If collusion is more frequent in concentrated industries, the loss incurred by a deconcentration policy, which even in this case shifts output away from the more efficient firms in concentrated industries, may be offset by any price reductions resulting from the greater difficulty of colluding. But such offsetting gains are likely to be slight, since the data reveal that medium-sized firms in concentrated industries are unlikely to be setting prices much above *their* unit costs. That is why there appears to be no significant positive correlation between profit rates and market concentration for small and middle-sized firms. If U.S. policy continues to seek deconcentration, the net effects are likely to be a reduction in economic efficiency.

The two alternative explanations for these data are pictured in figures 1 and 2. Figure 1 illustrates how economies of scale combined with "restrained" collusion could produce these data. Large firms collude to set price at p, which is more than sufficient to cover the unit cost of these firms at

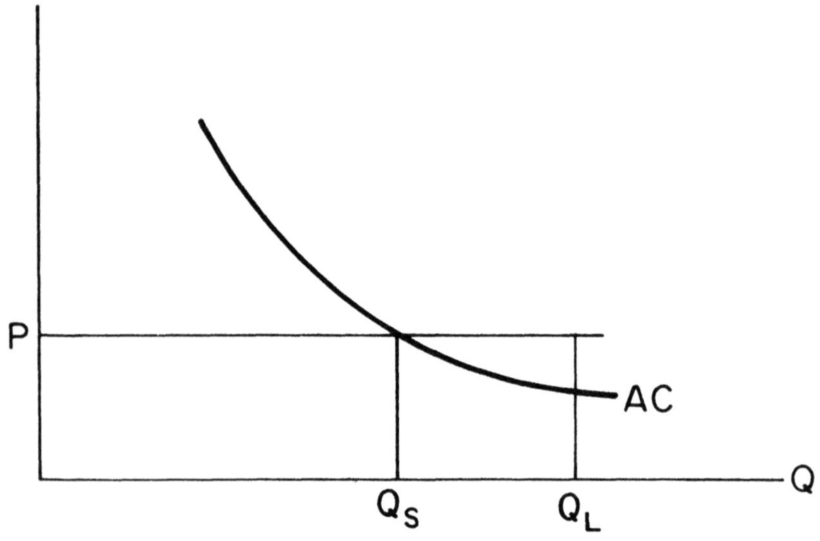

Figure 1

output rate Q_L but just sufficient to allow smaller firms to break even at output rate Q_S. The profit-rate pattern produced would appear as in the last row of table 1. Deconcentration, by shifting output from the larger firms to the smaller, would increase unit cost and would not significantly reduce price. If the markets underlying these data are correct descriptions of economic markets, so that the price received by all firms is the same, then the profit rate of large firms relative to small provides an unbiased index of the superior efficiency of the large firms. If large firms, however, receive a lower price for their product (after adjusting for quality), then this index would understate the advantages of large size; and if large firms receive a higher price, the advantage of large size would be overstated.

Deconcentration in the presence of such scale economies would be followed by a renewal of forces leading to the expansion of a few firms. To prevent concentration from reappearing, or to control price when it reappears, it would become necessary to substitute regulation for antitrust. The use of such regulation, given our extensive experience with it, is likely to result in greater, not less, monopoly power of firms in these industries.

There are data, however, that cast suspicion on the scale-economy rationalization of what is going on. If scale economies are at work, oligopolistic industries should become even more concentrated, but extensive and numerous investigations of the market concentration data fail to reveal any general or systematic trend toward increasing concentration.

Figure 2 explains these data without reference to scale economies. Some firms are able to find or stumble upon superior methods of producing a given quality of product. These firms have generally lower cost than their smaller rivals, but at the margin, the marginal cost for all firms is approximately the same. The failure of accountants to capitalize the superiority of the larger firms causes the economic rent they receive to appear in accounting statements as profits. The pattern of profit rates will then correspond roughly with the data we have been examining. Neither collusion nor scale economies need to be operative in order to explain the data. This explanation is consistent with the failure of concentration to increase still further, as seems to be required by the scale-economies explanation. With either explanation, a serious attempt to continue on a deconcentration course is likely to court the danger of imposing a net loss on the economy.

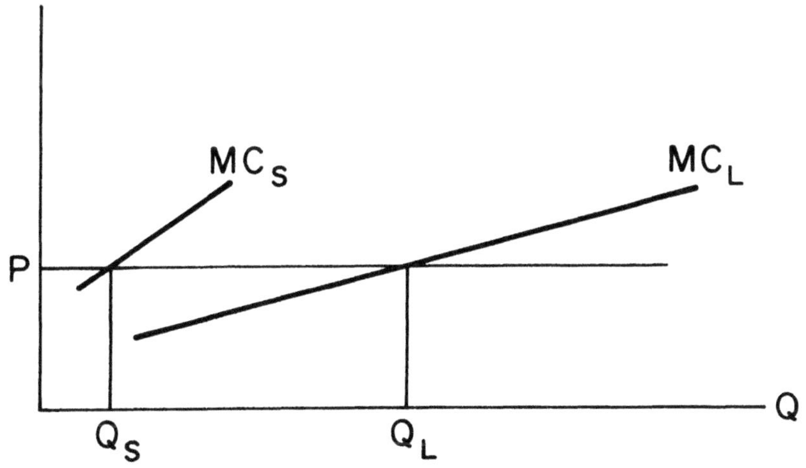

Figure 2

A similar problem arises with regard to the attempt to prohibit or restrict the use of various marketing practices for fear they will lead to monopoly. Price discrimination may represent an effort to compete in pricing by first lowering price to some customers. It may also result in a larger and more efficient output rate than would be true with uniform pricing to all customers. Tie-in arrangements, where the purchase of one good is conditioned upon an agreement to purchase another good from the seller, are likely to reflect attempts to discriminate in pricing more successfully than would be possible without the use of the tied good as a metering device. Prohibition of these marketing practices does not offer a clear efficiency gain because the imposed greater uniformity in price that results may make it difficult to begin to reduce price in order to compete or to expand output to larger rates than would a monopolist who can set only a uniform price. On the other hand, tolerance of price discrimination may increase the profitability of monopoly and hence may encourage the use of more resources to acquire monopoly. This problem has not yet been explored systematically by economists. In any case, price discrimination and tie-in sales have been severely restricted by antitrust decisions. Also, there has been a (partial) restriction on the use of requirement contracts, by which the purchaser agrees to meet all his requirements for the product for a stipulated period of time by purchasing from the seller with whom he contracts.

The disturbing aspect of these prohibitions is that they restrict the use of these marketing and pricing techniques for a generally incorrect reason—that they are designed to create (additional) monopoly. When one examines the instances in which antitrust has been used to prohibit the use of these techniques, there is little basis for suspecting that their purpose or effect was to create (more) monopoly. The use of tie-ins, for example, seems to have been much more a case of earning larger revenues and probably increasing output by facilitating price discrimination when some monopoly power already existed. Tying punch cards to the rental of computer equipment is hardly likely to lead to a monopolization of the punch card industry, since the seller who ties punch cards generally would be indifferent as to whether he produced the punch cards or purchased them from someone else. The antitrust prohibition of the use of such marketing devices is at least as likely to generate inefficiency as it is to inhibit the growth of monopoly.

There also has been a tendency in antitrust to penalize competitive pricing when this seems likely to yield a concentrated industry structure. The Alcoa case (1946) and early decisions in the recent IBM case fully reveal this tendency. Again, such policies pose a threat to efficiency and also to competition in the short run. Whether these policies forestall monopoly in the long run is an open issue. Economic theory sheds little light on *nongovernmental* sources of monopoly power. Our theory explains how a monopolist will price, but not the techniques (if any) that he can use to acquire monopoly in the first place.

That antitrust will be used to penalize competitive efficiency is no mere speculative possibility. Consider the treatments accorded U.S. Steel and Alcoa. The United States Steel Corporation escaped dissolution by refraining from competitive pricing, thus avoiding any charge that it used its power to make life difficult for smaller rivals; but Alcoa was found to violate antitrust laws because it behaved competitively. Alcoa had claimed that it never excluded competitors, but Judge Learned Hand clearly described the source of illegality in his reply: "We can think of no more effective exclusion than progressively to embrace each new opportunity as it opened, and to face every newcomer with new capacity already geared into a great organization having the advantage of experience, trade connections, and the elite of personnel."

Predatory pricing has been discounted in the literature as a rational way to acquire monopoly power. Merger or outright purchase of rivals would seem more effective, since the losses of a ruinous price war are thereby avoided, especially when new entrants can appear upon the scene after such a war has forced other rivals to capitulate. Predatory pricing makes more sense when mergers are forbidden, as is true in many instances of antitrust since the Celler Antimerger Act was passed two decades ago. Predatory pricing makes still more sense when new firms can be blocked from entering the industry. The latter condition is more closely approximated in the regulated industries, where entry tends to be severely restricted. Given our antimerger policy and legal barriers to entry in regulated industries, it may well be that we have created more fertile conditions for the use of predatory pricing to gain monopoly power.

Vertical price-fixing arrangements also create a dilemma for antitrust enforcement. Often, it has been held to be a violation of antitrust for a manufacturer to attempt to fix the price at which retailers may resell products that they have bought from him, on the grounds that the manufacturer was seeking to extend his monopoly to the retail level. The manufacturer, however, may only have wanted that retailer to provide certain information, displays, or demonstrations to further the sales of his product. In the absence of vertical price fixing, the provision of such services would dwindle. Prospective buyers would shop in outlets that offered these services and that asked a price sufficient to cover the additional cost of providing these services, but then would purchase the item at a lower-price discount outlet not offering these services. Under such conditions, the provision of services deemed useful from the viewpoints of both manufacturer and customer must dwindle. Fixing the price at the retail level for all outlets deprives the customer of any incentive to pass through a retail outlet providing the service, only to purchase at a discount elsewhere. The removal of this incentive makes the provision of a useful service possible where it might not otherwise be viable. Vertical price fixing may be a practice consistent with competition, since competition among manufactures (all of whom might fix their *own* prices vertically) may eliminate any substantial monopoly power, at the same time as it facilitates the production of desirable services.

Once antitrust policy moves beyond the penalizing of conspiracy and into matters of industry structure and marketing practices, the desirability of policy becomes much less sure and increasingly subject to the possibility that perseverance will reduce the efficiency of the economy. These problems must give pause to the onward rush of antitrust into these areas, at least until the theoretical and empirical economic issues are more firmly settled.

The alternative of substituting economic regulation for antitrust has great problems of its own. We now know that economic regulation has generally reduced efficiency in the American economy and has prevented beneficial competition from rising. Evidence that has been accumulating in recent years must increase our estimate of the importance of government intervention as a device to protect industries from competition. It is possible, I think, to give good reasons for believing that this evidence is indicative of underlying truth. Government, through regulation, makes available to industry resources supplied by taxpayers, not by customers or shareholders, and these can be deployed more effectively by virtue of the government's greater power to coerce. Entry can be blocked, and violators of regulator schemes can be prosecuted at taxpayer expense. Moreover, these actions can be directed only at those firms seeking to undermine the collusive agreement. Without government intervention, such competitive behavior could be punished only at great cost to those firms who seek to collude. The use of government to aid collusion is further facilitated by the right to collective petition for government services. Firms attempting to collude privately would be in violation of antitrust laws, but collusion to secure government aid is not. For these reasons, as well as the statistical evidence now available to us, it would seem that monopoly could be curtailed most effectively by limiting government involvement in markets to the search for collusive agreements to control price.

Michael C. Jensen**

Toward a Theory of the Press*

The major social problem we face today is how to control the political process that is destroying the free enterprise market system. Although I am pessimistic that we will in fact ever obtain a solution to this problem, we will surely never solve it unless we develop a viable positive theory of the political process. Such a political theory will not be complete until we also have developed a theory that explains why we get the results we do out of the mass media.

This paper is a first step in an attempt to develop a formal analysis of the behavior of the "press" (a term I use as a shorthand reference to all the mass media, including not only newspapers but news magazines, magazines, radio, and television).

I apologize to the reader in advance for the complete lack of any formal evidence in the paper. Furthermore, in this preliminary effort, I'm afraid I have accomplished little more than the elucidation of many issues I believe are important to the development of a viable theory of the press. What follows lacks a tight logical structure and does not, I believe, warrant yet the appellation "theory of the press." My hope is that it will provide the appropriate stimulation for a useful discussion of the issues.

The American press has played a major role in driving two recent presidents from office and is a major determinant

---

* Presented at the Third Annual Interlaken Seminar on Analysis and Ideology, Switzerland, June 1976.

** I am deeply indebted to William Meckling for many long and continuing discussions on these and other issues. His contributions are difficult to distinguish from those of a coauthor. Unfortunately, I bear full responsibility for all errors.

in shaping the opinions of individuals toward myriad issues such as the proper function of government and the causes of various social problems like inflation, unemployment, and "shortages" of oil and natural gas.

Webster's defines *romantic* as

> 1: consisting of or resembling a romance 2: having no basis in fact: imaginary 3: impractical in conception or plan: visionary 4a: marked by the imagination or emotional appeal of the heroic, adventurous, remote, mysterious or idealized. . . .[1]

Surely no better word can be found to describe the content of the press.

In 1920 the author and newspaperman H. L. Mencken described the press in the following words:

> The *average* American newspaper, *especially* of the so-called better sort, has the intelligence of a Baptist evangelist, the courage of a rat, the fairness of a Prohibitionist boob-bumper, the information of a high-school janitor, the taste of a designer of celluloid valentines, and the honor of a police-station lawyer. Ask me to name so many as five papers that are clearly above this average—challenge me to nominate five that are run as intelligently, as fairly, as courageously, as decently and as honestly as the average nail factory, or building and loan association, or Bismarck herring importing business—and I'll be two or three days making up the list. And when I have made it up and the names are read by the bailiff, a wave of snickers will pass over the assembly after nearly every one. These snickers will come from newspaper men who know a shade more about the matter than I do.[2]

In more recent times, the press has often been characterized by conservatives as a tiny enclosed fraternity of liberals who control the content of the news received by 40 or 50 million Americans over the television networks and major press outlets such as the *New York Times* and the *Washington Post.* It is asserted that the members of this small group control the content of the news in such a way as to serve their own purposes regarding what the news is and what the outcome of the political process should be. Former Vice President Agnew's famous attack on the network news pro-

1 *Webster's Seventh New Collegiate Dictionary* (1976).

2 H. L. Mencken, "On Journalism," *The Smart Set,* April 1920, reprinted in *A Gang of Pecksniffs,* ed. Theo Lippman, Jr. (New Rochelle, N.Y.: Arlington House, 1975), pp. 63–64.

grams and political commentaries is a good example of this phenomenon. I argue below that this "conspiracy theory" is fundamentally wrong.

Another theory of the press that from time to time receives popular expression is what I label the ignorance theory. This is the hypothesis that we get the results we do out of the press because those who gather and interpret the facts are ignorant.[3] While this may be an accurate description of the state of affairs at any time, it does not explain why these individuals remain so, why they refuse to become informed, or why others who are better informed don't replace them.

In 1976, for instance, Mr. Hobart Rowan, a nationally syndicated columnist on economic affairs, argued that taxpayers throughout the nation should help bail New York City out of its latest fiscal crisis. One of the arguments he offered to support this position was that New York City's welfare burden was exceptionally high because the city had more than its share of poor people. As evidence, he cited data indicating that 49 percent of the people in New York City had incomes that were less than the *median* income for the country as a whole. Need I say more?

I believe there are good reasons for the existence of such ignorance in the news media, and the sooner we understand them the sooner we will understand why the press behaves as it does.

Components of a Theory of the Press

I propose to analyze the behavior of the press in a way that is basically similar to the analysis of any other market composed of individual REMMs,[4] all acting so as to maximize their own self-interest. I begin with the assertion that we get an equilibrium in this market that is independent of the attitudes of the particular individuals serving as editors, newspaper reporters, TV newscasters, or commentators. Al-

3 See, for example, Herbert Stein, "Media Distortions: A Former Official's View," *Columbia Journalism Review*, March–April 1975, pp. 37–41.

4 *R*esourceful, *E*valuative, *M*aximizing *M*an, as William Meckling and I have labeled him. REMM is to be distinguished from sociological man, psychological man, and political man. For a detailed discussion of these issues, see William H. Meckling, "Values and the Choice of the Model of the Individual in the Social Sciences," *Schweizerische Zeitschrift für Volkswirtschaft und Statistik* 4 (1976): 545–60.

though, as usual, this matter of personal tastes is not irrelevant to the theory, I'm convinced that it does not determine the major thrust of the industry. Furthermore, the argument does not imply that the personal values of the individuals playing major roles in the media will be representative of a random drawing of the population as a whole. What I do assert is that the particular biases and the relative uniformity of biases of the people in the industry are endogenously determined by the system through self-selection and survival. Thus, these attitudes and tastes *reflect* the more basic underlying characteristics of the system and are not themselves a determinant of the behavior of the system.

A fruitful way to begin to model the characteristics of this industry (like any other industry) is to analyze the demand faced by the producers of news such as radio, TV, newspapers, and magazines. On the other side, we want to analyze the factors that enter into the determination of the supply of such news. Bringing these two together, we can then better understand the characteristics of the resulting equilibrium. Thus I reject the simplistic notion of the media as a conspiracy of any kind and believe the ignorance issue is not causal but the result of maximizing behavior of all individuals—both demanders and suppliers.

I ignore in the following discussion the distinction between news, sports, financial news, etc., generally observed in the industry and use the word *news* to refer to the entire nonadvertising component of newspapers, magazines, TV newscasts and special news shows, radio newscasts, and public affairs broadcasts.

Some questions that I hope we will eventually be able to answer with the aid of a well-developed theory of the press are:

> When will a prominent figure (political or private) be "protected" by the press? When will sensitive matters in his personal life (sex, financial matters, drinking habits, etc.) be kept out of the press? What is it that determines the point at which producers of the news feel free to attack him in full, as happened recently with Willy Brandt, Richard Nixon, Lyndon Johnson, and Wilbur Mills?
>
> How can we explain the role of syndicated columnists,

especially muckrakers like Drew Pearson and Jack Anderson?

Why is the news seemingly so often presented in terms of personal conflict between individuals?

Why is the news presented in the form of simplistic hypotheses (usually involving good versus evil) rather than the outcome of a complex equilibrium system, which I believe is far more accurate?

Why are businessmen and business in general given such little attention in the news? Why, when they are given attention in the news, are they usually treated as scapegoats for some scandal?

Why do markets and the free market system generally receive such unfavorable treatment by the press?

Some Elements Influencing the Demand for News

We must understand some of the basic characteristics of consumer preferences, which play a major role in the demand conditions facing the news media. To the extent that consumers have tastes for human interest stories, have favorite politicians or folk heroes, and have preferences for some formats over others, they will tend to reward those media sources that cater to their demands by purchasing, reading, or watching their product.

I assert that most of the demand for the product of the various "news" services derives, not from individuals' demands for "information," but rather from their demands for *entertainment*. In that sense, the news media are in competition with drama, soap operas, situation comedies, fictional writing, sports events, and so on. Observing the almost overwhelming devotion of the news media to political events, quasi events and non-events, it is easy to delude oneself into believing that people have a demand for *information* about the political sector. Downs, in his classic book on democracy, argues persuasively, however, "that for a great many citizens in a democracy, rational behavior excludes any investment whatever in political information *per se*."[5] Further-

5 Anthony Downs, *An Economic Theory of Democracy* (New York: Harper & Row, 1957), p. 245.

more, since the mere assimilation of free information consumes resources such as time and intellectual effort, I hypothesize that almost all of the information that most individuals in fact assimilate from the free data available to them comes primarily as a by-product of their consumption of entertainment. Once we understand that the primary function of the news media is to provide entertainment of a specialized form, we are in a position to understand why the press reports as it does. By entertainment, of course, I mean the phenomenon that is reflected in the demand for horror stories, burning skyscraper movies, romantic adventures and so on.

The Intolerance of Ambiguity

A fundamentally important fact about the demand for news is that people (especially those who are not members of the scientific community) have an enormous *intolerance of ambiguity*. That is, they demand answers or explanations to problems, puzzles, or mysteries—even if one is not available. They will pay people to provide such answers; the evidence from the history of man on this point seems overwhelming. I believe this factor is one of the fundamental elements explaining the worldwide and eternal demand for religions (and one of the major products of most religions). But the evidence goes far beyond this. Consider the function of medicine men, astrologers, gurus, security analysts, politicians, and many consultants.

In a very real sense the press plays the role of the modern medicine man. Given the consumers' demand for answers, it pays newsmen to dream up answers to problems—what causes inflation, unemployment, the energy crisis, high food prices, poverty, criminal behavior, etc. Since journalistic ethics generally prevents the newsman from offering his own opinions in the news columns, what he in fact does is to search out people who will offer these answers. Moderate perusal of almost any paper, TV news program, or popular magazine indicates that it is not necessary that these answers be consistent with available evidence; or, what is worse, it doesn't even seem to matter if they are contradicted by available evidence. In fact, evidence and careful logical reasoning are almost impossible to get past the average newsman or editor and seldom appear in any papers or newscasts. Some magazines occasionally seem to indulge the reader in such exercises, but very seldom. The reason, I believe, is that the average consumer doesn't find such material interesting (read: entertaining), and thus the producers have a positive incentive to suppress it. Most people basically reject the methods of science when it comes to matters that have very little direct and immediate payoff to them. Thus, emotionalism, romanticism, and religion play a large role in the demand for news.

H. L. Mencken, a newsman for 40 years, understood these issues quite well.

> What ails the newspapers of the United States primarily ...is the fact that their gigantic commercial development compels them to appeal to larger and larger masses of undifferentiated men, and that the truth is a commodity that the masses of undifferentiated men cannot be induced to buy. The causes thereof lie deep down in the psychology of the *Homo boobus,* or inferior man—which is to say, of the normal, the typical, the dominant citizen of a democratic society. This man, despite a superficial appearance of intelligence, is really quite incapable of anything properly describable as reasoning. The ideas that fill his head are formulated, not by a process of ratiocination, but by a process of mere emotion. He has, like all the other higher mammalia, very intense feelings, but, like them again, he has very little genuine sense. What pleases him most in the department of ideas, and hence what is most likely to strike him as true, is simply whatever gratifies his prevailing yearnings—for example, the yearning for physical security, that for mental tranquillity and that for regular and plentiful subsistence. In other words, the thing he asks of ideas is precisely the thing he asks of institutions, to wit, escape from doubt and danger, freedom from what Nietzsche called the hazards of the labyrinth, above all, relief from *fear*—the basic emotion of all inferior creatures at all times and everywhere. Therefore this man is generally religious, for the sort of religion he knows is simply a vast scheme to relieve him from a vain and painful struggle with the mysteries of the universe. And therefore he is a democrat, for democracy is a scheme to safeguard him against exploitation by his superiors in strength and sagacity. And therefore, in all his miscellaneous reactions to ideas, he embraces invariably those that are the simplest, the least unfamiliar, the most comfortable—those that fit in most readily with his funda-

mental emotions, and so make the least demands upon his intellectual agility, resolution and resourcefulness.[6]

What Mencken did not understand (or if he did, did not mention in this passage) is that his model of the individual (*Homo boobus*) is not an accurate description of the way man behaves in his everyday life. The evidence indicates that in everyday life the individual is an REMM. Furthermore, Downs provides us a good analysis of why, in his demand for political information, our REMM will in fact be led by rational calculating action to behave like Mencken's *Homo boobus*—it doesn't pay him, in general, to behave otherwise.

Thus, I believe this apparently schizophrenic behavior on the part of individuals is in fact the result of consistent and rational *maximizing* behavior. For lack of a better term, we might label it the Dr. Remm–Mr. Boobus phenomenon. Furthermore, it suggests a reason why so many people tend to believe that individuals are not in fact REMMs, but fools such as Mencken's *Homo boobus*. They observe what people say, the behavior of crowds, and the apparent ease with which people are misled on seriously pressing issues of the day, and they conclude that this behavior cannot possibly reflect the behavior of REMMs. Downs provides the basis for the argument that it is.

Consumer Preferences and the Devil Theory

There is much informal evidence to be gained from the study of the history of mankind—its religions, drama, literature, operas, and fairy tales. If we assume, as I think we must, that the content of the history of these areas reflects consumers' preferences (i.e., demand conditions), then this material provides evidence that is relevant to consumers' demand for the product of the news media. This history indicates to me that people like to have stories told and problems explained in the context of Good versus Evil. I like to summarize one major theme of this history under the rubric of the *devil theory*. This theory is remarkably simple in form and remarkably descriptive of how the press packages its "news." The devil theory holds that bad events are brought about by evil men with evil intentions and never by good

6 Mencken, "On Journalism," pp. 64–65.

men with good intentions. It has a corollary, too: good things are never done by evil men with evil motives. Again, the reason I assert that this characteristic of the press is attributable to the preferences of consumers (that is, demand conditions) and not to peculiarities on the supply side is that this is a good description of the content of most drama, literature, and children's fairy tales and of the way in which much religious material is presented.

This devil theory is a major explanation of why we observe in the news so little of what I would call analysis. Governmental programs never fail because they are badly designed with inappropriate incentives (welfare, urban renewal, foreign aid, and Medicare are all examples). Such programs almost always fail, according to the media, because evil men with evil motives pervert the system for their own ends. It also explains, I think, why the press evidences such enormous concern for the motivation of individuals involved in newsworthy controversy. Evil motives—or, what is the same thing to the consumer and therefore to the press, selfish motives—never lead to good consequences. Therefore, we seldom observe in the news any analysis of substantive issues. Analysis of the motives of the parties involved suffices as a substitute.

There exists another, slightly more subtle, version of the devil theory. It does not hold that all bad is done by evil men. Rather, it is the theory that the "system" (usually, but not always, the market system) induces men to behave in a selfish manner and that this leads to evil.

There are several other facets of consumer preferences that are related to the devil theory and that also have a substantial impact on the behavior of the media. The first is that consumers have a strong interest in *people* and therefore in stories about personal confrontations. The media, then, seldom present controversy in terms of the conflict between opposing ideas or theories but often go out of the way to convert such controversy into confrontations between people. One side is usually portrayed as self-interested (evil) and the other as altruistic (good). The environmentalist versus the corporate executive, the citizen oppressed by a governmental official or bureau, are two examples.

The second human trait that plays a major role in the consumers' demand for news is the commonly observed preference of humans for gossip. The sociologist Robert E. Park 50 years ago said: "The first newspapers were simply devices for organizing gossip, and that, to a greater or lesser extent, they have remained."[7] This preference for gossip is reflected in the society and entertainment columns' focusing on the personal lives of celebrities as well as in the usual "news" sections of the newspapers and broadcast media. It is also consistent with the simplistic theories of good versus evil generally offered by the press instead of more complicated stories about incentives and the resulting equilibrium of opposing forces. The office or hometown gossip similarly simplifies most stories, and in this sense Mr. Park was correct in his assessment of the press.

The Family and Antagonism Toward Markets

Why do we so often find the press carrying glowing stories of the benefits derived from governmental programs such as urban renewal (oftentimes, even when they are in the process of failing miserably)? And why are we so seldom treated to glowing reports by the press about how a housing developer, for example, has improved the standard of living of 5,000 families by planning and completing a new subdivision of 5,000 homes?—a feat made no less remarkable (as compared to urban renewal) through its accomplishment by voluntary exchange! Or, to put the issue in its starkest form: Why is it that the public at large and the press that reflects its views are so basically antagonistic toward markets in general?

I believe a major element in the determination of these attitudes is the structure of the family—in particular, the way in which we raise children—and the reflection of these values in religious dogma. Consider the family environment. We instill in our children early in life (or attempt to) a strong set of values regarding their duties and obligations to other menbers of the family (brothers, sisters, parents, etc.). In almost all societies we endow them with a strong set of values indicating that each individual is to do things for other members of the family without compensation. This carries over into adulthood and is reflected in the prevailing attitude

7 Quoted by Dennis J. Chase, "Foregrounding the News," *Reason*, August 1975, p. 17.

of people that one should be good and kind and perform services for one's fellow man without expecting direct compensation. As a result, many (if not most) people seem to believe that in some sense a society in which every man is his "brother's keeper" is the *good* society, and a society in which individuals perform services or help others only in exchange for payment (in dollars or in kind) is crass, materialistic, basically selfish, and most certainly undesirable. There exists in people a historic longing for ideal communities or utopias populated with unselfish, loving people, and I believe the family tradition is a major source of these longings.

If we step back for a moment, however, and analyze the family situation, we can see that a nondirect reward system has many characteristics that make it viable there. But these same characteristics will cause it to fail miserably as a way of organizing human cooperation in many other circumstances—especially in a highly specialized, mobile, and therefore unavoidably impersonal modern society. It is in this latter situation that explicit exchanges organized through the market system with immediate balancing payments (usually, but not always, in the form of general purchasing power) are likely to be much more successful in organizing human interaction and cooperation. Why?

The family is characterized by very long run relationships among individuals. Thus, if the exchanges between individual members of the family become seriously unbalanced or "unfair," as judged by either party, the "exploited" party has many opportunities to withhold his services or cooperation from a too "selfish" or offending party in the future. Individuals (husband and wife, for example) are continuously engaged in a series of exchanges, and I hypothesize that the relationship is such that it is simply too costly to try and put all those exchanges on a quid pro quo basis. Yet the exchanges are there nonetheless.

I consent to the wishes of my wife on occasion (for instance, by accompanying her to a movie or concert she wishes to attend) to make her happy and to maintain good relations—goodwill that I can draw upon the next time I unexpectedly bring home a colleague for dinner (or, worse yet, forget to come home for dinner). If I ignore her preferences too flagrantly, or she mine, the "exploited party" can retaliate in this game of life by voluntarily withholding future services or favors in many dimensions of the relationship.

Thus, there is a built-in incentive for the interacting parties in close personal relationships to reach an informal accommodation to each other's preferences. Furthermore, these principles extend not only to children, grandparents, etc., but to relationships with neighbors in a stable community and to social organizations. If you doubt this, I ask you to contemplate the last time you engaged in the following conversation with your wife. It almost always begins with the wife saying: "Dear, we just have to have the 'Johnsons' over to dinner. We've been to their house three times in the last 'six' months, and we haven't invited them back." Furthermore, these considerations of exchange extend to the employer-employee relationship in the business world—for example, the executive and his secretary.

In fact, all of life is a series of exchanges between individuals, and if those exchanges become too unbalanced (as viewed by one of the parties) cooperation stops. The question we want to answer is, why does it turn out to be more efficient to organize some of these exchanges on a quid pro quo basis (barter or money are examples) and others through a system of indirect and "unbalanced" exchanges through time? I say "unbalanced" exchanges for lack of a better term to refer to what I believe is the crucial phenomenon at issue—whether the exchanges are continually balanced from transaction to transaction (i.e., on a quid pro quo basis) or whether the books are balanced only over the long run.

Consider, for the moment, an example drawn from the other end of the spectrum from the nuclear family—a tourist environment in which the contacts between individuals are generally of a much shorter (almost momentary) duration. In this situation, the possibility of non-quid pro quo exchanges between people is much more limited than in the family or in a neighborhood. For one thing, the frequency of contact between two individuals may be very small (in the limit, once); in this situation, unless the offsetting favors can be performed immediately, the party wishing service has little or nothing to offer in the way of rewards or penalties. Imagine the plight of an Englishman in passage to Los Angeles trying to persuade a New York taxi driver to take him from Kennedy to La Guardia if he is prevented from engaging in a quid pro quo transaction. Furthermore, in such situations it is likely, if we are to put any weight on observed evidence, that these quid pro quo transactions will be most efficiently accomplished if they are allowed to take the form of monetary exchange for service, rather than barter. Thus it seems clear that if we disallow not only monetary exchanges but quid pro quo exchanges in these situations, we will vastly reduce the cooperation between individuals (and, in the case at hand, significantly increase the amount of walking by Englishmen).

Nevertheless, people seem to carry over their training from the home, supported and formalized in most religious traditions and the Golden Rule, to the outside world. They apparently find it difficult to see that the informal, long-run, non-quid pro quo exchange mechanism appropriate to the family environment is simply an inefficient mechanism for organizing exchanges when the frequency of contact is much lower and where the opportunity for symmetric provision of favors is nonexistent. Why?

How do we explain the fact that REMMs placed in Kennedy Airport and wishing to meet a plane departure at La Guardia would invent a system of quid pro quo exchanges to get them there if none already existed while, simultaneously, most of these same REMMs, if asked how the "good" society should be organized, would probably express sympathies for unselfishness, the Golden Rule, and "brothers keepers"? I think the reason is similar to the explanation regarding why these REMMs also behave like Mencken's *Homo boobus* when it comes to the press and why they will not, in general, invest resources in obtaining political information on which to base their vote. It doesn't pay them to seriously consider the issues involved (i.e., expend resources) in deciding how to organize the "good" society, any more than it pays them to expend resources to discover how a presidential candidate would in fact run the country. Their opinions and actions *as individuals* cannot possibly have any impact on the outcome. Their actions and discussions with the taxi driver, however, will most certainly have an impact on the rapidity of arrival at La Guardia. Hence, they will expend resources on organizing the latter exchange and give little or no attention to analyzing the former question. Instead, they emote, evidencing fond memories of family life, motherhood, apple pie, and *(short-run)* unselfishness—another example of the Dr. Remm–Mr. Boobus phenomenon. These emotional attitudes are reflected in their demands on the press and thereby in the news content produced by the press. Another triumph for consumer sovereignty!

Some Elements Influencing the Supply of News

There has been considerable analysis in the past regarding the news media, but it has tended to focus almost exclusively on what I think of as industrial-organization questions: property rights and the allocation of the frequency spectrum, economies of scale in production, joint ownership, FCC license renewal policies, market shares, advertising rates, etc. I want to focus here on a subject that has received little formal analysis as yet—the production situation faced by the individual reporter, editor, columnist, commentator, etc. Undoubtedly, there are important distinctions in the production situation facing each of these people, but I shall by and large ignore such differences here.

Rewards and Penalties

The supply of news is costly. The question that few have addressed in any analytical detail is, How does news get produced? There is a vast supply of "news" produced formally by the public relations industry for clients and by public relations departments of various organizations, including corporations, universities, eleemosynary organizations, the executive and legislative branches of state, local, and federal government, and many governmental bureaus at all levels. The Federal Energy Agency alone was reported to have about 140 public relations personnel on its staff at the time it was formed. The fact that these organizations voluntarily and at their own expense produce news releases for use by the media is evidence that they perceive benefits from what they consider to be the "right" kind of publicity. Much of this self-produced news is made to appear as though it were in fact produced by a disinterested reporter. Again, self-interest attributed to the source of such news reduces its value as publicity.

News reporters will have an interest in maintaining a long-term relationship with their sources of news, and they can offer both rewards and penalties to those sources as motivation for cooperating. The producers of news are thus engaged in a continuing series of exchanges designed to maintain their news sources' cooperation. The rewards seldom seem to be in the form of direct monetary payment but rather take the form of favorable publicity and recognition. The threat of unfavorable publicity can and does serve as a means for the news media to elicit cooperation—and on occasion the threat is direct and open.[8] We can also expect reporters to grant favors to important news sources by avoiding the publication of material the news sources would find harmful. One of the implications of this exchange process is that those newsmen or producers who have greater rewards to offer potential news sources will be less likely to cater to the preferences of those news sources than will papers, magazines, or TV stations with smaller rewards to offer.

On the other side, news sources with monopolistic control over information of value to newsmen will tend to demand and receive more favorable treatment by the news media. If we can identify those individuals who possess such monopolistic access to information, this analysis predicts they will less often be criticized in the news or have unpopular or damaging aspects of their personal lives revealed. Richard Daley, Mayor of Chicago and Boss of the last of the big-city political machines, is a good example of this. In my stay in Chicago from 1962 to 1967, the press played a very active role in discovering and disclosing fraud and corruption in the city. I was continually amazed that none of this was ever attributed in any way to Daley personally; the wrongdoing was always attributed to some lower-level functionary. All this even though it seemed generally accepted that little of importance occurred in city government without Daley's knowledge.

---

8 Thomas Griffith reports the experience of Eli Lilly, approached by NBC in 1972 for information on a story about the use of prisoners and other volunteers for the testing of new drugs. Lilly refused because on a previous occasion it felt its story had not been fairly presented by an NBC-owned station. The Lilly executives were told that a reporter would be filmed in front of a hospital saying, "Here's where a company admittedly experiments on prisoners. When we called Eli Lilly to see whether the prisoners were being mistreated, we were refused admission." Lilly then agreed to admit a reporter to the hospital. She found no mistreatment of prisoners, and nothing about Lilly appeared on the air. "Must Business Fight the Press?" *Fortune*, June 1974, pp. 220 ff.

What is it that suddenly determines the point at which the producers of the news media feel free to attack a prominent official or personality in full? This seems to happen relatively frequently with public officials; Willy Brandt, Lyndon Johnson, and Wilbur Mills are examples. In each of these cases the press suddenly seemed to break its "self-restraint," and aspects of the individual's personal life such as sexual activities, financial affairs, and drinking habits became featured news. I hypothesize that this will tend to occur when the individual in question loses control over his monopolistic access to information and loses his popularity with consumers of the news—or, in more general terms, when the benefits of the disclosures are larger than the present value of the costs (primarily the future benefits of the exchange relation with the news source that will be lost). A complete answer to this issue will involve more detailed knowledge about the demand for muckraking.

On the other hand, those individuals or groups with great popularity with readers and viewers will tend to receive more favorable treatment by the press simply as a result of the press's own interest in its marketing problem.

The greater is the power of the particular news agency, the lower is the likelihood that the agency (paper, magazine, newspaper, TV station, or network) will sacrifice its own short-run advantage to cater to the preferences of any given news source. The *New York Times, Fortune,* and the *Washington Post* are in a strong position in this regard.

To the extent that there is competition on the news-gathering side, individual news sources (government officials, etc.) with monopolistic access to information will have more power. And that power will be greater if the situation is such that the source can selectively exclude members of the press from obtaining information on a timely basis. The careful use of exclusive interviews or off-the-record conferences by such a news source can prove useful in providing incentives for all newsmen to curry his favor in order to avoid exclusion and increase the likelihood of their receipt of an exclusive news break.

Entrepreneurial Aspects of Journalism

People seem to love crises, apparently because of their entertainment value. If this hypothesis is true, and if it increases

TV and radio news audiences and newspaper and magazine readership, these media cannot be expected to remain passive bystanders reporting on the pathos cast up by life. In this sense, the press has strong incentives to foster sensationalism rather than calm dispassionate recounting of facts. But the incentives are for far more than mere sensational reporting. The media have strong incentives to help manufacture such crises. As Mencken, in 1920, so adequately describes the press:

> The problem before a modern newspaper, hard pressed by the need of carrying on a thoroughly wholesome business, is that of enlisting the interest of this inferior man, and by interest, of course, I do not mean his mere listless attention, but his active emotional cooperation. Unless a newspaper can manage to arouse his *feelings* it might just as well not have at him at all, for his feelings are the essential part of him, and it is out of them that he dredges up his obscure loyalties and aversions. Well, and how are his feelings to be stirred up? At bottom, the business is quite simple. First scare him—and then reassure him. First get him into a panic with a bugaboo—and then go to the rescue, gallantly and uproariously, with a stuffed club to lay it. First fake him—and then fake him again. This, in substance, is the whole theory and practice of the art of journalism in These States. In so far as our public gazettes have any serious business at all, it is the business of snouting out and exhibiting new and startling horrors, atrocities, impending calamities, tyrannies, villainies, enormities, mortal perils, jeopardies, outrages, catastrophes—first snouting out and exhibiting them, and then magnificently circumventing and disposing of them. The first part is very easy. It is almost unheard of for the mob to disbelieve in a new bugaboo. Immediately the hideous form is unveiled it begins to quake and cry out: the reservoir of its primary fears is always ready to run over. And the second part is not much more difficult. The one thing demanded of the remedy is that it be simple, more or less familiar, easy to comprehend—that it make no draft upon the higher cerebral centers—that it avoid leading the shy and delicate intelligence of the mob into strange and hence painful fields of speculation. All healthy journalism in America—healthy in the sense that it flourishes spontaneously and needs no outside aid—is based firmly upon just such an invention and scotching of bugaboos. And so is all politics. And so is all religion.[9]

---

9 Mencken, "On Journalism," p. 65.

Mencken's description fits the newspaper and network news activities of the 1970s as well as it did the newspapers of the 1920s.

Moreover, so well did Mencken understand this process of crisis creation and the attack on public figures that as early as 1914 he laid out the details of its anatomy, its likeness to a sporting contest, and its formula for success:

> In assaulting bosses, however, a newspaper must look carefully to its ammunition, and to the order and interrelation of its salvos. There is such a thing, at the start, as overshooting the mark, and the danger thereof is very serious. The people must be aroused by degrees, gently at first, and then with more and more ferocity. They are not capable of reaching the maximum of indignation at one leap: even on the side of pure emotion they have their rigid limitations. And this, of course, is because even emotion must have a quasi-intellectual basis, because even indignation must arise out of facts. One at a time!
>
> . . . a newspaper article which presumed to tell the whole of a thrilling story in one gargantuan installment would lack the dynamic element, the quality of mystery and suspense. Even if it should achieve the miracle of arousing the reader to a high pitch of excitement, it would let him drop again the next day. If he is to be kept in his frenzy long enough for it to be dangerous to the common foe, he must be led into it gradually. The newspaper in charge of the business must harrow him, tease him, promise him, hold him. It is thus that his indignation is transformed from a state of being into a state of gradual and cumulative becoming; it is thus that reform takes on the character of a hotly contested game, with the issue agreeably in doubt. And it is always as a game, of course, that the man in the street views moral endeavor. Whether its proposed victim be a political boss, a police captain, a gambler, a fugitive murderer, or a disgraced clergyman, his interest in it is almost purely a sporting interest. And the intensity of that interest, of course, depends upon the fierceness of the clash. The game is fascinating in proportion as the morally pursued puts up a stubborn defense, and in proportion as the newspaper directing the pursuit is resourceful and merciless, and in proportion as the eminence of the quarry is great and his resultant downfall spectacular.[10]

---

10 Mencken, "Newspaper Morals," *Atlantic Monthly*, March 1914, reprinted in *A Gang of Pecksniffs*, ed. Lippman, pp. 47–49.

I ask you to reread his description as you contemplate the Woodward-Bernstein success story. Watergate has made these reporters wealthy men, and they seem to have understood this strategy well. Consider also the anatomy of such other recent "crises" as the New York City default, energy, and inflation.

William Meckling and I have argued elsewhere that politicians also have a strong vested interest in the creation of crises.[11] It provides them the opportunity to justify their existence (by "saving" us) and to expand their powers by using the resulting hysteria to transfer rights from the private to the public sector. They thereby increase the demand for their services and their realm of influence. Thus, there exists a natural and close alliance of interests between the political sector and the news media in the creation and care and feeding of crises.

The business community does not seem to have a similar interest in the promotion of crises. Also, businessmen are not as inclined to court the media as are political figures. Why? My hypothesis is that the publicity that the media can hand out as rewards is not as valuable to the nonpolitician. When the *Homo boobus* who consume the news purchase a house, auto, meat, etc., they behave as we expect REMMs to behave in allocating their own scarce resources. There is little of the Dr. Remm–Mr. Boobus phenomenon reflected here, as there is in the way they cast their votes for political office.

The incentives facing the business community in its relations with the press appear to be changing, however. As the political sector grows larger at the expense of private markets, the damage that the media has shown it is capable of inflicting on the owners of corporations is now providing a much stronger incentive for businessmen to cater to the news media. For example, J. Walter Thompson in recent times has begun to offer a two-day seminar to teach executives how to handle the press and TV interviews.[12]

---

11 William H. Meckling and Michael C. Jensen, "Can the Corporation Survive?" *Financial Analysts Journal*, January–February 1978.

12 Griffith, "Must Business Fight the Press?" and Edith Efron, "The Free Mind and the Free Market," *Reason*, August 1975, pp. 24–31.

Politicians, however, are not the only group with interests in common with the press in the promotion of crises. Scientists also rank high on the list and can be found actively aiding in the creation and feeding of most recent crises such as the savings of the cities, the food "problem," the energy "problem," and environmental "problems," and I believe a survey of the results will indicate that they have been quite successful in increasing the support for scientists by the public sector. In that sense, they are no different from almost any other special interest group I can think of. In addition, most governmental agencies—NIH, ERDA, Agriculture, Geological Survey, NSF, the Army Corps of Engineers, NASA, and HEW—also participate actively in the promotion of their own special interests through the press and often in conjunction with another existing or predicted or created "crisis."

Further Considerations

1. The muckraking industry contains some interesting aspects that are not well understood now and are worthy of consideration. Will it pay individual news organizations to avoid having muckrakers on their staffs in order to reduce the costs that might be imposed on them by those powerful individuals they criticize—costs that would take the form of reduced access of their news reporters to information from these sources? Perhaps by syndicating muckraker columns and thereby diffusing that cost over many newspapers, these side effects on any given newspaper can be reduced. But this suggests that any given newspaper that refuses to run such a column would be able to benefit from this exclusion.

2. As Coase has pointed out, the press takes a very different view of the appropriate role of governmental regulation in the market for goods and the market for ideas.[13] Producers of the news defend a completely unregulated press under the First Amendment with a vigor approaching fanaticism (a view that is not inconsistent with their own self-interest and a view that is not consistent with their general position on the appropriate role of government in the regulation of the market for goods). One currently contro-

13 R. H. Coase, "The Market for Goods and the Market for Ideas," *American Economic Review* 64 (1974): 384–91.

versial issue in this realm concerns the rights of newsmen to refuse under the First Amendment to disclose news sources. Granting newsmen such rights provides them the ability to bestow benefits on some information suppliers by reducing the potential costs they might bear from dealing with the press. It is not clear, however, that such a policy is in fact desirable. But the full implications of the incentive effects of alternative rules on this issue have not yet been analyzed.

3. In many respects, the relationship between the individual news reporter and the editors and publishers has some similarities to the relationship between professors and their universities. Professors can increase their own welfare by behaving somewhat like independent entrepreneurs in marketing their talents and services to the world at large; and for those who do so, conflicts often arise between their interests and those of the universities employing them. Many news reporters are in a similar situation; and to the extent that they can gain personal renown by their actions, they can increase their independence from their particular media employer and transfer some of the benefits from their activities to themselves. They may also, on occasion, be able to generate benefits for themselves by actions that impose costs on their employers. A detailed analysis of the structure of this agency problem might well yield some additional insights into the behavior of the media.

GPSR Compliance

The European Union's (EU) General Product Safety Regulation (GPSR) is a set of rules that requires consumer products to be safe and our obligations to ensure this.

If you have any concerns about our products, you can contact us on ProductSafety@springernature.com

In case Publisher is established outside the EU, the EU authorized representative is:

Springer Nature Customer Service Center GmbH
Europaplatz 3
69115 Heidelberg, Germany

Batch number: 10823817

Printed by Printforce, the Netherlands